100 TURNING POINTS IN AMERICAN HISTORY

100 Turning Points in American History

Alan Axelrod

Guilford, Connecticut

An imprint of Globe Pequot, the trade division of
The Rowman & Littlefield Publishing Group, Inc.
4501 Forbes Blvd., Ste. 200
Lanham, MD 20706
www.rowman.com

Distributed by NATIONAL BOOK NETWORK

British Library Cataloguing in Publication Information available

Library of Congress Cataloging-in-Publication Data available

ISBN 978-1-4930-3743-8 (hardcover)
ISBN 978-1-4930-3744-5 (e-book)

ISBN 978-1-4930-5947-8 (paperback)

♾™ The paper used in this publication meets the minimum requirements of American National
Standard for Information Sciences—Permanence of Paper for Printed Library Materials, ANSI/
NISO Z39.48-1992.

CONTENTS

focus on what *drives* the story, which is called "plot," and what *propels* the plot, which are any number of *turning points*.

In history, as in a big novel or a big movie, what most compels us in the long run are not the *things, events,* and *causes* but the turning points: the decisions, acts, innovations, errors, ideas, successes, and failures on which the contours of the nation's life—*our* lives—depend. Turning points create what we call "destiny" or "direction." They spin off our "values" and "ideals" as well as our "flaws," "foibles," and "faults." Turning points are like the peaks of an electrocardiogram—an EKG. They mark the very pulse of the nation's history.

This book, then, does not claim to present "American History," let alone the "Most Important Things, Events, and Causes in American History." Instead, it identifies one hundred points at which the national path we share turned on its way to where we find ourselves more or less in the present. If you prefer, think of these *turnings* as *fulcrums* on which the levers of national belief, effort, and endeavor lift us or let us down. In either case, they are the features of our shared story that keep us glued to the narrative, that keep us from slamming the book cover shut or taking our popcorn and walking out of the theater. They are the points, the moments, at which those who came before us could have gone this way or that. And so, we are better off knowing about them and recalling them and thinking about them than remaining unaware of them, forgetting them, or ignoring them.

Columbus Arrives in the "New World" (1492)

Over the past three decades or more, a laudable evolution toward increased respect for human rights has created a growing backlash against Christopher Columbus, who, upon "discovering" America, tried to promote to his patrons, Spain's King Ferdinand and Queen Isabella, the enormous value of Native American slave labor. The Spanish monarchs had authorized Columbus's voyage on April 29, 1492, the very day on which they issued their Edict of Expulsion, banishing all Jews from their kingdom. Yet, even the demonstrably intolerant Ferdinand and Isabella rejected as immoral Columbus's views on slavery. As if the modern condemnation of Columbus as a racist conquistador is not criticism enough, many commentators have long pointed out that he did not "discover" America at all. Nearly five hundred years before him, around 1000, Norse captain Leif Ericson, out of Greenland, struck land in present-day Newfoundland, establishing a village he called Vinland, the first European colony in North America. A few years before this, in 986, another Norseman, Bjarni Herjólfsson, became the first European to set eyes on the Americas. For that matter, geographers believe that people from Asia had entered North America as early as 10,000 BC via a land bridge that existed where the Bering Strait is now.

These criticisms and corrections matter. Yet, whether Columbus was a good man or deeply flawed and whether he "discovered" anything or not, he unquestionably created the first great American turning point. When, on October 12, 1492, after seventy perilous days at sea, one of his sailors sighted land, the New World began to open to the Old. The earlier migrations, sightings, and even settlements made no impact on the empires of Europe. But the impact of Columbus's first and subsequent three voyages (1492, 1493, 1498, and 1502) was profound. They began the Spanish colonization

Portrait of a Man, Said to Be Christopher Columbus was painted del Piombo in 1519 and today hangs in New York's Metropolita
METROPOLITAN MUSEUM OF ART

of the Americas, which was followed by the colonial proje
England, and other European states. America rapidly e
nomic, cultural, political, and military realm of Western Civ

crew, was a work of bold fiction. The other, in which he
the progress of the voyage, he kept hidden.

The deception was not discovered, but it soon wo
10, just two days before the cry of *Land ho!* was finall
all three vessels verged on mutiny. But then, on Oct
island its inhabitants called Guanahani (believed t
Island) hove into view. The ships landed, Columbus
the name of the Spanish sovereigns, and he exercise
to give Spain's new possession a proper Christian na

On this first voyage, Columbus went on to probe
Cuba, and the island of Hispañola (divided toda
the Dominican Republic). On that large island, he
Navidad. Coincidentally, on Christmas Day—Navi
Santa Maria was wrecked in a storm.

Leaving behind a garrison to occupy the fort, C
to Spain on January 16, 1493. No sooner had his m
horizon than the garrison began pillaging the ho
natives and ravaging the women. Columbus, who r
late in 1493 on his Second Voyage, found no tra
Indios ("Indians"), as Columbus called them, had
It was the first "war" of European conquest in the

En route back to Spain from the First V
stopped at the Canary Islands on February 15,
dispatched a letter to Luis de Santangel, describin
and breathless detail. Luis immediately had the le
for all practical purposes, published throughout
was to prompt Pope Alexander VI to issue two
Inter Caetera II, which were followed on June 7
Tordesillas. These documents divided possession
had "discovered" between Spain and Portugal.
edgeable geographer-mariners, most notably
and cartographer Amerigo Vespucci, concluded
found a shortcut to the riches of the Far East bu
what Vespucci called a *Mundus Novus*: a "Ne

the German mapmaker Martin Waldseemüller named most of the vast region after Amerigo himself, calling it America.

We do not know if Ferdinand and Isabella were disappointed that Columbus had not found a short route to the riches of the East. But we do know that, very quickly, all Europe thrilled to the prospect of a *New* World—because opportunity in the Old was waning. Kingdoms and properties and royally patented enterprises were finite. Columbus had told tales of lands of limited resources, laden with gold, and populated by natives who could be pressed into service as miners. Equally important was the prospect of whole populations to be conquered for Christianity in a great harvest of souls.

There was instantly born in this America what would later be called the American Dream. It was the promise of new beginnings. Europe was in thrall to the concept of primogeniture, the ironbound system in which all wealth and all titles passed to the first son of any great family, leaving younger offspring with limited opportunity. Now these dispossessed had a New World in which to make their own destinies. As for those born into families that were neither great nor wealthy, the New World offered even more miraculous prospects for a prosperity impossible in Europe. A hopeful voyager to the lands across the ocean could dream great dreams and claim as much as his intrepidity, strength, and wit would accommodate. Suddenly, Europe became the realm of the past, and America the promised land of the future. This was the paradigm that guided American history for the next half a millennium.

Jamestown Is Founded (1607)

The Spanish started colonizing the Americas within a few years of Columbus's 1492 voyage. The English did not get started until Queen Elizabeth I knighted Humphrey Gilbert and sent him off to the New World in 1579. His first fleet broke up in a storm at sea, and he was forced to limp home. It was June 1583 before he tried again. This time, he reached St. John's Bay, Newfoundland, claimed the territory for his queen, but was lost at sea on his return to England when his overloaded vessel foundered, sparing no one.

Gilbert's half-brother, Walter Raleigh, inherited his royal charter and in 1584 sent a small reconnaissance flotilla to what would later be named Croatan Sound in the Outer Banks of North Carolina. The advance party returned to England with cheerful reports of a land populated by "most gentle, loving and faithful" Indians, who lived "after the manner of the Golden Age." Raleigh got a knighthood and, in return, named the land Virginia, after his "Virgin Queen."

That was the last good luck his venture had.

In 1585 and 1586, Raleigh sent parties of settlers under Sir Richard Grenville. Early in 1587, Sir Francis Drake found them starving, begging him for passage back to England. Undiscouraged by their return, Raleigh immediately launched another three ships, bearing 117 men, women, and children. They landed at what is now called Roanoke Island, off the North Carolina coast, late in 1587. Their leader, John White, set them up in a swamp before returning to England to fetch supplies Raleigh had promised to send. In London, White learned that the supply vessels had been delayed by the attack of the Spanish Armada's attempted invasion of England. He returned to the colony, bearing supplies, in 1590. Where a rude settlement had been, he found only a few rusty items of hardware—and the name of a neighboring island carved into a tree: CROATOAN. The colonists had vanished.

England was off to a dismal start in America. At last, in 1605, two groups of merchants, one calling itself the Virginia Company of London (aka the London Company) and the other the Plymouth Company, vied for a royal charter to establish a colony in the territory of Raleigh's patent. Elizabeth's successor, James I, authorized the Virginia Company to colonize southern Virginia while the Plymouth Company was assigned northern Virginia.

The Virginia Company moved first, recruiting 144 settlers, which included rich and poor. The rich paid their way upfront. The poor obtained their passage to America and the right of residence in the colony by "indenturing" (binding) themselves to labor for the Virginia Company for a period of seven long years. Both rich and poor set off in December 1606 aboard the *Susan Constant*, the *Discovery*, and the *Goodspeed*. Thirty-nine died before reaching Virginia. On May 24, 1607, the 105 who survived the voyage touched land at the mouth of a river they named the James and immediately began clawing "Jamestown" out of the wilderness.

St. Augustine, Florida, founded by Spanish admiral Pedro Menéndez de Avilés in 1565, today claims distinction as the oldest European-established settlement in the United States. Jamestown, founded forty-two years later, is usually described as "the first permanent English colony" in the New World. But "permanent" is something of an exaggeration. To begin with, Jamestown was planted in a malarial swamp. To make matters worse, the town got started far too late in the season for planting crops. Besides, the rich "gentlemen"—those who were not indentured—refused to do the manual labor needed to hack a colony out of the wilderness. Half the tiny colony was gone within a few months, either dead or fled into the arms of the local Indians.

What saved them all from ghoulish extinction was a former crusader and pirate turned soldier of fortune whom the Virginia Company had hired to supervise the military defense of the colony. Back in December 1607, Captain John Smith was foraging for food along the Chickahominy River when he was captured by Indians, who took him to the village of Chief Wahunsonacock. (The English soon dubbed him Powhatan, calling his people the Powhatans.) As Smith tells it, this encounter was nearly lethal. He was about to be clubbed to death when Powhatan's daughter, eleven-year-old Pocahontas, impulsively laid her head upon his. "At the minute of my execution, she hazarded the beating out of her own brains to save mine," Smith wrote. Released, Captain Smith offered himself up for adoption by the tribe and in this way cadged sufficient corn and yams from the Powhatans to delay absolute starvation—for a time.

But only for a time. As perilous as 1607 and 1608 were, the year 1609 was terrible enough to earn the title of the "Starving Time." Wretched human skeletons cannibalized the sick. Indeed, even the dead did not escape, as the colonists looted the new graves of their fellows. Much to the horror of the Powhatans, they also dug up freshly interred Indians. Confronted by a village of ravenous cannibals, Smith imposed martial law on the colony. He laid down one simple law: those who worked, ate. Those "gentlemen" who disdained work, starved.

Smith's stark discipline carried Jamestown through the Starving Time, but the colony's continued survival, let alone any hope of its eventual prosperity, depended on friendship with the Powhatans. Trouble was, the Englishmen were far from cordial. Determined to intimidate Chief Powhatan and his people into sharing more of their food and crops, a leading settler, Captain Samuel Argall, abducted Pocahontas in 1613 and held her hostage. For her part, Pocahontas was more fascinated than frightened by the English. She rapidly learned their language and was soon functioning more as an ambassador than a prisoner. In 1614, she secured the blessing of her father to marry the tobacco planter John Rolfe. It was a union that brought eight desperately needed years of peace, a period that saw the arrival of more colonists from England. Jamestown and all southern Virginia took root.

While Captain Smith was concerned to maintain good relations with the Indians, the leading men of the colony were eager to curry favor with the royal court and others back in England. Accordingly, Rolfe carried his bride back to the mother country, where she became a great favorite with London society as well as the court of King James I. Tragically, twenty-two-year-old Pocahontas contracted a fatal ailment abroad, to which she succumbed on March 21, 1617.

Nevertheless, the combination of the Powhatans' charity and the favorable impression Pocahontas made in England garnered much political and economic interest in the colonial venture. Jamestown did begin to flourish, its economy driven by a highly successful cash export, tobacco, which the Indians taught the settlers to plant. As all Europe rapidly developed the tobacco habit, the prospect of growing rich from the cultivation of the weed attracted a steady stream of settlers to the colony.

While the wealthy became even wealthier as planters, the "poor" settlers worked off their indenture obligations and were given ownership of their land. At first, there were enough indentured servants to grow and harvest tobacco for the plantation owners. But as more and more indentured servants worked off their obligations, the planters became desperate for new sources of labor. As early as 1619, a few began buying laborers from Dutch traders, whose merchandise of choice were human beings "imported" from Africa.

The First African Slaves Are Sold
in America (1619)

Racism ruled European hearts and minds even at the height of the high-minded Renaissance and the start of the Enlightenment. In 1492, Columbus wrote to his patrons Queen Isabella and King Ferdinand that the meek natives of the Caribbean would make excellent slaves for the Spanish Empire. Although the royal pair demurred when it came to casually enslaving Native Americans, Columbus and the conquistadors who followed him nevertheless usurped native land, looted native property, and, for all intents and purposes, did make slaves of the Indians. As for the English settlers who came later, the land grabbing and the looting were on a smaller scale, but war with Indians became common. As for slave labor, the English preferred another source.

Some dozen years after the founding of Jamestown, Virginia tobacco growers began trading with Dutch merchants for a new import: African slaves. The Dutch were actually new to the slave trade. In 1562, John Hawkins, a gentleman mariner, scion of a prominent family of Plymouth in Devon, England, commenced what he called the "traffick in men" by opening regular slave trading between Guinea on the western coast of Africa and the West Indies off the American mainland. This was the foundation of a system that came to be called the Triangular Trade, by which slaves were carried from western Africa to the Americas, which used their labor to cultivate tobacco. Soon, sugar, cotton, and indigo dyestuffs were added; all were very profitably exported to Europe. The Europeans sent such manufactured goods as textiles and rum to Africa and used the profits to buy African slaves for sale in the Americas. (A variation on the Triangular Trade shipped slaves from Africa to the Caribbean, where they labored on sugar plantations. The sugar was exported to New England, which used it to make rum, which—along with other trade goods—was sent to Africa for the purchase of more slaves.)

Slavery became so central to the Southern economy and way of life that the region broke away from the Union to preserve what Southerners called their "peculiar institution" and even featured an engraving of slaves on the $100 1862 Confederate banknote. More than 670,000 of these notes were issued. WIKIMEDIA COMMONS

The Triangular Trade became the basis of the early American colonial economy. By the beginning of the seventeenth century, the Dutch and the French were in the business as well. By the time Jamestown made its first purchase of twenty slaves from Dutch traders, the Spanish and Portuguese were already holding over a million enslaved blacks in the colonies they had established in the Caribbean and South America.

The Jamestown settlers either paid their own passage to America, if they had wealth, or purchased passage by indenturing themselves to seven years' labor in Virginia. After those seven years were up, the indentured servants either established themselves on their own farms or demanded wages to continue working for the former holders of their indentures. This created a labor crisis in the colony and motivated the purchase of slaves. Slaveowners owned their slaves in perpetuity. Death offered no liberation, since the owner was entitled to any children his slaves bore. Perpetuity truly was forever.

Slavery took a while to become fully established in America. The purchase price of human property was too dear for most early planters. But for those who could pony up a small fortune, the investment in eternity was a bargain. As the slave trade multiplied and the American colonies became increasingly populated, including by American-born slaves, the price of slaves imported from Africa steadily declined. With the lower prices and the continued development of the colonies, demand for slaves rose—but so did domestic supply.

South Carolina, which began in 1665 as the Carolina Colony, led the other American colonies in making slavery absolutely essential to its economy. By the 1730s, its most important cash crop was rice, with large plantations spreading over the tidal and inland swamps of the Low Country along and adjacent to the coast. Inland from these wetlands, in conditions less congenial to rice, indigo—a versatile dyestuff—thrived. The colonists grew accustomed to thinking of their slaves as property, not people. The swampland climate in which they worked was rife with disease, especially mosquito-borne malaria. Slaves were fed as cheaply as possible, so malnutrition often added to the assaults on their health. By the mid-eighteenth century, slaves were becoming so cheap that many planters worked them to exhaustion and early death. It was cheaper to purchase new human property than to invest cash and conscience in looking after those they already owned.

South Carolina law was wholly on the side of the slaveowners. Draconian slave codes gave masters license to treat their property as they saw fit. The slaves had no recourse. Many plantation owners lived in genteel but exciting Charleston rather than in a plantation house stuck in the middle of a dull and noxious swamp. They entrusted day-to-day operations to an overseer, whose allegiance was to the bottom line. The overseer's continued employment and the magnitude of his compensation were determined by the quantity of the harvests, not by decent treatment of plantation labor. The brutality of overseers soon became proverbial.

By the middle of the eighteenth century, despite high mortality rates, the black slave population outnumbered the white population of South Carolina. This fact began to prey on white minds in this colony and wherever else slaves were numerous. The possibility of a violent slave uprising began to loom large in the Southern imagination.

But the South was not the only region where livelihoods depended on slavery. New England would, in the nineteenth century, become a center of anti-slavery activism, but, in the seventeenth and eighteenth centuries, the region's shipping industry thrived on the importation of slaves. Moreover, as an anchor of the Triangular Trade, New England not only benefited from the shipping business but also from the exportation of the rum the region distilled. Nor was the marketing of the slaves themselves confined to the South. Bustling slave markets were found in New England as well as in New York and other Atlantic port towns all across the northern Atlantic seaboard.

Because plantation agriculture was so labor-intensive yet so profitable, especially in international trade, slavery flourished as an economic system. The wealthiest Southern planters were richer than the wealthiest Northern industrialists through the first half of the nineteenth century. True, there was little trickledown of wealth to the mass of the Southern white population, but the planters were nevertheless looked upon as benevolent despots. Except for terrible thoughts of slave revolt, Southern society was orderly and settled. A system of strict racial control developed, designed to institutionalize racial inequality and segregation. This suppressed most individual moral qualms, especially as the export revenues kept rolling in. While an abolition movement developed in the North, based on moral and religious motives, American politicians favored regional compromise—at least until the vast western frontier of the United States began to yield to settlement. This opening of the frontier created opportunity for many poor white Southerners, who readily relinquished their regional allegiance. Amid Western expansion and the rise of the Industrial Revolution, slavery became less and less an indispensable aspect of the nation's economic life and more an exclusively Southern phenomenon. Southerners themselves began to call it the "peculiar institution," and it was indeed increasingly perceived as "peculiar" to a single region. As economic imperatives in favor of slavery shrank during the nineteenth century, the moral imperatives opposing it grew. Conflict became inevitable, and the nation tore itself apart in a civil war.

The *Mayflower* Arrives (1620)

Every American has heard about "the Pilgrims" who arrived in America aboard "the *Mayflower*." Beyond this, few, if asked, can explain just who they were and why their arrival matters.

The English Protestants who became known as Pilgrims were a sect within another sect, the Separatists, who were themselves a splinter group of the Puritans. On November 10, 1517 (October 31, by the "Old Style" calendar in use at the time), the German monk and theologian Martin Luther published *Ninety-five Theses*, a document that began the great schism in European Christianity known as the Protestant Reformation. In 1534, England's King Henry VIII, failing to persuade the Pope to annul his marriage to Catherine of Aragon, separated the Church of England from the Catholic Church. Within a few years, reformers who became known as Puritans—because they sought to "purify" the Anglican Church—rejected much of the ceremony of the Church of England as tainted by Roman Catholicism. Some Puritans, the so-called Separatists, gave up on the cause of reform altogether and simply broke with the Church of England. The most extreme of these Separatists suffered persecution in England and either went underground or fled the country. These were the Pilgrims.

A small band of Pilgrims from the village of Scrooby in Nottinghamshire voyaged across the English Channel and found a home in Leyden, Holland, a country celebrated for its religious tolerance. There they were no longer persecuted, but these Pilgrims felt themselves to be strangers in a strange land. They missed the sound of the English language, and while they had a deep grievance against the Anglican Church, they loved England. They feared that raising their children in Holland would soon erase a heritage they held second only to their religion. The only alternative, they decided, was to seek absolute autonomy by establishing their own colony in America, where they could live as subjects of English monarchs, yet separately from the corrupt tyranny imposed by the Church of England.

Most of the Pilgrims were yeoman farmers and tradespeople. They were neither rich nor powerful. To gain passage to the New World, they had to strike a frugal deal with London merchants to split the cost of a voyage to royal lands in New England. The compromise they made was to take with them a number of non-Pilgrims—indeed, faithful members of the Church of England. Whereas the Pilgrims sought to establish a righteous kingdom of God in America, their fellow travelers, whom they called "Strangers," wanted nothing more than economic opportunity—a chance to prosper in their own land.

Unsurprisingly, the voyage on the small ship *Mayflower*, with Christopher Jones as quarter-owner and captain, was roiled with dispute. The Company of Merchant Adventurers, from which the Pilgrims secured passage, had given them permission to establish a settlement in the Virginia colony. In tempestuous seas, however, Captain Jones veered northward from the upper limit of the colony. Some say that he did this simply because the weather prevented his sailing south to Virginia (which then extended to the present-day southern border of Pennsylvania). Others believe that the Pilgrims and Strangers were at each other's throats so that mutiny was imminent. Eager to eject his troublesome passengers, Jones landed via the nearest available harbor. Yet another theory is that the Pilgrims bribed Jones to deposit them in a place where they would be free from the authority of the Merchant Adventurers—free, that is, to govern themselves.

Land—today's Cape Cod—was sighted on November 9, and while the *Mayflower* briefly turned south, it ended up returning to Cape Cod, anchoring in present-day Provincetown Harbor. The "Strangers," realizing that they would soon be left outside of the Company's jurisdiction, were alarmed. For their part, the Pilgrims were none too happy living among some fifty "Strangers." So, as the vessel rode at anchor, the two groups sat down and drew up an outline of a self-government they could agree on. They called what they created a "Civil Body Politic," and they promised to abide by the few laws they set down for the common good of the colony. This "Mayflower Compact" was the first constitution written in North America. It established three things: First, this settlement would be a community of law. Second, although the Pilgrims wanted to create a holy place, the Strangers were not to be coerced into any religious belief or doctrine. Third, the Mayflower Compact foreshadowed the political nature of the United States itself, which would be created around its own "compact," the Constitution. At the heart of the Pilgrims' settlement was the same thing that is at the heart of the United States to this day: a firmly stated and agreed-upon *idea* of order.

Tisquantum—Squanto—Saves the Pilgrims (1621)

Whether due to bad weather and rough seas, or Captain Christopher Jones's great eagerness to eject his apparently mutinous passengers from the *Mayflower*, or a Pilgrim bribe to the good captain, or a providential act of the Lord, Pilgrim and Stranger—religious zealots and those just looking to make a living—came ashore together at present-day Provincetown, Massachusetts, in November 1620. They would later settle at a place they named Plymouth, after the English port from which they had sailed.

While still riding at anchor off Provincetown, the Pilgrims and Strangers made one extraordinary preparation for living together. They drew up the Mayflower Compact, the first Constitution in the New World, designed to protect their common rights and responsibilities.

The document showed great wisdom and foresight, but these, it turned out, were not enough. The arrival of the *Mayflower* in late fall had been ill-timed. It was far too late to plant, and these voyagers, to whom the abrasive weather of Old England was long familiar, were about to discover how much harsher was New England's. A resupply ship was not due until the spring of the following year, 1621, and between November 1620 and spring of the next, lack of adequate shelter, semi-starvation, and a variety of diseases—the most prevalent being scurvy, a painful wasting disease caused by lack of vitamin C—took a horrific toll. Of the 102 *Mayflower* passengers who landed, 45 were buried on Cole's Hill before that first winter was done.

No wonder the Pilgrims viewed as a blessing from God in the spring of 1621 the appearance of Tisquantum, whom they called Squanto. He was a member of the Patuxet tribe and was, with an Abenaki sagamore (chief) named Samoset, among the first Native Americans who made meaningful contact with the Pilgrims and Strangers. Squanto, who spoke fluent English, took the lead in helping the new arrivals plant winter crops and build serviceable, if rude, winter shelters.

Born about 1580 near Plymouth, Squanto is believed to have been abducted in 1605 along the Maine coast by Captain George Weymouth. The captain was sailing on a commission from the owner of the Plymouth Company, Sir Ferdinando Gorges, to explore the coasts of both Maine and Massachusetts. His motive for abducting Squanto—along with four Penobscot Indians—was to obtain Native American specimens to bring back to England for the amusement and edification of Gorges's investors. Squanto and the other four Indians were given reasonably comfortable accommodations on the voyage to England, and from 1605 to 1614, Squanto lived with Gorges, who taught him English, grooming him as an interpreter and guide.

Squanto returned to Massachusetts in 1614 with Captain John Smith, for whom he may have served as a guide. Unfortunately, he was again captured, this time by the English explorer Thomas Hunt. He was sent back to Europe not in comfort, but in chains, to be sold on the Spanish slave market. He managed to escape, however, and found refuge with monks, among whom he lived for several years until he took passage yet again for America in 1619. On his arrival home, he was devastated to discover that his native tribe, the Patuxet, was no more—dead to the very last person, except for himself. All had fallen victim to smallpox. Introduced into the population by the English, the disease was almost invariably lethal among populations who had absolutely no resistance to it. Now without house or homeland, Squanto went to live with the nearby and generous Wampanoags.

The winter of 1620–1621 nearly halved the *Mayflower* immigrants. Squanto and Samoset showed them what to do to prepare for the next winter. Squanto demonstrated the Indian method of planting, which used rotting fish—abundant in this seaboard region—as fertilizer. The method succeeded in squeezing crops even out of the stony and parsimonious soil of New England. Squanto educated the *Mayflower* settlers in the construction of weathertight shelters, to be used until more ambitious buildings were constructed. In all this, he may have felt duty-bound to pay forward to the English the life-saving kindness the Wampanoags had shown him. Indeed, the Pilgrims judged his intervention as the benevolent presence of the hand of God. Subsequent generations of American historical popularizers have portrayed Squanto's "charity" as either the act of a rustic "natural" Christian or as proof that even a "savage" can model the best of civilized behavior.

For some three hundred years, Euro-Americans have worked infinite variations on the theme of the Noble Savage. Yet, by the time he encountered the Pilgrims, Squanto of Massachusetts had already proved himself to be, like Pocahontas of Virginia, a wily survivor and a brilliant ambassador. He served the Wampanoag chief Massasoit as an interpreter of and negotiator with the newcomers. His brief from the chief was to establish profitable relations with these people who, poor and miserable as they might now appear, had been sufficiently skilled and daring to journey to America and begin to scrape out a settlement from the soil. Soon, their homeland across the sea would send them goods to trade, including tools and weapons. Massasoit wanted to put himself and his people ahead of competitors for the English settlers' commerce and, perhaps, even a military alliance.

Thanksgiving became an official national holiday by proclamation of President Abraham Lincoln on the final Thursday of November 1863. Most Americans, however, think of it as a tradition first celebrated by the Pilgrims and their Indian "friends" to give thanks for the harvest Squanto had made possible. Its abundance that autumn of 1621 was a joy, especially after the deadly dearth of the previous year. It boded a far more merciful winter. The Pilgrims and Wampanoags accordingly celebrated jointly with a feast, which Squanto, for his part, must have regarded as a triumph of statesmanship. Nevertheless, he was no impersonal statesman. In 1622, he earned the deeply personal gratitude of the Pilgrims when he helped them find a missing child, and, once again, he lent both his hand and his expertise in more planting and fishing.

Yet Squanto was also interested in establishing himself as a powerful figure in this new hybrid society of white and Indian. His fluency in English was a great asset, as was his intimate knowledge of English ways and manners. Among his Native American associates, he did not scruple to grossly exaggerate the influence he wielded over the English. On one occasion, he threatened that if he did not get his way from local chiefs, he would direct the English to unleash the plague—smallpox, presumably—which, he said, they stored in a pit.

With the passage of time, more Pilgrims immigrated to what was now called Plymouth Plantation. Accompanying them was a new breed of Strangers. They were called Particulars, because they did not belong to the joint-stock company, instead financing their own voyage. Like the earlier Strangers, they were neither Pilgrims nor even especially religious. Their chief interests were commercial. The towns that rose in and around Plymouth, Massachusetts, were not exclusively Pilgrim, but each did have at least one radical Puritan church congregation, independent of all the others, which exercised an outsized influence over both the religious and secular lives of all townspeople. Still, unlike the Puritans who founded the Massachusetts Bay Colony in 1628, they did not bar the unconverted from playing a role in the colony's secular affairs. True to the Mayflower Compact, the Pilgrims fostered a settlement of broad enfranchisement, which encompassed Strangers and Particulars as well as people like themselves. Doubtless acting out of a variety of motives, Squanto was instrumental in the survival of this theologically strict yet politically tolerant settlement, and he thereby fostered a liberal tradition that would become the most distinctive theme in the American story. Squanto himself did not live to see the growth of this tradition. While serving as a personal guide to Plymouth's governor and early historian, William Bradford, he succumbed to a fever in November 1622.

A Massachusetts Settler Kills an Indian, Touching Off King Philip's War (1675)

Chief Massasoit of the Wampanoags, ally of the Plymouth colonists, died in 1661 at the age of eighty-one. His son Wamsutta, whom the English called Alexander, succeeded him as the Wampanoag sachem and continued friendly relations. However, under his leadership, Wampanoag loyalties became divided between two competing English colonies, Plymouth and Rhode Island. Plymouth militia major (later governor) Josiah Winslow arrested Alexander and took him to Duxbury to answer conspiracy charges, demanding that he prove his loyalty to Plymouth by selling certain lands to that colony instead of to Rhode Island. While a prisoner, Alexander fell ill and died. His twenty-four-year-old brother, Metacom or Metacomet, whom the English called King Philip, succeeded him as sachem. Philip believed that Winslow had poisoned his brother. Well, who knows? What is certain is that relations between Plymouth and King Philip had indeed been poisoned.

Early in 1671, outraged by an encroachment upon his land, Philip staged a threatening show of arms. He was summoned on April 10, 1671, to Taunton, seat of Plymouth's government and, under threat, signed the "Taunton Agreement," which compelled him to collect and surrender his people's arms. At the end of September, having failed to disarm his tribe, Philip was brought to trial. Fined £100, he was further humiliated by a requirement that, henceforth, he obtain colonial permission before buying or selling land or waging war against other tribes. Stoically, he accepted the verdict, but for the next three years he secretly forged anti-English alliances with the Nipmucks and the Narragansetts.

In January 1675, John Sassamon (or Saussaman) a so-called Praying Indian—a Christianized Native American—who had been Philip's private secretary, tipped off colonial authorities to the sachem's plotting.

This engraving of a Wampanoag raid on settlers during King Philip's War was created for an 1886 book commemorating the 250th anniversary of the Providence Plantations, forerunner of the state of Rhode Island. WIKIMEDIA COMMONS

Before the end of the month, Sassamon's body was found on the ice of a frozen pond. Philip was immediately charged with conspiracy to murder, but he won release for lack of evidence.

Months passed. On June 11, three days after other Indians were executed for Sassamon's murder, word reached the English that Wampanoags were arming near Swansea and Plymouth Town, which were adjacent to Wampanoag territory. Instances of cattle killing and looting began to be reported, and panicky settlers started fleeing some towns, including Swansea. As Indians freely appropriated the abandoned property, one angry settler shot and killed a "looter."

The incident hardly seemed a turning point in the still-young history of Anglo-America, but what resulted from it, King Philip's War, was a catastrophe for New England's colonists and Native Americans alike. Between 1675 and 1676, half of the region's towns were mauled and a dozen utterly destroyed, requiring the work of a generation to rebuild them. The fragile colonial economy suffered devastating blows, due both to the direct cost of the war—some £100,000—and to the disruption of the fur trade with the Indians and the virtual cessation of coastal fishing and the West Indies trade. Not only did the war siphon off the manpower customarily devoted to these industries, many men never returned to their peacetime occupations, as one in sixteen male colonists of military age died. Many others—men, women, children—were also killed, captured, or starved. In proportion to New England's population of 30,000, King Philip's War was the costliest conflict in American history. As for the Indians, at least 3,000 perished, and many of those who did not die were deported and sold into slavery.

The early English colonies were more rivals than allies. Only grudgingly did Massachusetts Bay, Plymouth, and Rhode Island raise a joint army, which mustered during June 21–23, 1675, at Miles's Garrison just opposite Philip's stronghold at Mount Hope Neck, Rhode Island. By the time the force was assembled, Wampanoags had raided Swansea and other towns in Massachusetts and Rhode Island. Connecticut joined in the war effort on July 1, even as Philip was negotiating an alliance of his own, with Weetamoo, the "squaw-sachem" of the Pocaset tribe. In Rhode Island, the headstrong militia captain Benjamin Church led twenty men in pursuit of Philip. In a place known to history only as Captain Almy's "pease field," he and his party were set upon by three hundred Indians. Church and his band fought desperately for six hours, until they were evacuated by an English river sloop.

The war escalated quickly so that by mid-July, much of New England was awash in blood, as Wampanoags were joined by Narragansetts and Nipmucks. Discouraged by the militia's performance against the Indians in hand-to-hand combat, colonial leaders broke off pursuit of Philip and built a fort to besiege him. This strategic blunder prolonged the war. While the English were busy building the fort, Philip escaped from the Pocasset swamp on July 29 and made for Nipmuck country to the northeast so that, by the end of August, fighting had spread into the upper Connecticut Valley, the Merrimac Valley, New Hampshire, and Maine. Philip led raid after bloody raid. Repeated attempts at negotiating peace or even a truce failed. Worse, formerly friendly Indians now turned on the colonists.

By late autumn 1675, the Narragansett tribe concluded a new treaty in Boston. Despite this, on November 2, Connecticut's colonial council decided to make a peremptory strike against the Narragansetts. Plymouth and Massachusetts joined in, and the army of the United Colonies—as this band of one thousand called itself—assembled at Wickford, Rhode Island, under the command of Plymouth governor Josiah Winslow. On December 18, they marched to battle in a frigid snowstorm, aiming to capture the stronghold of the Narragansett sachem Canonchet in a frozen swamp at Kingston, Rhode Island. In fierce combat on December 19, eighty of Winslow's army fell, and about six hundred Narragansetts— half of them women and children—died. Over the protests of a badly wounded Benjamin Church, who pointed out that the battered English would need the shelter of the Indians' wigwams for the bitter winter night, the colonials put the encampment to the torch and then withdrew instead of pursuing the surviving Narragansetts, who escaped to Nipmuck country and lived to fight another day.

The "Great Swamp Fight" inflicted heavy losses on the Narragansetts but also served to strengthen desperate anti-English alliances among the Wampanoags, Nipmucks, and Narragansetts. With the new year, Philip attempted to extend his alliances beyond New England, taking many of his people to Mohawk country near Albany, New York, in search of ammunition and provisions in addition to friends. New York governor Edmund Andros persuaded the Mohawks not only to spurn the alliance but also to attack Philip, who fled back to New England. Andros succeeded in blocking a grand Indian confederacy, but the New England forces were too exhausted to press the fight to a finish. The Indians rallied and renewed their offensive, raiding many settlements in Massachusetts, Rhode Island, and Connecticut. The early spring of 1676 marked the low point of the colonists' fortunes. The English footprint in New England contracted, despite emergency laws forbidding the evacuation of towns. Outlying settlements around Boston lay abandoned.

By late spring of 1676, colonial forces began to take the offensive. In western Massachusetts, Captain William Turner, leading a force of 150 mounted men, attacked an Indian encampment at the Falls of the Connecticut River above Deerfield, Massachusetts, on May 19. It was not so much a battle as it was a massacre: the soldiers poked their muskets into the wigwams and shot the Indians—including many women and children—as they slept. Although the Indians were routed, Turner failed to pursue, and the surviving warriors turned a retreat into a counterattack, killing about forty men, Turner among them.

At last, the colonists became increasingly aggressive. Responding to reports of "hostiles" fishing in the Pawtucket River near Rehoboth, Captain Thomas Brattle led a combined force of colonists and their Indian allies in an attack that killed about a dozen of Philip's warriors. On June 2, Connecticut major John Talcott launched a combined Indian-English assault against Philip in western Massachusetts. Early the same month, Benjamin Church was authorized to build a new army on behalf of the United Colonies, using white and Indian soldiers. Still, Philip fought on, launching a massive but unsuccessful assault against Hadley, Massachusetts.

At Nipsachuck, Rhode Island, on July 2, John Talcott dealt the Narragansetts two crushing blows when he attacked a band consisting of 34 men and 137 women and children, killing all the men and 92 of the women and children. On the next day, at Warwick, he slew eighteen men and twenty-two women and children, taking twenty-seven prisoners as well. While Benjamin Church prevailed in skirmishes at Middleborough and Monponsett on July 11 and, a week later, skirmished with Philip's men in and around Taunton, Major William Bradford pursued Philip himself, narrowly failing to run him to ground on July 16.

On July 30, 1676, Church led an army of 200, including 140 friendly Indians, in pursuit of Philip. This mixed force killed Philip's uncle on

July 31 and, the next day, captured the sachem's wife and son. Philip himself escaped, but the demoralization of his warriors had become too much to bear. In August, a deserter from Philip's camp approached Church, offering to lead him and his men to the sachem. Church deployed his men around the camp after midnight on August 12 and moved in at first light.

Philip took to his feet, just as an English soldier fired—and missed. The marksmanship of an English-allied Indian called Alderman was better. Benjamin Church ordered the slain sachem's body butchered, awarding the head and one hand to Alderman. The remainder of the corpse was quartered and hung on four trees, customary practice in an execution for treason.

With King Philip's death, the war named for him came to a quick end. In its aftermath, many Native Americans professed abject submission to the English. Others, however, fled to Canada, New York, and the Delaware and Susquehanna valleys, where they meditated a revenge that exploded in a long series of raids and guerilla actions culminating in the French and Indian War. The North American theater of the Seven Years' War of 1756 to 1763, it was a vast conflict many scholars describe as history's "real" first world war.

Salem Tries Its People
for Witchcraft (1692)

The winter of 1691–1692 was a typical New England winter, bitter and life-threatening. Heaped upon that misery was the death of friendly relations between colonists and Native Americans—destroyed by King Philip's War in 1675–1676 and replaced by mutual resentment, fear, and menace. Oppressed by hardship and anxiety, the people of the predominantly Puritan settlement of Salem, Massachusetts, clung close to their Church for comfort and guidance. It was critical that this imperiled frontier community remain godly and pure. And that is why Salem Village minister Samuel Parris was terrified by what was happening to his daughter and his niece.

Elizabeth Parris and Abigail Williams had taken up fortune-telling. It was, of course, the devil's work, and that was bad enough. But soon after they had fallen into this filthy habit, the pair fell ill, convulsing, spewing streams of demonic speech, and assuming obscene contortions of body. Reverend Parris resorted to prayer, confident that this would cure them. When it did not, he summoned physician William Griggs. The doctor quickly confirmed the pastor's worst fears. The girls suffered from no physical ailment. Rather, they were in the grip of the "Evil Hand," victims of witchcraft.

Parris called on the village elders, who subjected the girls to relentless questioning—not concerning their own condition but about who had cast the spell upon them. They demanded that Elizabeth and Abigail identify the witches. And when they began naming names, the Salem authorities commenced judicial proceedings on February 29, 1692, against the accused.

It proved but the first droplets in a torrent of accusations. The Salem witch trials, which spanned February 1692 to May 1693, remain

This nineteenth-century engraving depicts the trial of a Salem, Massachusetts, woman accused of witchcraft. One of her young victims appears to writhe under her spell. WIKIMEDIA COMMONS

to this day a subject of American fascination, history, popular lore, and debate. But neither the witchcraft outbreak nor the trials were unique to Salem. Prior to 1692, more than seventy witchcraft cases had been tried elsewhere in New England, resulting in eighteen convictions. In Old England and throughout Europe during the seventeenth century—and before—accusations of witchcraft were common. Some resulted in trial and punishment, including torture and execution. Modern analysis of the best-documented cases demonstrates that the typical accused witch was a poor, elderly woman with neither means nor property. Occasionally, similarly marginalized men were also accused. Beyond low-economic status, the suspected witches were almost always social pariahs, people described by their neighbors as disagreeable and quarrelsome. Usually, they were quite isolated, with neither friends nor family. In effect, "witches" were members of a persecuted minority.

Salem *was* hardly alone in accusing people of witchcraft, but it was unique in the sheer volume of accusations. In 1692 alone, more than 140 people were accused, 107 of them women—and this out of a village of 600 residents. Moreover, not all of the accused fit the social stereotype that prevailed elsewhere. Some were prominent men of property and their wives. Tellingly, as the trials progressed, the most vulnerable to accusation were those who raised voices in protest against the Reverend Parris's zeal on behalf of the prosecution. He and some seventy other Salem residents, almost all of them members of his congregation, bore witness to corroborate the testimony of those either diagnosed as victims of witchcraft or who complained of being possessed.

Quite quickly, the Salem crisis drew the attention of the new royal governor of Massachusetts, Sir William Phipps. Not content to leave in village hands what had become a grave judicial issue, Phipps established a special Court of Oyer and Terminer to try the cases. The new court's first session convened in June, with more than seventy cases on its docket. During that summer and into the fall, fifty of the accused pleaded guilty to practicing witchcraft. Of the rest, who maintained their innocence, twenty-six were tried and convicted and nineteen executed. Most controversial in the proceedings was reliance on what was called "spectral evidence"—evidence that, by definition, was invisible and intangible. It "existed" solely in the claims of witnesses who complained of being tormented by the accused. Spectral evidence could be neither objectively corroborated nor objectively demonstrated.

Spectral evidence satisfied most Puritan clerics, but it did not sit well with Governor Phipps. Nor did the sheer volume of convictions. He dissolved the Court of Oyer and Terminer in the fall and turned over the remaining cases to the permanently established Superior Court of Judicature. From October through the end of the year, this court heard fifty cases, binding over for trial twenty-one defendants, of whom just three were convicted. And even these convictions were overturned the following year. As for defendants whose cases were still pending at the beginning of 1693, Phipps issued unconditional pardons. Then he went further, declaring in concert with the Superior Court that witchcraft was henceforth not to be regarded as a criminal offense. With this, the Salem witchcraft trials were permanently at an end.

The trials were over—but their grip on the American consciousness has never been entirely loosed. In modern Salem, witchcraft has long driven a modest tourist industry, but it was in 1953 that the left-leaning playwright Arthur Miller put his finger on the turning-point significance of the Salem trials. He used them as the plot of his now-classic Broadway play, *The Crucible*, a compelling allegory that condemned the anti-Communist "witch hunting" of the House Un-American Activities Committee (HUAC) and, in the Senate, that of Joseph McCarthy. Why did these 261-year-old events work so compellingly against injustice in a modern nation professing dedication to freedom of speech and dissent? Precisely because the play showed that social and political hysteria, mob mentality, and tribal prejudice were never far below the surface of American civilization, despite high-minded laws and noble aspirations. In 1692–1693, there was a turn toward irrationality followed by a turn back toward rational enlightenment and reverence for law. The American history that leads from the trials is a road of sharp turnings away from law, justice, and humanity followed by just as many curves back toward liberal democracy.

Young George Washington Ignites the French and Indian War (1754)

By the early eighteenth century, America was a frequent European battleground. King William's War (1689–1697) ended the seventeenth century, and Queen Anne's War (1702–1713) began the eighteenth. King George's War (1744–1748) came next. All three were North American aspects of European conflicts, chiefly involving the English and French. Native Americans participated in them as well as in numerous smaller wars in between these major conflicts. The treaty of Aix-la-Chapelle ended King George's War on October 18, 1748, bringing a fleeting peace to the American frontier. Then, on March 16, 1749, England's King George II granted vast western tracts to the Ohio Company, a powerful syndicate of British traders and speculators. This reignited conflict with both the French and several Indian tribes, who believed that the new royal charter meant invasion of their lands.

Their fears were entirely justified, as an influx of British traders flooded territories that had been the exclusive trading province of the French. In response, the governor of New France, Jacques-Pierre de Jonquière, marquis de La Jonquière, built new forts and strengthened old ones. In 1752, the English negotiated the Treaty of Logstown with the six Iroquois tribes and the Delaware, Shawnee, and Wyandot, by which these Native Americans gave the English rights to all of the vast Ohio country in exchange for trading privileges and for defense against the French. At this point, the western frontier was already a packed powder keg boding a new war between France and England. The Logstown Treaty put a match to that powder. A new French governor, the Marquis Duquesne, hurriedly built a string of forts up and down the Ohio country, and the English-allied Indians were thoroughly intimidated. Thus, with a major war looming, the English lost most of their Native American military assets.

In August 1753, even as England's Indian alliances were falling apart, Lord Halifax, from the safety of London, urged the king to declare war against France. In preparation, Cabinet and crown authorized Virginia lieutenant governor Robert Dinwiddie to evict the French from territory under his jurisdiction. Dinwiddie commissioned twenty-one-year-old George Washington to carry an ultimatum to Captain Jacques Legardeur de Saint-Pierre, commandant of Fort LeBoeuf (at present-day Waterford, Pennsylvania). Washington, with a small delegation, set out from Williamsburg on October 31, 1753, and did not reach Fort LeBoeuf until December 12, 1753. He delivered the eviction notice, only to be politely rebuffed by Captain Legardeur. Governor Dinwiddie responded by ordering militia captain William Trent to build a fort at the forks of the Ohio (site of present-day Pittsburgh). On April 17, 1754, a superior French force seized the newly completed fort. On this very day, Dinwiddie sent George Washington with 150 militiamen to reinforce a position that, unknown to both Dinwiddie and Washington, the English no longer held.

While on the westward march, Washington received news of the fort's surrender. He decided nevertheless to continue his advance and engage the French. On May 28, having sighted a thirty-three-man French reconnaissance party, he led forty of his militiamen and a dozen Indian warriors against them. His intention was to deliver a violently forceful message that the French were not welcome in the Ohio country.

Unaware of Washington's presence, the French encamped in what Washington described as a "bower." He led his forces to within 100 yards of the French position. He then looked to his right and to his left. Satisfying himself that all men and weapons were in place and ready, he rose to his full height, drew his sword, stepped into a clearing, and gave the command to advance. At about fifty yards from the bower, he gave the command to fire.

Those among the French who were loitering outside the cover of the bower ran back to fetch their muskets. The two sides exchanged fire, and men began to fall. At fifty yards, a three-quarter-inch-diameter one-ounce ball had more than sufficient muzzle velocity to tear a large hole in a man. The entrance wound was little larger than the diameter of the ball. The exit might have been three or four inches across.

Amid the falling men, Washington felt mounting exhilaration. He later wrote to his brother, John Augustine Washington, "I fortunately escaped without a wound, tho' the right Wing where I stood was exposed to & received all the Enemy's fire and was the part where the man was killed & the rest wounded. I can with truth assure you, I heard Bulletts whistle and believe me there was something charming in the sound."

Washington pressed the attack, and the French began to give ground. Some broke and ran, only to be summoned back by their commander. They returned, meekly, hands in the air. A casual observer might have marveled at their obedience, but Washington understood that the men had seen his Seneca Iroquois allies. It was far preferable to surrender to the Virginians than to run into the arms of Indian warriors. Washington let the Seneca have their way with the wounded, whom they summarily scalped. Washington wanted his allies to satisfy what he saw as their natural bloodlust. Besides, he had no desire to be burdened with the care of the enemy's wounded. He did draw the line, however, at the Indians' demand for similar vengeance against the twenty-one unhurt prisoners of war.

Of the thirty-three French engaged in the battle, twenty-one survived unwounded to be taken prisoner; one wounded man, somehow overlooked, escaped death at the hands of the Indians; and another soldier, a man named Mouceau, escaped altogether and returned to Fort Duquesne, as the French called the outpost they had earlier captured from the English. There he told the tale of the fight.

This was George Washington's maiden battle. In itself, it was a skirmish. For Washington, it was a personal turning point. But for the history of North America, it was a major inflection point. Among the slain was the commander of the French force, Joseph Coulon, Sieur de Jumonville, whom the French claimed was an ambassador on a peaceful mission. His death was sufficient reason to go to war—and, so, historians consider this fifteen-minute exchange of fire the first battle of the French and Indian War.

Spanning 1754 to 1763, it was the American theater of the Seven Years' War (1756–1763) and thus involved the American colonies in a global struggle between the British and the French for greater empire. At stake in North America was control of a vast continent. Unforeseen at the outbreak of the war was the manner in which the conflict would also shape alliances and enmities between the Native Americans and the Euro-Americans and would create a political, cultural, and military environment in which the seeds of yet another war were sown—a colonial rebellion in 1775–1783, which wrested from England independence for a United States of America.

The Boston Massacre Is Followed by a Trial (1770)

Boston was not a happy place in 1770. Economically, the city was especially hard-hit by a depression sweeping Britain's colonies. Politically, restless Boston felt sorely oppressed. The first misery was evidenced by widespread joblessness, the second by the despised presence of British soldiers, the Redcoats.

The British soldiers' lot was no better and almost certainly worse than that of working-class Boston civilians. Mercilessly flogged for the least infraction—Bostonians often called them Lobsterbacks—they were paid a starvation wage. So, it was not unusual that, on a blustery March 5, 1770, an off-duty soldier appeared at Grey's ropewalk, a wharfside maker of ship's ropes, looking for a part-time job. He was not alone. Ragged Boston men sought wages as well, and the presence of one of His Majesty's Lobsterbacks competing for work rightfully theirs was sufficient to touch off a small-scale riot.

The melee swelled but soon subsided; the mob, however, never went home. The men roamed the streets, more joining them as they walked. By nine that evening, about sixty were seen advancing in the direction of the Customs House, one of the despised centers of British authority. They stopped in front of the building and jostled close to one Hugh White, a Redcoat sentry.

What had sent them to White was word of a fresh outrage against the working people of Boston. Edward Garrick, apprentice to a local wigmaker, had loudly complained to White that his company commander stiffed his master for a wig he had ordered. White responded by beckoning the accuser forward. When Garrick stepped up, White smashed him in the center of his face with the butt of his musket. Hands clasped to

The great American silversmith and patriot Paul Revere created this 1770 engraving as propaganda intended to stir revolutionary outrage over the "Bloody Massacre" in Boston. War, however, did not erupt for another five years.
NATIONAL ARCHIVES AND RECORDS ADMINISTRATION

his bleeding visage, Garrick fled, pursued by another soldier at the point of a bayonet. Thus, a small riot grew large.

The mob began pelting White and other soldiers with hard icy snowballs. As they did so, other Bostonians joined them. British officers arrived but could gain control neither of their men nor of the mob. Fearing that White would be torn to pieces, Captain Thomas Preston quickly mustered seven soldiers and led them to the sentry's rescue. Seeing this, Henry Knox, a local bookseller who would become a general in the Continental army and, later, President George Washington's secretary of war, ran up to Preston.

"For God's sake," he told the captain, "take care of your men. If they fire, they die!"

"I am sensible of it," Preston quietly replied. With that, he turned toward the besieged White and loudly ordered him to fall in with the seven-man detail he led.

White was quick to obey, but the mob suddenly surged to block him. Preston and his men found it impossible to break through the throng. The captain ordered them to fall back and form a defensive line where they stood. This impressed the Bostonians as a fresh outrage. Gathering up more ice balls, they shouted taunts, hurled their cold missiles, and dared the troops to open fire.

Stymied, Preston sent a solider to fetch Justice of the Peace (JP) James Murray. The captain asked the official to read the Riot Act, hoping that hearing a list of the harsh penalties for public disorder would bring the mob to its senses. Instead, the recitation provoked a renewed barrage of ice balls, most now aimed at the JP.

Then came a more serious missile. Someone in the mob hurled a heavy wooden club at the line of soldiers, knocking Private Hugh Montgomery off his feet. With effort, he rose, but he uttered no curse—indeed, no word of any kind. Montgomery silently cocked his musket, leveled it, and fired.

The round went wild. Perhaps Montgomery intended it as a warning only. Perhaps he missed. The shot did, however, goad a merchant named Richard Palmes to lash out at Montgomery with the wooden billet he gripped in his fist. Instinctively, the Redcoat thrust back with his bayonet, sending Palmes into retreat. Seeing this exchange, Private Matthew Killroy took aim at Edward Langford and Samuel Gray. He hesitated.

"God damn you, don't fire!" Gray warned. Whereupon Killroy pulled the trigger. Unlike Palmes, his aim was flawless. A musket ball smashed through Samuel Gray's skull and tore into his brain.

At nearly the same moment, another musket spoke. It was but a single report, but the soldier, apparently jittery, had loaded and rammed two balls. We know this, because history records that two rounds found their mark in the chest of Crispus Attucks, aged forty years, a fugitive slave from Framingham. The twin projectiles killed him where he stood. Gray, the first man hit, died later. But the end came instantly for Attucks, who is therefore remembered as the first man killed in this prelude to revolution.

The death of Crispus Attucks was followed by more musket fire and the deaths of three more Bostonians, two instantly, a third mortally wounded. After this, the stillness was punctuated only by the well-drilled *click* and *click* and *click* of a firing line reloading. Unafraid, the Bostonians surged forward again. In response, the muskets were leveled—again. This time, however, Captain Preston strode along the line, knocking each man's barrel upward.

"Don't fire!" he snapped. "Don't fire."

So ended Act I. Act II began with the arrest and indictment, by a colonial court, of Captain Preston and six of his men. The charge against all was murder. The officer and his soldiers believed they were done for, about to be conveyed into the hands of a mob. And so the local advocates of revolution would have had it. Samuel Adams, leader of the Sons of Liberty, and his friend, Dr. Joseph Warren, furiously fanned the flames of Boston's rage.

That is when two of the city's most admired attorneys, Josiah Quincy and John Adams, stepped forward to provide the accused with a defense. "Council," Adams declared, "ought to be the very last thing an accused person should want [be denied] in a free country."

John Adams was outraged by what was already being called the Boston Massacre, but he wanted the king in London as well as leaders across all Europe to witness how men and women aspiring to become citizens of a free country went about determining guilt and innocence. Give rein to mob justice, John Adams believed, and Americans would, in the eyes of the world, forfeit their moral right to independence.

On behalf of their clients, Adams and Quincy presented pleas of not guilty by reason of self-defense. In a closely watched trial, the two lawyers acquitted themselves with dignified brilliance. For their part, the Boston juries showed themselves to be people of justice. Captain Preston and four of his men were acquitted. Two others were found guilty—though not of murder but of the lesser crime of manslaughter. Their punishment was painful—both were branded on the thumb and summarily discharged from military service—but not lethal. Together, the two acts of the Boston Massacre drama revealed a people on the verge of both revolution and the creation of a free and just nation.

A Minuteman Fires the Shot Heard 'Round the World (1775)

General Thomas Gage, son of the 1st Viscount Gage, grew up on the Sussex estate his family had owned since the fifteenth century. He purchased a lieutenant's commission in the 1st Northampton Regiment in 1741 and began a long career as a British army officer. By the 1750s, he was lieutenant colonel of the 55th Foot Regiment (later renumbered as the 44th) and in 1755 was sent with it to North America, where he fought in the French and Indian War alongside a young Virginian named George Washington, against whom he would later do battle in the American Revolution.

In 1774, Gage was appointed military governor of chronically rebellious Massachusetts. He replaced the unpopular Thomas Hutchinson but was assigned a mission hardly destined to make him more popular. King George III and Parliament directed him to bring the troublesome New England colonials to heel by whatever means were necessary.

On the evening of April 18, 1775, Gage started some seven hundred troops on the march from Boston to Concord, Massachusetts, to secure a known rebel arsenal there. His intention was to preclude the development of an organized *armed* colonial rebellion. Part of his operation, however, involved ordering the arrest of two prominent ringleaders of what seemed no more than an incipient antitax movement. They were John Hancock and Sam Adams. Gage had badly underestimated three things. First, he did not understand that the colonists were not merely objecting to certain taxes. They were moving toward independence. Second, he had no idea of how extensive the network of spies and informants the Sons of Liberty, a pro-independence secret society, had assembled. The Sons quickly learned about the arrest order, and this additionally alerted them to Gage's military operation to disarm Concord. That brings up the third thing Gage did not know. He was aware that informal colonial "militias" had sprung up throughout

Massachusetts, but he did not grasp how numerous and well coordinated they were. He had no idea that they were popularly known as "Minutemen," because they had all agreed to be prepared for action within a minute of receiving the call. The Sons of Liberty dispatched two of their most trusted couriers, Paul Revere (a brilliant local silversmith) and William Dawes (a militiaman specializing in artillery), along with others to alert Hancock and Adams to the arrest order and to summon the Minutemen to arms.

Before dawn on April 19, British grenadiers and light infantrymen disembarked from boats at Lechmere Point on the Cambridge bank of the Charles River. When they were surprised by colonial musket shots, Lieutenant Colonel Francis Smith and Major John Pitcairn sent riders back to Boston to summon reinforcements. In the meantime, some ten miles northwest, in Lexington, militia captain Jonas Parker dressed the ranks of the seventy or so citizen-soldiers who had mustered on the village green, which fronted the road to Concord. Parker's mission was to intercept the Redcoats. History records that one of his men murmured loudly enough to be heard, "So few of us. It is folly to stand here." Parker, it is said, roared back: "The first man who offers to run shall be shot down." Some sources say that he continued, "Stand your ground. Don't fire unless fired upon. But if they want to have a war, let it begin here!"

Maybe Parker said this. Maybe not. In any case, quite a few militiamen, seeing the approach of what looked to be a great scarlet wave, simply walked away. Close enough to note this, Pitcairn shouted to the remaining militiamen, "Lay down your arms, you rebels, and disperse!"

Parker responded by ordering his men to fall out—that is, to depart the green but to take their weapons with them. Seeing this, Pitcairn repeated his command to disarm. Parker said nothing in return, and in the vacuum of command on both sides, someone—it is unknown whether Redcoat or Patriot—fired. More shots followed, and a Redcoat was slightly wounded in the leg. Two balls grazed Pitcairn's horse.

But no one knows which shots were from British and which from American muskets.

Nevertheless, a British officer ordered a volley, which was instantly followed by Pitcairn's order to cease fire and surround the green. For some reason, however, his men fired a second volley.

Those militiamen who had not walked off or run away, returned fire. This sent the Redcoats charging with their bayonets. All but Captain Parker fled. Wounded, he was fumbling to reload when a British bayonet cut him down. He was one of eight Minutemen killed at Lexington. Ten more lay wounded. Except for the British regular hit in the leg, Pitcairn's soldiers suffered no casualties. And so, the Battle of Lexington, first engagement of the American Revolution, ended—in defeat.

The next battle went better for the Patriots.

By the time the British arrived in Concord, about seven miles northwest of Lexington, some four hundred Minutemen, commanded by local resident James Barrett, occupied a ridge overlooking the town. Below, Lieutenant Colonel Smith took no notice of them. He sauntered into a local tavern with his staff officers and bought dinner and drinks while his grenadiers searched house-to-house for hidden arms. Discovering some gun carriages, they set them ablaze.

Seeing this, one of Barrett's officers demanded of his commander, "Will you let them burn the town down?"

Barrett responded by ordering his four hundred men down from the ridge to defend Concord. Seeing their approach, a British light infantry captain formed up his men and opened fire. Most of the shots fell short—though two found targets in Captain Isaac Davis and Private Abner Hosmer, both killed instantly.

According to the most popular account, the first American shots came in response to the command, "Fire, fellow soldier! For God sake, fire!" Years later, in his "Hymn Sung at the Completion of the Concord Monument, April 19, 1836," the philosopher-poet Ralph Waldo Emerson wrote of Concord's "embattled farmers," one of whom fired the "the shot heard round the world."

It was not the first shot of the American Revolution but the first shot of the first revolutionary battle in which the Americans prevailed. For the Patriot militia at Concord proved far more formidable than that at Lexington. The fighting was over by ten o'clock in the morning, ending with the headlong retreat of the Redcoats. But the more significant fighting—shocking to the British regulars—came as large numbers of Minutemen and other armed colonists harassed and sniped at the British column retreating from Concord and at the fourteen hundred regulars and Royal Marines marching in the opposite direction, from Boston, to reinforce them.

To the British, it seemed that armed men were coming from every village and every farm between Boston and Concord. They did not stand and fight in neat ranks like the Redcoats but fired from behind stone walls and trees or even from inside houses. The road between Boston and Concord became a gauntlet of fire, mile after mile. In the end, both the retreating forces and the would-be reinforcements headed in the same direction: toward Boston. Seventy-three British regulars were confirmed killed and twenty-six listed as missing, presumed killed. An additional 174 were wounded. The colonials lost forty-nine killed, five missing, and forty-one wounded. Even as the battle and its aftermath were being fought, the newly created Continental Congress voted the mobilization of 13,600 troops. Two village skirmishes signaled the beginning of the long, painful birth of a new American nation.

The Continental Congress Adopts the Declaration of Independence (1776)

No American turning point is more famous than the day the United States declared itself born, and no American day is more famous than July 4. But these are not one and the same day. On July 2, 1776, the Second Continental Congress approved a resolution to the effect that "these United Colonies are, and of a right ought to be, free and independent States." Nearly a month had passed since Richard Henry Lee of Virginia introduced it on June 7 in what was then the colonial legislature for the province of Pennsylvania, commandeered by the Continental Congress as a convenient place of assembly. Today, it is known as Independence Hall.

The resolution came as no surprise. After all, Americans had been fighting a revolution since the opening shots at Lexington and Concord on April 19, 1775. But it was not universally welcomed. In fact, many of the delegates had been sent to the Second Continental Congress with explicit orders to vote against independence. Pennsylvania's John Dickinson and South Carolina's Edward Rutledge were typical of the conservatives. They saw no problem with fighting for full representation in Parliament and more self-governance. They even supported the idea of an alliance with France. They believed the colonies should unite in a confederation. But making a complete break with the mother country? It was too dangerous—and almost certainly foolhardy. Fight the revolution to gain an advantageous political position but postpone any talk of independence—lest King and Parliament, confronted with so bold a declaration, deal the colonies a crushing blow.

But outside of their meeting place, especially in New England, the movement toward total independence was growing daily, stirred up by the likes of Boston's Samuel Adams and the recent English émigré Tom Paine, who published *Common Sense* in January, a grandiloquent and

The American painter John Trumbull depicted the five framers of the Declaration of Independence—the principal author, Thomas Jefferson, tallest among them—presenting their handiwork to the Continental Congress. The painting was later engraved on the back of the $2 bill, and the original hangs today in the Capitol Rotunda. LIBRARY OF CONGRESS, ARCHITECT OF THE CAPITOL COLLECTION

highly persuasive argument for leaving the empire behind. Lee was Sam Adams's man in Congress, and the Bostonian believed that the Virginian would succeed in moving the great assembly to make the most important decision Americans could ever make—the decision to take hold of their own destiny.

As for fighting without declaring independence, a number of delegates pointed out that this was a losing strategy. First, only an independent government could form meaningful international alliances. Second, the war was not going well. General Washington needed a rallying cry to inspire his troops. They needed a goal, a prize, a reason to fight and, if need be, die. There was no better reason than creating a nation.

As the delegates wrangled, Sam Adams was assigned to a committee putting together articles of confederation. His cousin, John Adams, chaired the committee composing a treaty with France. He was also called on to collaborate with Benjamin Franklin, colonial polymath, a man of international reputation, to compose a declaration of independence. And lest Adams and Franklin become overly enthusiastic, Congress put New York conservative Robert Livingston and Connecticut Yankee Roger Sherman on board as ballast.

A fifth member was wanted—but agreement on who that should be proved elusive. Lee seemed too radical, while his fellow Virginian, Benjamin Harrison, seemed too conservative. But a Virginian was desirable to have, and there was a thirty-two-year-old gawky redhead who was not much of a public speaker, but those who knew him, knew he could write with eloquence, wit, and intelligence. Both the Adamses liked him—and, besides, old Ben Franklin was ailing and John Adams was preoccupied with the French treaty. In the end, John Adams recruited Jefferson to draft the document by presenting three blunt reasons: "Reason first—You are a Virginian, and a Virginian ought to appear at the head of this business. Reason second—I am obnoxious, suspected and unpopular. You are very much otherwise. Reason third—You can write ten times better than I can."

Although Jefferson was very worried about his sick wife back in Virginia—a frail young woman, Martha Wayles Jefferson would die in 1782 at thirty-four—but he wrote with great speed and, clearly, under remarkable inspiration. Years later, in 1825, he wrote in a letter to Henry Lee just what he had been trying to accomplish in the declaration. It was not an attempt to "find out new principles, or new arguments, never before thought of," but "to justify ourselves in the independent stand we are compelled to take" and to "appeal to the tribunal of the world . . . for our justification." He intended the document "to be an expression of the American mind, and to give to that expression the proper tone and spirit called for by the occasion." He drew on "the elementary books of public right, as Aristotle, Cicero, Locke, Sidney, etc." Of these, the seventeenth-century British philosopher John Locke most influenced Jefferson. Locke had enumerated the basic rights of human beings—life, liberty, and property—which Jefferson echoed in his declaration: "We hold these truths to be self-evident, that all men are created equal, that they are endowed by their Creator with certain unalienable Rights, that among these are Life, Liberty and—." He stumbled over "property" and instead wrote "the pursuit of happiness." In this phrase, he may have come closest to capturing a true "expression of the American mind," the essence of what later generations would call the "American dream." For Jefferson, an independent America would be a place for human fulfillment—or, at the very least, its pursuit.

Seeking to justify the break with Britain to the world, Jefferson included a bitter condemnation of King George III for having, among other acts of injustice, "waged cruel war against human nature itself, violating its most sacred rights of life & liberty in the persons of a distant people who never offended him, captivating & carrying them into slavery in another hemisphere, or to incur miserable death in their transportation thither." Jefferson was a Virginia planter who owned slaves, but he found the slave trade evil, and he believed its condemnation should be part of the Declaration of Independence. Jefferson proudly laid his handiwork before Congress on June 28, 1776. His fellow Southerners quickly struck the condemnation of slavery but deleted little else from the document—although just enough to offend Jefferson's authorial pride.

John Adams was ecstatic when, on July 2, Congress unanimously voted that the American colonies were from that day forward free and independent states. He wrote to his wife, Abigail, that the second day of July would "be celebrated by succeeding generations as the great anniversary festival . . . It ought to be solemnized with pomp and parade, with shows, games, sports, guns, bells, bonfires and illuminations from one end of the continent to the other, from this time forward forever more."

Two days were consumed in dotting *is* and crossing *ts* so that it was July 4 before the Continental Congress approved the document for publication. The signing, however, was kept secret lest the act endanger the signatories' lives. It was not until August 2 that a final fair copy was opened for "public" signature. John Hancock signed it large and bold, reportedly remarking, "There, I guess King George will be able to read that!" Hancock remarked to fellow signer Benjamin Franklin, "We must be unanimous. There must be no pulling in different ways. We must all hang together." To which Franklin replied, "Yes, we must indeed all hang together, or most assuredly we shall hang separately."

America had declared its independence—a turning point in the history of the world itself. Within it, however, was a turn not taken. For the "unanimous Declaration of the thirteen united States of America" proclaimed those states' commitment to liberty and the inalienable human rights for everyone—with the exception of those they chose to enslave. This unturned corner was the Original Sin in the new American paradise and would be atoned for in a torrent of blood beginning in 1861, just eighty-five years after the founding document was signed.

Victory at the Battle of Yorktown Assures Independence (1781)

In the sixth year of the American Revolution, British commander Earl Charles Cornwallis engaged Patriot forces under the Marquis de Lafayette and General "Mad" Anthony Wayne at the Battle of Green Spring, Virginia, on July 6, 1781. Cornwallis eked out a very slim victory. Instead of pressing his advantage by pursuing the rebels, Cornwallis acted on instructions from General Henry Clinton, commander in chief of British forces in America, to occupy and hold a position in Virginia. He decided to capture and hold Yorktown, a backwater tobacco port on the small Yorktown Peninsula.

There is an old strategic adage about never putting your army's back against a body of water, and Cornwallis was putting his army on the edge of the York River and the Chesapeake Bay. But Cornwallis regarded this as a strategic asset rather than a liability. As he saw it, the position gave him access to support from the Royal Navy. To further secure a means of supply and escape, Cornwallis divided his forces, planting Banastre Tarleton's British Legion at Gloucester Point, on the opposite bank of the York from his main force.

By this time in the war, France had made an alliance with the emergent United States, and early in July 1781, the French army, under General Jean Baptiste Rochambeau, joined Washington's Continental Army above New York. The combined forces briefly engaged the British, but Washington, concluding that the Redcoats intended to defend the city fiercely, decided to focus on a major campaign in Virginia. With Rochambeau, he intended to reinforce Lafayette and Wayne against Cornwallis while French admiral François Joseph Paul de Grasse cut off the British general's contact with the Royal Navy, which was his seaborne means of reinforcement, communication, and supply. The plan was for

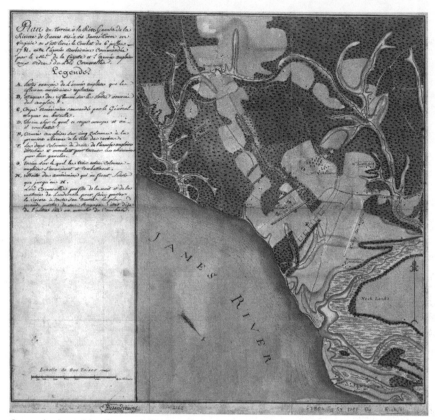

Commissioned by General Rochambeau, this French map by Jean Nicholas Desandroüins depicts the left bank of Virginia's James River and the Battle of Green Spring in the run-up to the culminating Siege and Battle of Yorktown.
LIBRARY OF CONGRESS, ROCHAMBEAU COLLECTION

de Grasse also to land three West Indian regiments for use in the ground campaign. By August 21, the Franco-American march to Virginia was on.

By September 1, General Clinton realized that Washington and Rochambeau were no longer bound for New York, but for Virginia. He dispatched a fleet under Admirals Samuel Graves and Samuel Hood from New York to intercept de Grasse's West Indian fleet and another French fleet, under Admiral Jacques-Melchior Saint-Laurent, Comte de Barras, supporting it. The French navy operated with a brilliance it had not earlier exhibited. De Grasse outran the British to the Chesapeake, and French cruisers were positioned in the James River to block Cornwallis from withdrawing to the south. Additional French ships set up a blockade of the York River at its mouth. De Grasse deployed the rest of his vessels to await the approach of the Royal Navy at the mouth of the Chesapeake.

At this point, the folly of Cornwallis's having positioned his army on the York Peninsula became apparent. He was bottled up at Yorktown. His army would still have had a chance, if Admiral Graves had acted boldly and scattered the French blockading fleet. Graves, however, was not a bold commander, and when the two fleets made contact on September 5, 1781, in Chesapeake Bay, Graves had lost the initiative. The Battle of the Capes, off the Virginia Capes, began at four in the afternoon and was over by six in the evening. Outnumbered twenty-four ships to nineteen, Graves and Hood withdrew from the engagement and did not stop sailing away until they were safely returned to New York.

As for Charles Cornwallis, he and some six thousand of his men were now cut off at Yorktown.

On September 9, de Barras's fleet appeared over the horizon and joined de Grasse in Chesapeake Bay. This secured total control over the great bay, which enabled de Grasse to land the troops his ships carried. Thus, when the Franco-American forces rallied at Williamsburg, Virginia, they numbered some sixteen thousand men facing nine thousand belonging to Cornwallis. Of this number, seven thousand were in and around Yorktown. The rest, including Tarleton's Legion, were posted at Gloucester, across the York River.

George Washington and Rochambeau proceeded with careful deliberation. On September 17, the two commanders held a council of war aboard the *Ville de Paris* to plan the Siege of Yorktown. What emerged was simple: While de Grasse maintained control at sea, the allied armies would envelop Yorktown and bombard it with artillery landed by de Grasse's ships. During the bombardment, French and American engineer troops were to dig trenches through which the infantry would approach Cornwallis's fortifications. In the meantime, on September 23, Cornwallis handed one of his couriers a message for Henry Clinton in far-off New York. "If you cannot relieve me very soon," it said, "you must be prepared to hear the worst."

By October 1, 1781, Washington's forces overran Cornwallis's outer fortifications. They installed artillery there and began pounding Yorktown at close range. Five days later, on October 6, General Washington, rarely ceremonial, made a great show of personally breaking ground for the first trench by which the attackers would close in on the now-battered British-occupied village.

On the night of October 14, the dashing young Alexander Hamilton, Washington's aide-de-camp, partnered with a French officer to lead a furious bayonet assault against defenders of two redoubts near the York River. After securing these positions, the digging of the approach trenches became more vigorous, and they were quickly extended all the way to the York, pinioning Cornwallis and his army in a small area in and around Yorktown. In final desperation, Cornwallis sent out a sortie of 350 men against a line of allied trenches on October 16. The American defenders retreated, but French grenadiers soon counterattacked, driving the British back into Yorktown.

After this defeat, Cornwallis resorted to one last move. He decided to attempt a breakout under cover of darkness. His plan was to cross the York River to Gloucester Point, where Tarleton's Legion was ensconced, and then hoof it by forced march northward nearly four hundred miles to British-held New York City. It was, in fact, less a plan than an act of desperation. Nevertheless, the first contingent of troops was loaded into boats. Their intention, after unloading at Gloucester Point, was to send the boats back for more troops. In this way, gradually, everyone would be transferred to Gloucester Point, from which they would make a quick march around Washington and Rochambeau.

But fortune did not favor Charles Cornwallis. A heavy storm stranded the first boats at Gloucester. Seeing no way out now, on October 17, 1781, Cornwallis was resigned to throwing himself and his army on the mercy of the Americans and the French. At about ten in the morning, a Lieutenant Denny of the Pennsylvania Line reported seeing "a drummer mount the enemy's parapet and beat a parley," the signal for a truce. With this, Denny reported, "an officer, holding up a white handkerchief," advanced toward the American lines. "The drummer accompanied him, beating."

Washington ordered his artillery to cease fire and sent an American officer out to meet the British representative. The officer tied a handkerchief over the Briton's eyes, sent the drummer back to Yorktown, and took the redcoat to a house in the rear of the American lines. There, the emissary asked for an armistice to discuss surrender terms. He promised that, before the end of a two-hour ceasefire, Earl Cornwallis would send his proposal. Washington agreed. What Cornwallis asked for was the parole of his troops and their safe conduct to England. Washington replied that he felt no need to bargain. Surrender, he said, must be without condition. Cornwallis delayed his response, but before the day ended, he had agreed.

On October 19, Washington and Rochambeau arrayed their victorious troops in a double column one mile long, Americans on the right, Frenchmen on the left. At the head of the line, Washington sat astride his horse. At the foot of the line, Rochambeau was mounted on his. At an agreed-upon moment, the army of Charles Cornwallis began its march out of their fort and between the two lines. They carried their colors "cased," tightly furled in token of their surrender. Grimly, each soldier threw down his weapon in a growing pile. To a man, the troops directed their gaze upon the left line, the column of Frenchmen, refusing so much as to acknowledge the Americans' presence on the right.

As for Cornwallis, he claimed illness so that he would not have to face surrendering in person to General Washington. He entrusted his sword to General Charles O'Hara, who offered the weapon to Washington. That commander silently stepped aside, allowing General Benjamin Lincoln, who had been forced to surrender Charleston, South Carolina, on May 12, 1780, to accept it in his stead. The sword presented, some seven thousand British soldiers marched off to prison camps. Only Cornwallis, with his principal staff, was allowed free passage to New York.

The Siege and Battle of Yorktown did not end the American Revolution. Indeed, it did not even end the British military presence throughout much of the United States. What it did extinguish was the

British will to continue the fight. When word of the defeat of Cornwallis reached London, Prime Minister Lord North gasped out, "Oh God! It is all over."

With England facing assault from the combined fleets of Spain and France, both allied with America, Parliament concluded on December 20 that it was time to negotiate peace. Fighting continued sporadically in the southern region, but negotiations nevertheless commenced in Paris on April 12, 1782, with Benjamin Franklin acting as lead treaty commissioner for the United States. By October 5, terms had been reached, specifying US boundaries, procedures for the evacuation of British troops, American access to the Newfoundland fisheries, and free trade and navigation of the Mississippi River—in addition, of course, to the Crown's acknowledgment of the full and absolute independence from the British Empire of its lower thirteen American colonies. On November 30, 1782, a provisional treaty was ready to be ratified by the belligerents, and, on September 3, 1783, the Treaty of Paris was concluded. The United States, bloodied, took its place among the world's family of nations.

Delaware Becomes the First State to Ratify the Constitution (1787)

Delaware's blue-and-buff license plate proclaims itself as "The First State." It was, in fact, the first state to ratify the new Constitution, on December 7, 1787. But it wasn't as if the thirteen states were shoving in line to accept the document as the law of the new nation. There was, in fact, great reluctance and worry.

In 1781, while the United States was still fighting for its independence, the states approved the Articles of Confederation, which were less a national constitution than a contract among thirteen separate rebellious colonies struggling to become independent states. The confederation gave governing authority largely to the individual states, deliberately keeping the central government weak. The inefficiencies created by this system soon became obvious and were driven home to many Americans by the outbreak Shays's Rebellion, which spanned August 31, 1786, to June 1787. It was a violent uprising among the farmers in western Massachusetts—later joined by others—who were barred from paying their debts with the worthless paper money issued by individual state governments. Continental Army veteran Captain Daniel Shays led a raid on the federal arsenal in Springfield, Massachusetts, to secure arms in an attempt to force the closure of the Massachusetts courts where debtors were being sued for repossession of their property. The economic and political instability created by a weak central government brought demands for a stronger national union. In 1786, Alexander Hamilton, who was a member of a five-state meeting in Annapolis, Maryland, to revise the Articles of Confederation, called for a larger convention to do a bigger job.

Delegates from every state except Rhode Island—which was vehemently opposed to altering the Articles—converged on Philadelphia in May 1787. Their assigned task was comparatively modest: revise the Articles of Confederation, the charter for the central American government that had been approved by the states in 1781. In debate, all but two convention delegates were quickly persuaded that the document required more than a revision. Some form of government that divided authority between the states and a relatively strong central government was needed. This realization quickly led to a philosophical discussion on the nature of government itself. Agreement was reached that America should have a republic that answered to its citizens. The structure of that republic, they decided, should be a balance among three branches: executive, legislative, and judicial. As John Adams believed, the most effective way to prevent a government from becoming drunk on power was to divide it so that power always checked and balanced power.

Having thus philosophized, the convention set about hammering together an entirely new form of government, one that had not been contemplated in the Articles of Confederation. Chiefly drafted by future fourth US president James Madison, the Constitution gave the federal government authority to levy taxes, to regulate interstate and foreign trade, and to raise and maintain an army. It withdrew from the states the authority to issue money, to make treaties, and to tax imports and exports. For the purpose of administering the new federal powers, the Constitution created a bicameral legislature composed of a Senate, to be filled by two delegates elected by each state assembly, and a House of Representatives, to be composed of popularly elected representatives. The number of representatives would be in proportion to the population of the states they represented.

Proportional representation raised an ugly problem. Obviously, a means of counting population had to be implemented. Should slaves be counted? The southern states said yes, because they wanted a higher proportion of representation. The nonslave states, up north, said no. The crisis was resolved with the so-called Three-Fifths Compromise, which provided that, for purposes of a census to determine representation in the lower house of Congress, slaves (the Constitution referred to them only as "other Persons") would be counted but at the discounted rate of three-fifths of a person. The same discounted method would also be used to determine the amount of taxes due from the states to the federal government. The compromise was the first of many concerning slavery.

As for the executive branch of government, the Constitution called for a president and a vice president, who were not chosen directly by popular vote but by "electors" appointed by the state legislatures. The number of electors for each state equaled the number of representatives the state sent to Congress. As for the powers of the president, they were broadly and loosely defined. The chief executive was charged with "faithfully executing" all laws, serving as commander in chief of the armed forces, overseeing all foreign relations, and appointing federal judges and other officials. Although the president was commander in chief, only Congress had the power to declare war, and while the president could veto legislation, Congress could override a veto by a two-thirds vote in both houses.

Slighted in the Constitution was the judicial branch, the powers of which were only very vaguely defined. The fourth chief justice of the Supreme Court, John Marshall, gave the judiciary its greatest power when he took it upon himself in 1803, years after the Constitution had been ratified, to declare in *Marbury v. Madison* a law unconstitutional, thereby voiding it. This introduced the enduring concept of judicial review.

When the document was complete, every state but Rhode Island called a ratifying convention late in 1787 or early in 1788. Five states—Delaware, Pennsylvania, New Jersey, Georgia, and Connecticut—quickly ratified the Constitution. Others took longer, and North Carolina voted against ratification. Massachusetts demanded a series of amendments to define individual rights. The Federalists—those who supported the Constitution as written—objected, but John Adams and John Hancock hammered out a compromise by which Congress would consider amendments when the Constitution went into effect. Most states accepted this promise, Massachusetts leading the way, followed by Maryland, South Carolina, New Hampshire, Virginia, and New York.

Having boycotted the Constitutional Convention, Rhode Island submitted the draft Constitution to town meetings, whose voters rejected it 2,708 to 237 on March 24, 1788. North Carolina's state convention, deadlocked through August 1788, adjourned without a decision. The Constitution went into effect despite these states, but when the Bill of

Rights was introduced as a bloc of ten amendments in 1789, both North Carolina and Rhode Island elected conventions that added their ascent, making ratification unanimous.

It was a turning point for American government, but, more importantly, for the history of human government. The ratification of the Constitution was the first known instance in which a people exercised the liberty to decide just how they would be governed.

The Bill of Rights Is Drafted (1789)

The convention that framed the Constitution was supposed to do no more than revise the dysfunctional Articles of Confederation. It quickly became apparent to most of the delegates that the scope of the problem was beyond revision and that a new document—really a new approach to government—was needed. So, everything was put on the table, with one exception. The delegates saw no need to lay out the very feature that most people today think of first when they think of the Constitution. They did not think it necessary to set out *individual* rights. It's not that they wanted to deny these rights, but, aiming to create a concise document, most of the delegates believed that the function of the Constitution was to "enumerate" the powers of the government. Since the government was barred from assuming authority that had not been explicitly provided for in the Constitution, it was barred from trespassing on the rights of individuals or, for that matter, the states.

Those who supported a strong central government—and therefore supported the Constitution—were called Federalists. Those opposed were anti-Federalists. As this second faction saw things, the concept of "enumerated powers" was dangerously open to interpretation; therefore, it was hardly a sufficient safeguard against the central government someday taking on tyrannical powers. Anti-Federalist delegates refused to ratify the Constitution without including in it a Bill of Rights—something like the equivalent of the Virginia Declaration of Rights (1776) or the English Bill of Rights (1689) or even the Magna Carta (1215). Federalists stubbornly refused to include such a section, but they agreed to a compromise proposed by the Massachusetts Delegation led by anti-Federalists Sam Adams and John Hancock. The Federalists promised to draft a Bill of Rights for amendment to the Constitution, once the main document had been ratified. In 1789, accordingly, Congress recruited James Madison to compose the necessary amendments. He resorted to such historical sources as the constitutions of several states as well as the English Bill of Rights and the Magna Carta. His principal model, however, was the Virginia Declaration of Rights, which had been adopted in 1776 by his home state.

Madison rapidly composed a dozen amendments, eight of which enumerated individual rights, two set certain limits to the federal government, and two more dealt with other issues and were therefore not presented as part of the bloc of ten amendments offered for ratification and known as the Bill of Rights.

The ten amendments were ratified by the states on December 15, 1791:

- The First Amendment guarantees freedom of religion, freedom of speech, freedom of the press, and the right of popular assembly for the purpose of petition for redress of grievances.
- The Second Amendment guarantees the right to bear arms.
- The Third Amendment limits the quartering of soldiers in private homes.
- The Fourth Amendment bars unreasonable searches and seizures and requires that search warrants be specific rather than blanket documents and that they be issued only upon probable cause.
- The Fifth Amendment mandates grand jury indictments in major criminal prosecutions, prohibits "double jeopardy" (being tried more than once on the same charge), and guarantees that no one need testify against themselves; it also bars seizure of private property for public use without just compensation and forbids deprivation of life, liberty, or property without due process of law.
- The Sixth Amendment guarantees a speedy public trial by jury and additionally mandates that accused persons be fully informed of the accusation, may confront witnesses who testify against them, may subpoena witnesses for their defense, and have access to legal counsel.
- The Seventh Amendment guarantees the right to jury trial in civil cases and inhibits courts from overturning jury verdicts.
- The Eighth Amendment prohibits excessive bail, unreasonable fines, and "cruel and unusual punishments."

The Ninth and Tenth Amendments are different from the first eight in that they define limits of government power rather than individual rights:

- The Ninth Amendment provides that the enumeration of rights in the Constitution must not be construed to "deny or disparage" other rights retained by the people.
- The Tenth Amendment sets out the "doctrine of reserved powers"—the principle that all powers not explicitly delegated to the United States are reserved to the states or the people.

The Bill of Rights was annexed to the Constitution only grudgingly by the Federalists. Call it a kind of glorious afterthought. Yet it is what most Americans consider the very essence of American liberty.

The Supreme Court Decides Its Supremacy (1803)

A dispute between a disappointed political appointee, William Marbury, and Thomas Jefferson's secretary of state, James Madison, ended up in the US Supreme Court on February 11, 1803. It certainly did not seem to have the makings of a historic case, let alone have the potential of being a turning point in American history and government. At the time, most people saw its only interest as being a legal cliffhanger, since the case put Chief Justice John Marshall in a tight spot. He had to choose between defying the president of the United States or weakening his court.

The backstory went like this. In the closing days of his presidency, John Adams appointed William Marbury as justice of the peace for Washington, DC. It was one of several judicial appointments Adams made and signed but that were not "distributed"—that is, were not made official by their formal delivery to the appointees. When Thomas Jefferson took office after Adams, he found the undistributed appointments on his desk, and he had to decide what to do with them.

Jefferson was a liberal—some would say a radical. Historians call the political party he created the Democratic Republicans, and they vehemently opposed the Federalists, the conservative party of Washington and Adams. The law that had made Marbury's and the other appointments possible, the Judiciary Act of 1801, was passed by the Federalist majority in Congress to help stem the tide of Jeffersonian "radicalism." The law established six new circuit courts and authorized the appointment of sixteen new federal judges as well as several attorneys, marshals, and clerks. Adams rushed to fill all these positions with conservative Federalists. Jefferson had to choose whether to honor the intention of his predecessor by duly seeing to the distribution of all his last-minute appointments. If he distributed them, Federalist influence in the government of which he had just become chief executive would remain strong. In the end, he chose to withhold the undistributed commissions.

William Marbury took the matter before the bar. He petitioned the Supreme Court for a "writ of mandamus," a court order to a public official (in this case, Secretary of State Madison) to do what his duty and the law required, namely to distribute his commission.

Chief Justice Marshall's dilemma? If he issued the mandamus, compelling Madison to distribute Marbury's commission (and, presumably, the others), he would put the Supreme Court in direct opposition to the president. If he declined to issue the writ, he would be quite properly seen as bowing to the president's will and thereby diminishing the authority of the court.

A brilliant man, Marshall devised a brilliant response of enduring and profound consequence. On February 24, 1803, he handed down a decision that found Marbury was indeed entitled to his commission; however, the decision continued, the Supreme Court could not legally compel the secretary of state to deliver it. The clause in the Federal Judiciary Act of 1789 that allowed writs of mandamus to be requested of the Supreme Court, Marshall declared, was unconstitutional because it gave the court authority that the Constitution did not explicitly authorize. For this reason, the clause was null and void, not just in this case but for all time.

On its face, it might appear that this decision diminished the Supreme Court by denying to it a power the 1789 act had given it. Quite the contrary, Marshall's decision established the legal precedent that created the foundation of the Supreme Court's true supremacy. While Marshall sacrificed poor Marbury, who never did get to be justice of the peace, the chief justice bequeathed to the Supreme Court awesome power. He established for the court the role of "judicial review" by which the high court was empowered not merely to review whatever lower court decisions litigants brought to it on appeal but also, in deciding an appeal, to determine the constitutionality of laws passed by Congress.

The Constitution established three branches of government. Articles I and II spelled out the powers of the Legislative and Executive Branches, respectively. Article III was not as specific concerning the authority of the Judicial Branch. Marshall's decision in *Marbury v. Madison* in effect "completed" Article III, elevating the judiciary to full coequal status with the other two branches and thereby perfecting the system of checks and balances essential to the American democracy.

Thomas Jefferson Purchases Louisiana from Napoleon (1803)

Spanish explorers under Panfilo de Narváez in 1542 and Hernando de Soto in 1543 were the first to claim portions of what became the Louisiana Territory. The Spanish crown quickly lost interest in the region, however, which left it open to claims made by French explorers. Most notable among these was René-Robert Cavelier, Sieur de La Salle, who, in 1682, named the vast tract Louisiana, after the "Sun King," Louis XIV.

Louisiana was mainly in French hands through the French and Indian War of 1754–1763. This conflict was fought, on the one hand, prinicipally between British imperial forces with British colonial aid and a few Indian allies and, on the other, between French imperial forces and a larger number of Indian allies. But late in that war, Spain allied itself with Britain. It did so just in time to claim a slice of the spoils produced by British victory. France ceded to Spain all of Louisiana. Yet Spain did little enough with most of the territory and, on October 1, 1800, concluded with Napoleon a secret treaty by which it returned Louisiana to France in exchange for certain portions of Tuscany. At the time, Tuscany was not Napoleon's to give away, but he promised that he would conquer it. Given his record, the Spanish crown considered conquest a sure thing.

The ink was barely dry on the secret treaty when Napoleon suddenly abandoned the war by which he could have won Tuscany for Spain. This triggered a bitter dispute between the French and the Spanish, during which time Spain continued to administer Louisiana. Spain had not only expected Napoleon to present the kingdom with Tuscany but also expected France to maintain Louisiana as a vast buffer zone between the American states and its own holdings. When France failed to do so, the Spanish administration revoked, in October 1802, the American traders' "right of deposit," terminating their valuable licenses to store goods in New

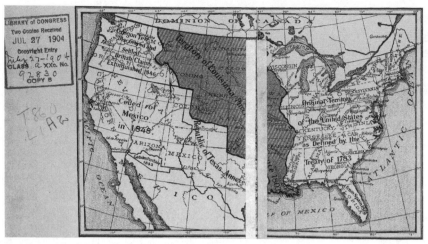

Published in 1904 for the Louisiana Purchase Exposition in St. Louis, this map illustrates the extent of the territory acquired from France in 1803. LIBRARY OF CONGRESS

Orleans for loading onto ocean-going vessels. The effect was to suddenly close off the Mississippi River to American trade. Spain's Catholic culture clashed with an American culture based on Protestant Christianity. The two groups were as oil and water on the western frontier.

The closing of the Mississippi River to American trade was a catastrophe for a US economy still in its infancy. To make matters worse, while the Spanish strangulation of western trade was crippling, the prospect of Napoleon controlling a major expanse of territory on the western frontier of the United States was downright terrifying. Granted, France, which had been instrumental in the American victory that ended the War of Independence, was still at least a nominal US ally. What President Thomas Jefferson feared was that war between France and England would prompt the British to seize the Louisiana Territory, thereby putting a sharp geographic crimp in an American independence so recently won.

Assailed by such thoughts, Jefferson threatened war on both France and Spain—even as he sent James Monroe, recently appointed minister to Great Britain, to Paris. His instructions were to offer to purchase the key port city of New Orleans. In the back of the president's mind was a good deal more than New Orleans. Some twelve years earlier, in 1790, Captain Robert Gray had become the first American citizen to circumnavigate the globe. On his return to Boston Harbor, Gray reported having made a major discovery that had eluded both the English and the Spanish during their explorations. It was a great, navigable western river flowing some 1,243 miles through the American Northwest, which Gray named after his ship, the *Columbia*. Jefferson reasoned that this twelve-year-old discovery gave the United States a plausible claim to territory on the Northwest Coast. If a US presence could be established at the mouth of the Mississippi—namely at New Orleans—the nation would have at least an arguable claim to everything between the Mississippi River and the Northwest Pacific coast.

It was an inspiration, even if the claim was tentative. But then the fortunes of war turned against Napoleon in a way that, as it turned out, favored America. In the West Indies, the French army, finding itself on the losing side of the Haitian Revolution, was falling prey to something far deadlier than Toussaint Louverture's freedom fighters. Yellow fever was decimating its ranks. Envisioning his great army languishing in a bog of disease, Napoleon decided to cut his losses and withdraw from the Americas—at least for now. He could not, however, afford to leave a vacuum on the North American mainland, one into which the British would doubtless rush. Moreover, he desperately needed an infusion of funds to finance his European wars. Louisiana suddenly loomed in his imagination as the proverbial stone that might kill two birds. Put the Americans in Louisiana, and the vacuum would be filled. Sell that territory to the Americans, and there would be plenty of cash in the French war chest.

On April 11, 1803, even before Monroe arrived in Paris to negotiate the purchase of New Orleans, Napoleon's wily prime minister, Charles Maurice de Talleyrand-Périgord, the Prince of Talleyrand, asked Robert R. Livingston, US minister to France, just how much Jefferson might offer for the *whole* of Louisiana. Instantly appreciating the magnitude of the opportunity, Livingston got the ball rolling, and negotiations proceeded in earnest as soon as Monroe arrived. A number was agreed on: sixty million francs—about fifteen million 1803 dollars. Even at today's value—roughly $276 million—this was a spectacular bargain for some ninety thousand square miles of trans-Mississippi territory. Per acre, it was about four cents, and Monroe hurriedly concluded a purchase treaty, which was signed on May 2, 1803.

Deal though it undoubtedly was, the actual extent of the property was rather in doubt. The Gulf of Mexico was fixed as the southern boundary of the Louisiana Purchase and the Mississippi as the eastern boundary, but not a soul knew for certain whether the real estate included West Florida (the region on the north shore of the Gulf of Mexico) and Texas. One more wee difficulty was the possibility that the purchase itself was unconstitutional, for the simple reason that the Constitution failed to make any provision for buying foreign lands.

No matter. The Senate ratified the treaty on October 20, 1803, and the United States took formal possession of the Louisiana Territory on December 20, thereby instantly doubling its national sprawl and putting itself in position to span the entire continent from sea to shining sea. More immediately, Jefferson saw it as a gift from the very heavens. What was called, circa 1800, "the West"—the expanse between the Appalachian Mountains and the Mississippi River—was filling up rapidly. Congress had rushed to enact legislation protecting the Indians against the depredations of ravenous settlers, but the federal government had no military muscle to enforce any limits. The answer? More space—either for white settlement or Indian relocation. Jefferson envisioned moving large numbers of Native Americans west of the Mississippi and thereby avoiding conflict with the insatiable land hunger of the frontiersmen. Such was Jefferson's vision. But most Americans greeted the Louisiana Purchase as the promise of cheap land, low taxes, less government, and a generally better life in what they pictured as the great Eden beyond the Mississippi. The American frontier was thrown wide open.

The British Burn Washington (1814)

Some wars are thrust upon a nation—as when Japan attacked US Navy and Army installations in the territory of Hawaii on December 7, 1941. Such conflicts are often called wars of necessity. Others are wars of choice. The 2003 decision to invade Iraq was such a war, and so was the War of 1812 nearly two centuries earlier.

Grade-school history books generally explain that the United States declared war on Britain because the Royal Navy, desperate to crew its ships fighting Napoleon, intercepted and boarded American merchant vessels to "impress" (abduct) sailors into the British service. Calling this an attack on American sovereignty and freedom of the high seas, the United States declared war on the British Empire on June 18, 1812. Yet the fact is that just two days earlier, on June 16, the British agreed to halt impressment aboard American vessels. No matter. The actual cause of the War of 1812 had little to do with freedom of the seas. It was, rather, the product of an insatiable hunger for land.

"Spanish Florida," territory extending as far west as the Mississippi, was loosely held by Spain in the early nineteenth century, a kingdom allied with Britain against Napoleon. If the Americans defeated the British in North America, this ally could be made to yield Spanish Florida to the United States. Southerners and Westerners were excited by the prospect, but New Englanders were opposed. In Congress, Kentucky's Henry Clay, leader of the congressional "War Hawks," used the impressment issue, complaints that the British were arming Indians against American frontier traders, *and* the acquisition of Spanish Florida to persuade a reluctant President James Madison to declare war.

With a standing army of just twelve thousand widely dispersed troops led by inept politically appointed officers, the War of 1812 was a losing proposition from the start. The Americans suffered massive defeats at Detroit, on the Niagara frontier, and in New York. The diminutive US

The capture and burning of Washington, DC, as depicted in an 1876 book commemorating the centennial of American independence. LIBRARY OF CONGRESS, ARCHITECT OF THE CAPITOL COLLECTION

Navy scored some surprising victories, however, and in 1813 Captain Oliver Hazard Perry won control of Lake Erie while, ashore, General William Henry Harrison defeated the British and Tecumseh's Indian confederation at the Battle of the Thames (in present-day Chatham-Kent, Ontario). But Americans badly overreached with doomed attempts to invade deep into Canada. Worse, in 1814, with Napoleon on the verge of final defeat, Britain could finally focus on North America.

The Royal Navy imposed a ruinous blockade, which sent the American economy toward destruction. On land, British threats came from Canada, up and down the eastern seaboard and along the western frontier. Under the combined economic and military pressures, some in New England, a region vehemently opposed to the war from the beginning, were agitating for the region's secession from the Union.

There was ample reason to believe the nation was falling apart when, in late summer 1814, a British army under Major General Robert Ross overran feeble state militia forces in Maryland at the August 24 Battle of Bladensburg. Commanded by the incompetent General William H. Winder, the inexperienced militiamen broke and ran as soon as Ross opened fire on them. Only a small contingent of US Marines resisted. But they were vastly outnumbered.

With the momentum of victory at his back, Ross advanced on Washington, DC. Had he been a more aggressive and imaginative commander, he would have devoted more time and effort to destroying the capital and might even have occupied it. Instead, he conducted what amounted to a hit-and-run raid—which, however, was bad enough. His men put most of the public buildings, including the Capitol and the White House, to the torch. Madison and the bulk of the government fled ignominiously into the countryside.

Unwilling to linger, Ross advanced north to attack Baltimore, which, as a major port, he considered far more important than the nation's unprepossessing capital. A Royal Navy flotilla supported Ross by bombarding Fort McHenry, the city's chief defense in Baltimore Harbor, during September 13/14, 1814. That event, of course, was witnessed by one of Baltimore's rising young attorneys, Francis Scott Key, whom the British had arrested and detained on a warship. Key anxiously watched through a night of ceaseless bombardment and return fire. Dawn's early light revealed to Key the spectacle of the "Star-Spangled Banner" still waving over the battered fort. Not only had it withstood the onslaught, Fort McHenry gave as good as it got, forcing the Royal Navy as well as Ross's army to withdraw.

The triumph at Baltimore overshadowed the raid on Washington, the verse Key wrote enshrining the later battle as a national salvation, especially when sung to an English tavern tune popular in America. (Neither Key's verse nor that tune, "To Anacreon in Heaven," became the *official* national anthem until March 3, 1931.) Yet the fact remained that while the wreckage at Washington smoldered and Baltimore recovered from the assault, ten thousand British veterans of the Napoleonic wars were advancing into the United States from Montreal. The American land force opposing them was small, but on September 11, 1814, a US Navy captain, Thomas MacDonough, did battle against a British squadron on

Lake Champlain, scoring a remarkable victory that severed the invading army from its line of communication and supply. With this, the invaders retreated into Canada, and the British offensive along Lake Champlain simply evaporated.

The victory on Lake Champlain prompted British agreement in December 1814 to a proposed treaty that had been hammered out in a peace conference under way in Ghent, Belgium, since August. Signed on Christmas Eve, the Treaty of Ghent ended the War of 1812 but not before Major General Andrew Jackson had scored America's only truly devastating blow against the British army when he defeated a force three times larger than his at the Battle of New Orleans (January 8–18, 1815). This triumph came before word of the treaty reached the United States, and while it did not undo the economic and physical devastation the young republic had suffered, it did make the War of 1812 *seem* to many like an American victory. Indeed, several generations of US historians have called the War of 1812 the "second war of independence," claiming that it created a sense of national identity and purpose. Yet this sentiment was not the turning point that some historians claim. The more significant turning point created by the War of 1812 was the very fact that Americans chose to celebrate the symbol of national triumph created by the endurance of Baltimore rather than mourn a charred Washington. Having chosen to fight a ruinous "war of choice," Americans nevertheless discovered their resilience.

Ground Is Broken on the Erie Canal (1817)

Born in 1752 and died in 1816, Gouverneur Morris was a signer of the Articles of Confederation and the Constitution that replaced them. He even wrote the Preamble to the latter document, for which service he was dubbed the "Penman of the Constitution." A staunch Federalist, Morris was among an early minority of American political activists who considered themselves Americans first and citizens of their state second. Most of his contemporaries thought of themselves as Virginians or Carolinians or New Yorkers. For many, a sense of national identity would not come until after the Civil War.

Morris was a statesman and a politician, not a builder, but in 1800 he had a vision. It was for New York State to fund the excavation of a great canal to link the Hudson River, which ran on the western border of New York City, to Lake Erie, which opened onto the waterways of the vast West. Such a canal, Morris argued, would save a fortune in money and time by providing a waterborne alternative to shipping overland to the Mississippi Valley. This would rapidly grow the manufacturing base of the East Coast and was reason enough to dig a canal. But Gouverneur Morris, American, had a more far-reaching vision. He believed the canal would tie the bustling East to the sparsely settled West and that, in so doing, would begin to build a nation that might one day span the continent. The canal would start the transformation of New Yorkers and Vermonters and Pennsylvanians into Americans.

Morris made his argument for the canal in a political climate that generally opposed using federal money to construct public "improvements," and it took seventeen years before the New York legislature finally approved the project. If anything, it might have been President James Monroe's staunch opposition to federally funding roads that stimulated development, using state money, of the nation's first great commercial link. It was a bold project that faced a formidable geographical hurdle,

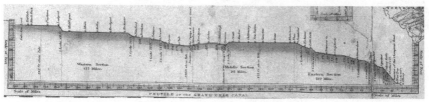

The Erie Canal was an engineering wonder that lifted vessels some 550 feet over the canal's 363-mile course from Albany in the east to Buffalo on Lake Erie in the west. This elevation profile of the canal was published in 1832. WIKIMEDIA COMMONS

since the land between the Hudson and Lake Erie rose some six hundred feet in elevation. No fewer than thirty-five locks were required to raise and lower canal boats across the terrain—a prospect so daunting that even Thomas Jefferson thought the canal foolhardy. But, heeding Morris, New York governor DeWitt Clinton championed the project. The first shovel bit into the earth in 1817, and the Erie Canal was completed in 1825. It ran for 363 miles, a testament to American engineering and American muscle. The $7 million that the Clinton-era legislature appropriated—a price so lofty that the "ditch" was christened "Clinton's Folly"—was repaid with astounding speed, and the canal began regularly producing profits averaging $3 million yearly.

The Erie Canal not only became a great commercial waterway. It was the chief route for immigrants traveling from the East to the Great Lakes country and beyond. So resoundingly successful was the canal that it ignited a great canal-building boom, which rapidly created a circulatory system uniting the Northeast with the complex of natural waterways throughout the West. By 1840, America was networked by 3,326 miles of canals, an infrastructure instrumental in ending the lingering economic recession that followed the largely disastrous War of 1812.

Did the Erie Canal and the other watery highways it spawned forge a nation out of disparate states? Yes—and no. It created a durable bond between the Northeast and the West but, in so doing, deepened the growing division between the free industrial North and the slaveholding agricultural South—a region with few connections to the West. The geography in which the Civil War developed was, in part, manmade.

South Carolina's John C. Calhoun Launches the Nullification Crisis (1828)

Andrew Jackson was inaugurated as the seventh president of the United States on March 4, 1829. He was the first "Western" president, the first who had not been born and raised among the "establishment" of the long-settled East Coast. His constituency was the "common man," who felt victimized by what they thought of as a corrupt political "aristocracy." The nation whose helm he took was roiled by bitter dispute over protective tariffs, which were designed to promote Northern industrialization at the expense of Southern agriculture, which relied on an export market that tariffs would surely diminish. America was also torn over tight credit—the rich liked it, the poor but rising people of the frontier found it oppressive. The nation argued over the price of western lands. Those in Northern states believed that the low prices set on western lands to encourage settlement would bankrupt the treasury. These same Northerners were the champions of high protective tariffs to curb imports and thereby protect their fledgling industries.

The Southerners wanted a chance to expand westward and, so, favored cheap land. They also needed large export markets for their cotton, indigo, and rice. High tariffs on European imports—finished fabric and clothing included—would curb demand for Southern export cotton. Among Southern export crops, cotton had taken the lead. Cotton cultivation was extremely labor-intensive and, as the South saw it, absolutely required the labor of slaves. The North, acting from motives of economic and political competition as well as genuine moral abhorrence of slavery, was in the early throes of what would soon be an unstoppable abolition movement. But it was the Southerners, whose planter class had the most to lose, who were quickest to express outrage—and act on it. Wedded to lucrative export crops, reliant on low tariffs to build the market for their produce, hungry for more land and low prices, and, most of all, dependent both economically and socially on the institution of slavery, Southerners believed that Northerners would not be satisfied until they had succeeded in suppressing, subjugating, and ultimately ruining the Southern way of life.

Southern politicians condemned the Tariff of 1828 as the "Tariff of Abominations." Foremost among these leaders was the South Carolinian John C. Calhoun, who served as vice president first under John Quincy Adams and then Andrew Jackson. As he grew older, he became an increasingly passionate and narrowly parochial champion of his native region. In the year of the Tariff of Abominations, he wrote and anonymously published the *South Carolina Exposition and Protest*, a pamphlet that presented a novel theory of Constitutional law. Any state, Calhoun wrote, had the right to deem a law unconstitutional and unilaterally declare it "null and void." The 1828 tariff, he wrote, was one such law.

To Calhoun's consternation, his nullification idea gained little attention, especially when the issue of the Tariff of Abominations faded with the election of Andrew Jackson. As a Southerner, Jackson ran on the promise of tariff reform, which was sufficient to mollify the South. But when the Tariff Act of 1832 was passed during the Jackson administration, it seemed to Southerners even worse than the Tariff of Abominations. With its enactment, Calhoun abruptly resigned as Jackson's vice president to accept election to the Senate. In the meantime, on November 24, 1832, South Carolina called a convention that suddenly revived Calhoun's 1828 proposal by voting up an "Ordinance of Nullification," which barred Carolina state officials from collecting federal tariff duties in the state.

While nullification was Calhoun's brainchild, another South Carolina senator, Robert Y. Hayne, presented nullification to the Senate. Hayne took Calhoun's theory a step further, arguing that not only could a state nullify a law it deemed unconstitutional, it could also, if need be, secede from the Union. This was the theory of states' rights, which, at bottom, not only allowed for the dissolution of the United States but also denied the very idea of a *United* States.

Daniel Webster, senator from Massachusetts, replied to Hayne with a memorable defense of the powers of the federal government as the basis of nationhood itself. "Liberty and Union," he declared, "now and forever, one and inseparable!" And, so, the battle lines were drawn. Hayne, Calhoun, and other advocates of nullification proclaimed that theirs was a fight for states' rights. In fact, it was a fight to protect and preserve slavery. Calhoun believed that, sooner or later, the antislavery North, more populous than the South, would achieve a majority in the House and the Senate. When that happened, Northern senators would legislate slavery out of existence. The only hope, Calhoun argued to his fellow Southerners, was to make states' rights more powerful than the collective political and moral will of the North. Fortunately, Calhoun reasoned, Jackson, as a Southerner, would ultimately back nullification and retreat on enforcement of the tariff.

John C. Calhoun misjudged the president—badly, as it turned out. President Jackson responded to the South Carolina nullification resolution on December 10, 1832, with an executive proclamation upholding the constitutionality of the tariff, denying nullification, and rejecting the presumed power of any state to block enforcement of any federal law. The proclamation threatened armed intervention to support the collection of federal duties. To show that he was serious, Jackson obtained from Congress passage of a Force Act, which authorized him to use the military to enforce the tariff.

In a show of bravado, South Carolina summarily nullified the Force Act, and many Americans believed they were now on the verge of civil war. In the nick of time, however, early in 1833, Congress passed a compromise tariff, which even South Carolina accepted. For now, civil war was averted, but the Nullification Crisis foretold its inevitability. The theory of states' rights and nullification summoned forth the genie of secession, and there would be no putting it back in the bottle. For the next twenty-eight years, the dissolution of the United States grew from a theory to a possibility to a probability and, finally, a reality when the Civil War broke out in April 1861.

Congress Passes the Indian Removal Act (1830)

As everyone knows, the conquistadors were not the first Americans. Nor were the settlers of Jamestown or the Pilgrims at Plymouth Rock. The first Americans were the Native Americans, the people Columbus misnamed "Indians." They are the people descended from a cohort believed to be the first immigrants to North America, people from Asia. Over thousands of years, beginning some thirty thousand years ago, they started a multigenerational migration across dry land that is now the Bering Strait. They settled throughout the Americas, from Alaska to Tierra del Fuego. Most of those who came much later—Spanish, French, English—wanted these Native Americans "removed" to someplace else, someplace beyond where the newcomers wanted to settle. Beginning with George Washington, every American president pondered some sort of plan to make "Indian removal" systematic and a matter of law. The idea was always to push the Native Americans west. It was John Quincy Adams, the nation's sixth president, who responded to an impending constitutional crisis by laying the foundation for specific removal legislation.

In 1828, the state legislature of Georgia passed a law placing all Indian residents under state jurisdiction. Other southern states prepared to follow suit. The objective was to lift federal protection from Indian lands and Indian rights to those lands. Slaveholding Southerners not only coveted the land, they also sought to end the flight of fugitive slaves into Indian country. When slaves escaped into Native land, the Indians often refused to return the "fugitives" to their "rightful" owners. Initially, J. Q. Adams refused Southern demands to institute an Indian removal program. When Georgia responded to the refusal asserted authority over the Indians within its boundaries, Adams threatened to deploy the US army to protect Native Americans against the actions of the state. With

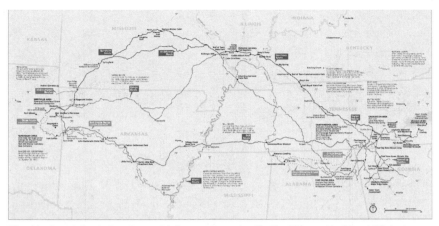

The National Park Service, which operates the Trail of Tears National Historic Trail, produced this map of the routes by which the American government marched Native Americans from their ancestral homes in the east to "Indian Territory" in and around what is today Oklahoma. US NATIONAL PARK SERVICE

states' rights already a burning issue because of slavery, civil war seemed a real possibility. To avert the destruction of the Union itself, Adams reluctantly agreed that federal legislation to remove the eastern tribes to the trans-Mississippi West was the only way to prevent civil war. Andrew Jackson's electoral victory over Adams in November 1828 gave the new president the responsibility for championing the necessary legislation.

In promoting the Indian Removal Act of 1830, Andrew Jackson did not set out to be evil. His intention was to solve what seemed to him and most Americans—Native and otherwise—an otherwise intractable problem, namely the fundamental incompatibility of "white" and "red" Americans. The legislation did not authorize seizure of land but mandated fair land exchanges. The idea was to give the removed peoples the equivalent of what land they had held—only in another, very distant, location.

The best of intentions aside, no plan is fair unless all parties freely agree to it. Nothing of the kind happened in the case of Indian removal. Officially titled "An Act to Provide for an Exchange of Lands with the Indians Residing in Any of the States or Territories, and for Their Removal West of the River Mississippi," the legislation was signed into law by President Jackson on May 28, 1830, and authorized the federal government to push many Eastern tribes west of the Mississippi, mainly to an area designated as "Indian Territory" in present-day Oklahoma and parts of Kansas and Nebraska. Few, however, wanted to leave their homeland for a place that looked different, had a different climate, had different soils, and would not support the level of farming and trade found along the eastern tier. When most resisted removal, Jackson's government implemented a removal policy that was ruthless and cruel.

As contemplated in this law, the process of Indian "removal" was to be a voluntary exchange of eastern lands for western ones. In practice, the process was very different. Government officials coerced or duped Indians into making the exchange. Typically, these officials secured the agreement of compliant Indian leaders, whom the federal government unilaterally deemed representative of the whole tribe. With these individuals, the exchange was made and then declared binding on all members of tribe. Once an agreement, however dubious, was concluded, the government moved the Indians off the land, often by force.

Alabama and Mississippi followed Georgia in passing legislation that abolished tribal government and placed Indians under state jurisdiction. This served to force the Native Americans out even faster as the states used the laws to appropriate Indian-owned lands. When some Native Americans appealed for federal protection, protesting that the state laws violated treaties made with the United States, President Jackson agreed—only to claim that he lacked the power to enforce treaty provisions on the states. The only solution, he said, was for the tribes to accept removal west of the Mississippi.

While some northeastern Indians were indeed peacefully resettled in western lands (dubbed "Indian Territory" and centered on present-day Oklahoma and parts of adjacent states), some one hundred thousand individuals of the so-called Five Civilized Tribes of the Southeast—Chickasaw, Choctaw, Seminole, Cherokee, and Creek—were moved by military force.

The Choctaws were the first tribe to yield to the relentless pressure, leaving Mississippi and western Alabama for the West in 1831 and suffering through a catastrophic winter, the rigors of which were multiplied by the corrupt disregard for the Indians' welfare. The Chickasaws signed removal treaties in 1832 and 1834, but the Creeks and the Seminoles resisted more fiercely. After the Creek War (1813–1814), some three-quarters of Creek land was ceded to federal or state governments. Creek holdouts allied themselves with the Seminoles in resistance, fighting the First (1817–1818) and Second (1835–1842) Seminole Wars. The second conflict sent most of the remaining Creeks on the trail to Indian Territory during 1836, but many of the Seminoles evaded federal authority. A Third Seminole War was fought as late as 1855–1858, and periodic military campaigns were mounted against groups of diehards. Many Seminoles remain in Florida to this day, and one band considered itself at active war with the United States as late as 1934.

When Cherokee removal proved slow—only two thousand having emigrated to Indian Territory by 1838, the deadline for removal—Jackson's successor, President Martin Van Buren, ordered the military to round up holdouts. While these Indians awaited forced removal under military escort, they were imprisoned in stockades, which were, in fact, concentration camps. Families were forced to abandon farms, livestock, and other property, and the troops guarding the camps abused their wards, even to rape and murder. "I fought through the civil war," one Georgia soldier later recalled, "and have seen men shot to pieces and slaughtered by thousands, but the Cherokee removal was the cruelest work I ever knew."

Except for a minority who hid out in the Appalachian Mountains of northern Georgia and North Carolina, the Cherokees were marched to Indian Territory during the fall and winter of 1838–1839. Fifteen thousand followed this aptly named Trail of Tears along its 1,200 miles. Four thousand died before reaching Indian Territory, a place as barren and resistant to cultivation as their southern homeland had been green and fertile. With Indian "removal," the US government chose persecution and oppression over justice and compassion.

Andrew Jackson Wages War on the Second Bank of the United States (1832)

The early nineteenth century was a tumultuous time for the economy of the young American republic. Although Major General Andrew Jackson's magnificent underdog victory against the British army in the Battle of New Orleans (January 8–18, 1815) made the disastrous War of 1812 look like an American triumph, the conflict had dealt the nation's financial health a heavy blow. The young federal government had taken on massive debt, which battered an economy legislators made even worse by enacting protectionist tariffs in 1816. Ruinous get-rich-quick schemes abounded throughout the land, including wild speculation in vast western tracts that had been opened to settlement by the war. Budding industrialists borrowed heavily even as foreign markets for American-made goods collapsed under the burden of the punitive tariffs.

For years, conservative political leaders had sought to stabilize the economy by supporting a national bank. Just before the War of 1812 broke out, a movement to recharter the Bank of the United States reeled under a barrage of challenges to the bank's constitutionality. This left the financial field to a horde of state banks, which lent money recklessly, thereby triggering epidemic inflation. As soon as the war began, the state banks—except for those in New England—suspended their practice of converting paper bank notes into gold or silver upon demand. This, naturally, caused the value of paper currency to collapse. With credit frozen and paper money all but worthless, Congress finally voted to charter a Second Bank of the United States in 1816. The hope was that this institution, if wisely managed, would bring the American economy much-needed stability and confidence.

That hope soon proved forlorn, as the Second Bank was from the get-go catastrophically mismanaged. And just when it seemed things could not possibly get any worse, Congress voted up the resumption of "specie payment" (on-demand conversion of banknotes to silver and gold). Instantly, a great many state banks, unable to make the conversion, were shuttered. As more and more banks failed, investors and debtors alike languished. At this point, the Second Bank of the United States clawed itself out of the hole by sharply curtailing credit and taking a hard line on existing debt payments. This began to salvage the credit of the nation, but as William Gouge, a Jacksonian-era economist, put it, "The Bank was saved, and the people were ruined."

Hardest hit in what was by this time being called the Panic of 1819 were the southern and western states, some of which rushed into law constitutionally questionable legislation to relieve debtors at the total expense of creditors. Everyone—debtors and creditors—seemed to rise up against the Second Bank of the United States, which Missouri's US senator Thomas Hart Benton christened "The Monster." The plight of the frontier states, which, throughout the nation's short history, had often been at loggerheads with the East Coast establishment, bitterly deepened regional differences in the United States and, more than four decades before the outbreak of the Civil War, revealed just how fragile the Union might be.

In the year of panic 1819, the state of Maryland sued James McCulloch, cashier of the Maryland branch of the Second Bank of the United States, for refusing to obey a Maryland law that levied an annual tax of $15,000 on banks chartered outside the state. The state sued McCulloch for payment. Five other states with similar laws taxing the Second Bank of the United States anxiously watched the progress of the suit, which quickly ended up in the US Supreme Court. In its decision in *McCulloch v. Maryland*, the court upheld the legality of the Second Bank of the United States, citing Congress's power to make "all laws . . . necessary and proper" to execute its specific powers outlined in the Constitution. The high court further held that, because the power to impose a tax implied the power to destroy the taxed entity, Maryland's law taxing the bank was unconstitutional. The Constitution gave no state the authority to destroy an entity created by Congress.

McCulloch v. Maryland bolstered the power of Congress. Of even greater immediate importance, it strengthened the economy by creating a legal climate in which the Second Bank of the United States suddenly flourished. With this, the economic center of gravity shifted back toward the East Coast establishment, and credit was tightened—at the expense of the nation's Southerners and Westerners. This development outraged Andrew Jackson, who won the presidency in 1828 on the votes from the southern and western frontier regions and who was both celebrated and derided as the champion of the Common Man.

In two terms—from 1829 to 1837—President Jackson introduced into American government a dramatically greater degree of democracy than Americans had enjoyed even under the likes of Jefferson, Madison, and Monroe. During the Jackson presidency, most states abandoned property ownership as a prerequisite for the right to vote, thereby vastly expanding the electorate to the ranks of the less-than-wealthy. States also enacted other legislation elevating the status of ordinary Americans. But Jackson understood that real power rested on money. That meant access to credit, and as long as the Second Bank of the United States remained a bastion of East Coast elitism and hoarded wealth, Jackson believed his southern and western constituency would suffer. Thus, when the bank's charter approached the time for renewal, Jackson vetoed the recharter bill that had been passed by Congress. This move was so popular that Jackson sailed to a second term in 1832. Feeling that he was riding a popular mandate, he issued an executive order summarily withdrawing all federal deposits from the bank.

Even though the charter of the Second Bank of the United States had four years left to run in 1832, the withdrawal of federal funds was a mortal wound. The "monster," humbled, limped along to the expiration of its charter in 1836. State banks once again took up the slack, and credit quickly became more plentiful. The flow of new cash triggered a rush of Western settlement. Jackson rejoiced. He had not so much opened the West as he had funded it, and the effect on the course of nineteenth-century American history was profound. Equally profound, however, was the curse put on the American economy for the final two-thirds of the nineteenth century. The United States became a nation of cyclical boom and bust, in which both great American enterprises and struggling American families were tossed about like tiny craft on a perpetually angry sea.

Samuel F. B. Morse Demonstrates His Telegraph (1844)

Samuel F. B. Morse lived three lives. Born in Charlestown, Massachusetts, in 1791, the son of a prominent clergyman, he was educated at Yale University and showed great early promise as an artist. Like any American with serious artistic ambitions in the early nineteenth century, he traveled to Europe to study painting in its full historical context. He was soon pronounced a highly accomplished painter but was profoundly disappointed to discover, on his return to the United States, almost no demand for his work. Not to be daunted, he returned to Europe in 1829 with the aim of earning artistic recognition abroad that would carry weight back home.

He was, yet again, disappointed. For he earned precious little recognition in Europe. Eventually, he would gain a modicum of fame as a painter—with portraits of John Adams, James Monroe, and cotton gin inventor Eli Whitney, as well as a magnificent tour de force called *The Gallery of the Louvre*. But he could not earn a sufficient living from art. Still, two fateful encounters in Europe sent Morse in radical new directions.

The first came while he was touring Rome and was struck by a soldier with sufficient force to knock him to the ground. His transgression? He had failed to kneel before a passing Catholic religious procession. The incident buried itself in Morse's craw, and when he returned to America, he dashed off a series of very widely circulated articles arguing that the Catholic Church was plotting to undermine and overthrow the American democracy by sowing the frontier West with hordes of Catholic immigrants. In this way, the frontier would be dominated by men and women loyal not to the United States but to the Pope in Rome. Morse's articles caught on in a big way, spawning or fueling anti-immigration and nativist movements that would become powerful in the mid-nineteenth century and would continue to exert measurable influence well into the twentieth.

The second encounter was both more laudable and more important, pushing Morse into a third life—as a technologist, an inventor, a code maker, and shaper of modern civilization. While sailing on the return voyage to America, Morse struck up a series of conversations with a scientist named Thomas Jackson. Jackson discoursed on electricity and electromagnetism. What he said gave Morse the idea of using electrical current as a medium through which communication might be transmitted. He was not the first to hit upon this technology. As early as 1753, a Scottish magazine had published an article about using static electricity as a vehicle for communication and up through the early 1830s a number of scientists and inventors tinkered. Spain's Francisco Salva Campillo invented a barely working device in 1804 and Germany's Samuel Thomas von Sömmering did a little better in 1809. Francis Roland of England returned to static electricity in 1816 but did not get very far; the Russian diplomat Pavel Schilling created an electromagnetic telegraph that sent and received signals from one apartment in St. Petersburg to another in 1832. The next year, Carl Friedrich Gauss and Wilhelm Weber, both distinguished German scientists, cobbled together an electromagnetic device that transmitted and received messages over a full kilometer. In England, in 1837, Sir William Fothergill Cooke and Charles Wheatstone patented a telegraph system that used needles to indicate the letters of messages. While this is often called the first commercial electromagnetic telegraph, it was highly impractical.

Morse's infatuation with the idea of an electromagnetic telegraph was overwhelming. He set his artistic career aside and went to work developing a practical telegraph system. In addition and simultaneously, he devised a coded system of "dots" and "dashes" that enabled rapid transmission of language using the device. He patented both in 1837, and since his system was quite different from that of Cooke and Wheatstone, there was no conflict. Besides, Morse not only had a certain genius as an inventor, he also possessed a vision of how his device could and should and would transform nineteenth-century civilization. Moreover, he possessed the expressive skills to convey his vision to the US Congress, which voted an appropriation to subsidize construction of the first long-distance commercial telegraph line, which ran from Washington to Baltimore, a distance of roughly forty miles. On May 24, 1844, Morse transmitted the first message across that line. It was from the Book of Numbers 23:23: "What hath God wrought?"

Americans might not appreciate art, but they understood space—the vast space of the American continent. They appreciated that distances were the nation's greatest resource and its heaviest burden. A big country, much of it thinly populated across a wide landscape, was very hard to govern, let alone unify. The legislators understood that Morse had found a way to collapse time and space, to bind the nation together with wire and current.

In 1844, the United States had forty miles of telegraph wire. A single decade later, twenty-three thousand miles networked the nation and, from here, multiplied, becoming what one modern writer on technology has called "the Victorian Internet." By 1858, a cable was laid beneath the Atlantic Ocean, connecting the continent of the Americas with that of Europe. A communications revolution had begun, and the United States was both its source and central node.

James Marshall Finds Gold
in California (1848)

Hernán Cortés invaded, devastated, overthrew, and looted the Aztec empire during 1519–1521. A decade later, Francisco Pizarro did the same to the Incas in Peru. Both depredations yielded tantalizing quantities of gold, enough to stimulate more Spanish adventures, this time north, into the borderlands above Mexico. This cohort of conquistadors found no civilizations comparable to that of the Aztecs or Incas, but they heard from the mouth of a Franciscan missionary, Fray Marcos de Niza, legends of gold, including references to Seven Cities of Cibola in a kingdom called Quivera. None of Spain's northern expeditions found any of the yellow metal, but hunger for it endured through the centuries and became part of the North American identity.

In 1838, Johann August Sutter arrived in California, a bankrupt German merchant in a four-year flight from European creditors. Americanizing his name to John, he repeatedly tried to restart his financial life and finally succeeded in building a sprawling ranch in California's astoundingly fertile central valley. Sutter not only did well but also managed to weather the US-Mexican War of 1846–1848. On January 24, 1848, one of his employees, James Marshall, stumbled over gold flakes in the race of one of the Sutter mills on the American River. With this, it would seem, John Sutter's American dream was a dream come true.

Or not.

Word of Marshall's discovery quickly spread through the ranch and beyond. By March, all of Sutter's ranch hands and other employees had abandoned their posts to look for gold in the American River's south fork. Worse, Sutter's claim to the property around his mill—land he had "leased" from local Indians in exchange for some food and clothing—was challenged. He tried to keep word of the discovery from spreading farther,

The original caption of this 1850 daguerreotype by R. H. Vance describes the image as showing James Marshall in front of the mill where he discovered gold in 1848. Historians believe the mill is authentic but find it unlikely that the figure depicted is Marshall. LIBRARY OF CONGRESS

but Sam Brannan, a Mormon elder with a distinctively non-Mormon zeal for self-promotion, attracted the attention of the entire nation and, indeed, the world.

Years earlier, Brannan had led a shipload of Latter-Day Saints from the East Coast to Yerba Buena via the long sea route that swung around South America's Cape Horn. His intention was to establish a Mormon settlement, but he was checked by Brigham Young, who had his own ideas about planting the seed of a Mormon empire in the Great Salt Lake Valley of the American Desert. In 1848, Young summoned Brannan to Salt Lake City and summarily excommunicated him. On his way back to Yerba Buena, which had been renamed San Francisco the year before, Brannan stayed at Sutter's ranch. That is where he heard about the gold. Back in his hometown, he used the *California Star*, a newspaper he owned, to start publicizing the discovery. He himself, it is said, ran through the town's few streets waving a quinine bottle full of yellow gold dust while crying, "Gold! Gold! Gold from the American River!"

Within two weeks, San Francisco's population fell from several thousands to a few score. Among those who left was Brannan, who opened up a general store next door to Sutter's mill and quickly made a fortune supplying prospectors with picks, shovels, pans, and other necessaries, all at exuberantly inflated prices. While Sutter was fighting a losing battle to make good his property claims, some 250,000 1848 dollars' worth of gold was taken out of the American River and environs—by, it seemed, everyone except him. It was brought into San Francisco and much of it shipped back East via Cape Horn, stopping along the way at ports in Mexico, Peru, and Chile. This brought to California a flood of veteran miners from South America. Mexicans also came overland from the gold fields of Sonora. By the end of 1849, miners swelled the population of San Francisco and vicinity to more than ten thousand. Storekeepers, mercantile entrepreneurs, and real estate speculators cashed in on filling a demand for goods that rapidly outpaced supply.

In December 1848, President James K. Polk, addressing Congress, confirmed the tales of golden nuggets waiting in riverbeds to be scooped up by the handful. Immediately, men left their jobs on the Atlantic seaboard, midwestern villages, and southern plantations. Shedding their former lives, they made their way to California—some one hundred thousand in 1849 alone. It was a mass migration—by ship, by wagon, by foot. The miners were called "Forty-niners," and the event was dubbed the Gold Rush of 1849.

San Francisco suddenly found itself a major seaport. The harbor was a forest of ship's masts. Some vessels were deliberately run aground, abandoned, and turned into instant hotels and stores. Every day, some thirty new houses were built as the city's population neared fifty thousand—mostly young men, many of them well-armed hard drinkers and foolhardy gamblers. During the year, the now-violent city would count more than five hundred bars and one thousand betting establishments. Eggs went for $6 a dozen in town and more than $3 apiece near the gold fields.

In those fields, the easy pickings—so-called placer gold, which lay near the surface of dry land or loosely on the beds of shallow rivers and streams—quickly petered out. Prospectors had to put in more and more hard labor to find less and less. Even among those willing to do it, few '49ers grew rich and many grew discouraged. They did not blame dame fortune or themselves for their famine but typically cursed the multitude of "foreigners" surrounding them, including South Americans, Frenchmen, Mexicans, and, especially, the Chinese. Local governments passed laws severely restricting the rights of these people. Nativist mobs took the law into their own hands, and lynching became commonplace.

There *was* money to be made in California. By 1852, gold production soared to its peak of $81 million for the year. This, however, was being mined not by small-time prospectors but by well-financed mining companies with armies of labor at their disposal. Some solo entrepreneurs still did very well. Collis Huntington and Mark Hopkins made legendary fortunes by cornering the market for shovels, blasting powder, and the like. Charles Crocker and mining-camp grocer Leland Stanford became bankers and grocers. Together, as California's "Big Four," they invested, putting most of their fortunes into a transcontinental railroad project.

Others also bought in. John Studebaker sunk $8,000 he had gleaned from his wheelbarrow business—miners needed wheelbarrows as much as they needed picks and shovels—to expand his family's modest Indiana-based wagon works until it became the nation's biggest carriage maker. Levi Strauss, immigrant from Bavaria, patented the use of copper rivets to reinforce the seams of work pants made from single bolts of canvas tenting. They became not only the miner's uniform but also a cowboy trademark second only to Stetson and boots. As for Philip D. Armour, he had gone West as a prospector but made far more money from a butcher shop he opened in the gold fields. With that stash, he returned to his hometown, Milwaukee, and became America's foremost meatpacker. Then, of course, there were Henry Wells of Vermont and William G. Fargo of New York, who started an express company, which provided both transport and banking services to gold country.

As a phenomenon, the California Gold Rush lasted just about a decade, producing a far smaller yield than later strikes in Nevada, the Dakotas, and the Colorado Rockies. But its fame outshone everything that followed. It was a turning point that was the paradigm for all the mineral "rushes" to come. More immediately, thanks to the Gold Rush and the businesses that it seeded, California's population exploded to a quarter million by the mid-nineteenth century. President Zachary Taylor, anxious to bypass the divisive controversy that would doubtless come over the question of extending slavery into the territories, proposed to annex California not as a territory but directly as a free state, as part of the Compromise of 1850, which, in turn, gave the slaveholding South a stronger fugitive slave law.

In the long term, the Gold Rush kick-started the trans-Mississippi West as an economic and heavy industry counterweight to the East Coast elite. Increasingly, the West would become the engine driving the expansion of the American economy.

Female Suffragists Meet in Seneca Falls (1848)

In one extraordinary respect, the US Constitution was radical and even unprecedented. It was the founding document and instruction manual for the first national government created essentially from scratch. The American nation was a nation founded not on allegiance to some ruling house or a tribal identity but on a set of ideas, to which all citizens and government officials pledged their allegiance. America at its constitutional founding was unprecedented both as an opportunity and as a challenge. The United States could be anything the founders wanted it to be.

Two things those founders chose *not* to be were a nation without slaves and a nation in which women had rights equal to those of men. By the mid-nineteenth century, some six decades after the Constitution had been ratified, however, a group of men and women—many of them abolitionists—met to address the rights of women. During July 19 and 20, 1848, 240 Americans gathered at Seneca Falls, New York, to hold the first ever public political meeting on this subject. At the end of their meeting, they drew up the "Seneca Falls Declaration of Sentiments," an inventory of the various injustices women suffered under a male-dominated government and society. The document was pointedly modeled on the Declaration of Independence. It held most specifically that men oppressed women by, above all else, denying them the right to vote, to own property, and to gain access to a wide variety of educational and employment opportunities.

The convention at Seneca Falls was quickly over, but it served as a prelude to a much larger meeting in Rochester, New York, just two weeks later. After this, women's rights meetings were held annually. Seneca Falls also introduced America and the world to the convention's two primary organizers, Elizabeth Cady Stanton and Lucretia Mott. A native

Women's rights advocate Elizabeth Cady Stanton owned this house at 32 Washington Street in Seneca Falls, New York. She was a principal organizer of the 1848 Women's Rights Convention in Seneca Falls. LIBRARY OF CONGRESS

of Johnstown, New York, Stanton joined the abolition movement after she graduated from the Emma Willard Academy. It was while she was attending the World Antislavery Convention in London in 1840 that she met Lucretia Mott, the most outspoken woman abolitionist in the United States. A Quaker by upbringing, Mott passionately abhorred slavery, and in 1833 she founded the Philadelphia Female Anti-Slavery Society. She was stunned in 1840 when the World Antislavery Convention denied her a seat at the convention based on her gender. This directed her toward championing the doctrine of equality of the sexes.

Following their collaboration at Seneca Falls, Mott and Stanton continued to work together on both abolition and women's suffrage. In the meantime, Susan B. Anthony, who had been a Seneca Falls delegate, began building a number of grassroots women's rights organizations throughout the state of New York. She also took direct political action. In 1860, she managed to persuade state legislators to pass the Married

Women's Property Act, which gave married women the right to hold property in their own name, along with the right to earn and keep wages and to petition for custody of children in the event of divorce. It was a milestone law, which served as a model for other states.

The Civil War interrupted the women's rights movement, even as it put such women as Clara Barton and Dorothea Dix in the forefront of movements designed to care for wounded soldiers and, after the war, veterans. When the Civil War ended, the women's movement picked up again, with Lucretia Mott gaining election to the chair of the American Equal Rights Association. Both Stanton and Anthony worked to join the cause of women's suffrage to that of African American male suffrage. Yet male political leaders resisted the linkage, and the Fourteenth and Fifteenth Amendments to the Constitution—the one granting full citizen rights to former slaves, the other barring states from denying the right to vote on the basis of "race, color, or previous condition of servitude"—made no provision for women's rights, including the right to vote. This caused Mott's American Equal Rights Association to divide into two factions. The New York–based National Woman Suffrage Association, which was founded by Stanton and Anthony, accepted only women members and opposed the Fifteenth Amendment. The Boston-based American Woman Suffrage Association, which was founded by Lucy Stone and Julia Ward Howe, welcomed men and supported African American suffrage—even without woman suffrage.

Despite the schism, the movement that had begun at Seneca Falls persisted, and suffragists continued to organize, demonstrate, and— sometimes—break the law well into the twentieth century. Yet even after the Nineteenth Amendment was finally ratified on August 18, 1920, extending the ballot to women, the women's movement marched on. Armed with the vote, women now organized to advocate for the more complete legal, social, and cultural equality of the sexes.

The Supreme Court Hands Down Its Verdict in *Dred Scott v. Sandford* (1857)

Dred Scott was a fugitive Missouri slave who had belonged to John Emerson of St. Louis. An army surgeon, Emerson was transferred first to Illinois and then to Wisconsin Territory. He took Scott with him to each of these posts. After Emerson's death in 1846, Scott returned to St. Louis, where he sued Emerson's widow for his freedom, arguing that he was now a citizen of Missouri, having been freed because of his residence in Illinois, where slavery was banned by the Northwest Ordinance, and in Wisconsin Territory, where the provisions of the Missouri Compromise made slavery illegal. After a Missouri state court ruled against Scott, his lawyers—financed by abolitionist groups—appealed to the US Supreme Court, which handed down its decision in 1857.

The Supreme Court's antislavery Northern justices, predictably, sided with Scott, while the proslavery Southerners upheld the Missouri court's decision. Chief Justice Roger B. Taney, a native of the slaveholding state of Maryland, had the final word. He held that neither free blacks nor enslaved blacks were citizens of the United States and, therefore, could not sue in federal court.

This determination alone settled the case—legally, that is. But Taney decided to use the Dred Scott case to go further. He held that the Illinois law banning slavery had no force on Scott once he returned to Missouri, which was a slave state. He further held that the law in Wisconsin was also without force, because the Missouri Compromise was unconstitutional. Taney found that it violated the Fifth Amendment, which bars the federal government from depriving an individual of "life, liberty, or property" without due process of law. A slave was property and could not be taken from his or her "rightful" owner without due process—which, Taney held, did not take place in this case.

Dred Scott was the fugitive slave who was the subject of
Chief Justice Roger Taney's infamous 1857 Supreme Court
decision that kept Scott a slave and made the Civil War
inevitable. NATIONAL ARCHIVES AND RECORDS ADMINISTRATION

The Dred Scott decision outraged antislavery activists and galvanized
the abolitionist movement. The abolitionists asked a profound moral
question: Had the nation come to this, that the highest court in the land
could use the Bill of Rights to *deny* freedom to a human being?

Why did Taney issue such a broad ruling, one that went beyond
what was necessary for a decision in the particular case of Dred Scott?
Shortly after his election in 1856, then president-elect James Buchanan
immorally if not illegally lobbied the Supreme Court to make just such a
ruling. He supported the South, which wanted to gain the admission of
Kansas to the Union as a slave state, whereas antislavery Democrats and
Republicans favored so-called popular sovereignty, whereby the people

of a territory becoming a state would decide by referendum whether the state would be free or slave. Buchanan believed that if the Supreme Court, final arbiter of law, decided against Dred Scott, the constitutional protection of slavery where it existed would be affirmed and a civil war thereby permanently averted.

Buchanan made the grave mistake of misreading the temper of those who opposed slavery. Not only did the Dred Scott decision create powerful moral outrage, by defining slavery as strictly an issue of property, a Fifth Amendment issue, the decision mandated that slavery had to be protected in all the states, including those that neither practiced it nor permitted it. In short, the Dred Scott decision put the issue of slavery beyond any further political compromise. As abolitionists saw it, if the rights of slave holders had to be universally upheld as long as slavery existed, then, universally, slavery had to be abolished. The only way to abolish slavery was by constitutional amendment—which no slaveholding state would ratify. This being the case, the only way to obtain the necessary amendment was to compel the Southern states to agree to it. That, of course, meant a military showdown: civil war.

Seeking to defeat the abolitionist argument and thereby avoid civil war by legally preserving slavery in those states where it existed, the Supreme Court, aided and abetted by the fifteenth president of the United States, shoved the nation into a fiery abyss. The clock instantly began to run out on the *United* States. As for Chief Justice Roger Taney, his name would forever be reviled. And James Buchanan? Until recently, with the election of Donald Trump in 2016, he figured in virtually every poll of professional American historians as the nation's worst president.

William Smith Strikes Oil in Titusville, Pennsylvania (1859)

Oil derived from animal fat and beeswax and plant oils derived from olives, sesame seeds, grape seeds, and the like have been used as fuel for illumination at least as early as the Upper Paleolithic period, between fifty thousand and ten thousand years ago. Oil lamps are among some of the earliest artifacts archaeologists have discovered. In Euro-America, such oils were in use from the beginning of the seventeenth century. By the early nineteenth century in America, whale oil, which burned clean and without odor, was greatly preferred in oil lamps. Demand for it drove a whaling industry centered in New England; however, a new oil, called rock oil, was gaining ground against whale oil, especially as the great sea mammals were being harvested to scarcity and near-extinction by the mid-1800s.

Rock oil was a kerosene product distilled from surface shale rock, and while it was inferior to whale oil as a means of illumination—it did not burn very clean, and it smelled, well, like kerosene—a New York businessman named John Austin had an idea to make it more appealing. As the price of whale oil climbed toward prohibitive territory, Austin discovered a new kind of lamp manufactured in Austria, which was expressly designed to burn kerosene—and to do so both cleanly and economically. Austin imported a few examples of the lamp and began tinkering with it until he had perfected the design. He began making and marketing his version of the kerosene lantern in the United States. The product caught on quickly, creating a major spike in demand for "rock oil." By the late 1850s, a good many rock oil enterprises were incorporated, among them the Pennsylvania Rock Oil Company of Connecticut, founded by Wall Street attorney George H. Bissell and his law partner, Jonathan Greenleaf Eveleth, along with five other investors.

Heavily retouched, this photograph, copyrighted in 1890, shows Edwin L. Drake (right) and the so-called Drake Well in Titusville, Pennsylvania. Drilled in 1859, it was the first commercial oil well in the United States. LIBRARY OF CONGRESS

At this point, little was known about where to look for oil—except based on what was visible on the surface. Bissell and Eveleth had been told that significant amounts of oil had been seen floating on water near Titusville, Pennsylvania. Before Austin's kerosene lamp, almost no one would have taken this as good news. Oil floating on water meant tainted water, period. But now it seemed like opportunity. The two nascent oilmen obtained a sample of the floating slick, which they took to Professor Benjamin Silliman Jr. of Yale University, the chemistry-professor son of another eminent Yale chemistry professor. Indeed, the senior Silliman had been the first person to use fractional distillation. In 1854, his son became the first American to use his father's process to fractionate petroleum by distillation. The younger Silliman was obviously the nation's authority on oil. He analyzed the sample and assured the lawyers that it would make very good kerosene for illumination.

That was enough for Bissell and Eveleth. They bought some property in Titusville, incorporated, and, having no desire to get their hands dirty, hired Edwin Drake, a businessman who had more practical knowledge about finding oil than just about any other American at the time. He dug a well on a small island in Oil Creek near Titusville, using the methods practiced by salt well drillers. He and a blacksmith named William A. Smith built a derrick and an engine house to shelter a six-horsepower steam engine, which drove the drill housed within the derrick. The work proceeded slowly—three feet per day at best—and by April 1859, just over a year after Drake had been hired, Bissell and Evelith were ready to throw in the towel. Drake personally signed for a $500 loan to keep the operation going.

At last, on August 27, 1859, the drill reached its maximum depth—sixty-nine feet, six inches. By the next day, oil was visible on top of the water five inches from the top of the well. Drake had not only built the nation's first oil well, it had also struck oil—the first time that oil was drilled for and tapped at its source. Soon, the Drake Well was producing twelve to twenty barrels a day—enough to create an oil boom that sent the price of rock oil plummeting so that Drake's pioneering well never turned a profit.

But the demand for oil continued to rise as kerosene lamps rapidly increased in popularity and variety. Cheap petroleum distillates very soon replaced whale oil as the illuminant of choice. During the next few years, Titusville and other western Pennsylvania towns sprouted wells—at first by the tens and then by the hundreds. The landscape was transformed.

Industrialists looked for new ways to use petroleum—for lighting, heating, lubricating, and, yes, for a variety of patent medicines. By 1884, oil drilling was a national industry.

Paramount among the most successful entrepreneurs of the early oil industry was John D. Rockefeller, the son of an Ohio con man, who discovered that he had a head for business and saw in oil a growth industry. With demand increasing by the month, Rockefeller focused on ways to take control of the new industry from exploration to drilling to refining to transportation. By the time the automobile began to emerge at the cusp of the twentieth century, Rockefeller and a host of smaller oil companies were well positioned to make a civilization-transforming leap. An age of coal and steam power began to give way to an age of gasoline and the internal combustion engine.

Abolitionist John Brown Leads a Raid on the Federal Arsenal at Harpers Ferry (1859)

Born in Torrington, Connecticut, in 1800, John Brown grew into something of a drifter. He settled briefly in Ohio, Pennsylvania, Massachusetts, and New York, cadging work catch-as-catch-can. He was by turns a sheep drover, tanner, wool trader, farmer, and land speculator. A white man living in a strictly segregated America, Brown nevertheless settled his family in a black community established in North Elba, New York, in 1849 on land donated by an abolitionist philanthropist named Gerrit Smith. While living there, Brown, a passionate abolitionist, yearned to devise some bold plan to begin the liberation of enslaved black Americans. He and five of his sons moved to the Kansas Territory in 1855, determined to throw in their lot with antislavery forces, which were vying with proslavery settlers for control of the territory. The idea was to ensure that Kansas would be admitted to the Union as a free state.

Brown and his boys settled at Osawatomie, which became the headquarters of local free-soil guerrillas. On May 21, 1856, a proslavery mob raided, sacked, and burned the abolitionist stronghold of Lawrence, Kansas. Believing God called on him to avenge the sack of Lawrence, Brown led a nocturnal raid against a proslavery camp at Pottawatomie Creek on May 24. He and his cohorts hacked five men to death.

Two years had passed after this attack when, in the spring of 1858, Brown convened a meeting of blacks and whites in Chatham, Ontario, Canada. He outlined to them his plan to create in the hills of Maryland and Virginia a stronghold in which fugitive slaves would not only find refuge from the Fugitive Slave Law but would also have a base from which they could launch a massive slave rebellion. Those attending the

John Brown, radical abolitionist leader of the 1859 raid on Harpers Ferry, was photographed in the late 1840s or early 1850s. NATIONAL ARCHIVES AND RECORDS ADMINISTRATION

meeting went on to outline a plan for a new provisional government of the United States, one founded on the absolute abolition of slavery. The meeting unanimously elected Brown commander in chief of the planned provisional government. With these credentials in hand, Brown secured the financial backing of Gerrit Smith and other Boston abolitionists to finance a military action for abolition.

In the summer of 1859, leading an "army" of sixteen white men and five blacks, Brown established a headquarters in a rented farmhouse in Maryland, across the Potomac River from Harpers Ferry, Virginia (today, West Virginia). The men spent the summer preparing to launch a raid on the Harpers Ferry federal arsenal and armory at the confluence of the Shenandoah and the Potomac.

On the night of October 16, 1859, Brown led his twenty-one-man army in a lightning raid that took the armory as well as Hall's Rifle Works nearby. This accomplished, the men hunkered down to defend their conquest, holding hostage some sixty locals, among whom was the great-grandnephew of George Washington. Brown delegated two of his black "troops" to recruit local slaves. He was confident that these two men would be able to stir a spontaneous army of thousands who would "swarm" the countryside.

In fact, not a single slave answered Brown's call, and when the fighting started—which it soon did—the first civilian Brown's men killed was a free black man.

That combat commenced on October 17 as the citizens of Harpers Ferry, surrounding Brown's position, opened fire and killed two of the abolitionist's sons. Desultory shooting continued through the morning and afternoon, at which point the surviving raiders barricaded themselves and their hostages in a firehouse adjacent to the armory. A militia company arrived to help the civilians, and in the meantime, President Buchanan ordered the nearest permanent federal troops, a company of US Marines, to put an end to the raid. He placed this unit under the command of Lieutenant Colonel Robert E. Lee, US Army, and Lee's former West Point student, Lieutenant James Ewell Brown "Jeb" Stuart, both of whom happened to be nearby. Lee, on leave at his estate in Arlington, Virginia—he was struggling to untangle the financial affairs of his late father-in-law—arrived on the scene in civilian clothing.

Lee moved cautiously. Letting the night of the seventeenth pass, he sent Jeb Stuart under a flag of truce in the morning to demand Brown's surrender. As expected, Brown refused. When Stuart emerged from the parley, he slowly waved his broad-brimmed cavalryman's hat in a wide circle. It was the gesture Lee had instructed him to make as a signal for the marines to charge.

They wasted no time. Rushing the firehouse, they quickly smashed in the door and stormed the room, doing what they could to protect the hostages. Two of Brown's men were instantly bayonetted, and Marine

Lieutenant Israel Green stabbed Brown with his saber and then pummeled him into submission with the flat of his blade. In the space of just three minutes, all but four of the raiders were killed. Four citizens of Harpers Ferry, including the mayor, also fell, as did a single marine.

Brown, taken into custody, rapidly recovered from his wounds. The state of Virginia, not the federal government, charged Brown and his surviving followers with treason—against *Virginia*—in addition to murder and "conspiracy to foment servile insurrection." Trial followed swiftly and, ten days after the raid began, all were sentenced to hang.

Back then, hangings were public affairs. Those in attendance included a cadet class from the Virginia Military Institute taught by Professor Thomas Jackson, who, within two years, would be far better known as "Stonewall" Jackson. Also in attendance on December 2, 1859, was a darkly handsome and very popular idol of the stage, John Wilkes Booth. If the assembled throng hoped to see a display of fear, grief, and contrition, they were profoundly disappointed. Brown met his fate quietly and with singular dignity, having already declared at his sentencing, "Now, if it is deemed necessary that I should forfeit my life for the furtherance of the ends of justice, and mingle my blood further with the blood of my children and with the blood of millions in this slave country whose rights are disregarded by wicked, cruel, and unjust enactment—I submit; so let it be done."

In truth, by hanging John Brown, Virginia gave the North a potent martyr to its most radical cause. The North was in no mood to negotiate with the South, which, having glimpsed the resolve of northern abolitionism, was now likewise bent on war.

The Confederacy Goes to War against the United States (1861)

The island on which Fort Sumter was built came from the North, as New England granite was transported to Charleston harbor and dumped there in 1829. The fort rose from it very, very slowly. It was, in fact, far from complete on the day after Christmas in 1860 when Major Robert Anderson led his garrison of two US Army artillery batteries—sixty-eight soldiers, nine officers, and eight bandsmen, along with a handful of civilian workers—out of nearby Fort Moultrie and into Fort Sumter. Six days earlier, South Carolina had seceded from the Union and dispatched newly minted Confederate troops to confiscate all federal property, especially forts and arms. Anderson determined that Sumter, out on its artificial island, was the more defensible position.

Not that he had enough men or firepower to defend it. The governor of South Carolina demanded of President James Buchanan that Sumter be surrendered. Buchanan refused, but he also refused to fortify the position significantly. Through the balance of his moribund term and during the first few weeks of Lincoln's, Anderson and his command were held under siege.

On April 11, 1861, siege was about to transition to assault. General Pierre Gustave Toutant-Beauregard arrayed what were now *Confederate* guns along the rim of the harbor at Morris, James, and Sullivan's Islands, as well as Mount Pleasant and Forts Moultrie and Johnson. All pointed at Fort Sumter. Beauregard was a graduate of West Point, trained in the artillerist's art by none other than Major Anderson. Now he put Colonel James Chestnut, a prominent South Carolina politician, and another man in a rowboat and sent them toward the fort under a flag of truce.

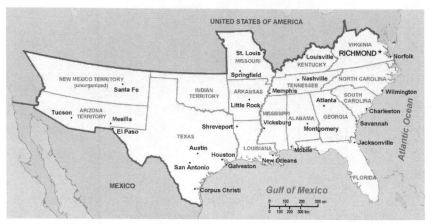

Created in 2005, this map shows the full extent of territory claimed by the Confederate States of America. Note, however, that much of Missouri, Kentucky, and the western area were never under effective Confederate control. West Virginia broke away from the rest of the state after Virginia enacted an Ordinance of Secession in 1861. It was formally admitted to the Union on June 20, 1863, in the middle of the Civil War. NICHOLAS FORTE, PUBLISHED ON WIKIMEDIA COMMONS

The emissaries delivered Beauregard's personal note to Anderson. It asked for—not demanded—the major's surrender, promising that all "proper facilities will be afforded for the removal of yourself and command, together with company arms and property, and all private property, to any post in the United States which you may elect. The flag which you have upheld so long and with so much fortitude, under the most trying circumstances, may be saluted by you on taking it down."

Anderson was not surprised by the chivalry of the note. He would have expected nothing less from a wealthy Louisianan. Indeed, Anderson admired the South, and he liked Southerners. He was a native of Kentucky married to a Georgia wife. He sympathized with Beauregard and others like him, but his allegiance, undivided, was to the US Army and the United States. He told Chestnut that the general's demand was one "with which I regret that my sense of honor, and of my obligations to my government, prevent my compliance." Then he sent the pair off with these words: "Gentlemen, if you do not batter the fort to pieces about us, we shall be starved out in a few days."

Just before one o'clock on the morning of April 12, 1861, Chestnut, this time with three others, again rowed to the fort. General Beauregard would hold his fire, they explained, on condition that Anderson provide a firm date and time on which he would withdraw. After conferring his officers, he handed Chestnut a note at 3:10 a.m. He would evacuate by April 15, unless President Buchanan ordered him otherwise.

Chestnut politely replied that the proposal was unsatisfactory. He took the note and wrote upon it a declaration warning that the bombardment of Fort Sumter would commence in one hour. Then he rowed away.

Chestnut related to his general the results of the parley. Beauregard offered Roger Pryor, who had earned a reputation as a southern "fire eater," a radical secessionist burning for war, the honor of firing the first shot of what would surely be a civil war. Beauregard had every reason to believe that Pryor would jump at the opportunity. After all, he had resigned from Congress on March 3, 1861, to rally to the Confederate colors.

"Strike a blow!" Pryor had repeatedly exhorted his fellow South Carolinians. "Strike a blow!" But now, to Beauregard, he replied that *he* "could not fire the first gun of the war."

It was nearly half past four on the morning of April 12, 1861. Chestnut had warned Anderson that the bombardment would commence in one hour. The assault was already going on a half-hour late. Tradition holds that Beauregard next offered the honor of pulling the lanyard to Edmund Ruffin, sixty-seven-year-old editor of a secessionist Virginia newspaper and a racist zealot on the subject of slavery. His dry white hair, uncut, flowed long and wild. His wide-set eyes burned with the fire of a much younger man.

As it turned out, however, Ruffin was the sole source of the story that *he* had fired the first shot of the Civil War. Historians agree that, Pryor having demurred, Beauregard simply ordered a Lieutenant Henry Farley, who commanded a two-mortar battery on James Island, to fire a small signal cannon precisely at 4:30. *That* was the first shot of some four thousand that followed.

Seeking to conserve precious ammunition, Beauregard ordered his batteries to fire one projectile at a time, in series, going around the ring of harbor emplacements in round robin. The serial bombardment continued nonstop all that Friday and into Saturday, April 13. Even at the relatively stately pace of fire, the experience must have been unnerving for Anderson and his garrison, who returned fire as best they could. With food, water, and powder dwindling, Anderson decided that having withstood a two-day bombardment without hope of reinforcement satisfied military duty and his own sense of honor. He ordered the lowering of the Stars and Stripes.

Instantly, Beauregard's guns fell silent. Fort Sumter was severely damaged. The masonry walls were battered down in many places, and most of the wooden structures within the fort had caught fire and burned to ashes. But not one of the four thousand rounds had so much as grazed a soldier of the garrison.

When the shooting ended, the gun-shy fire eater Roger Pryor was among the first to enter the remains of Fort Sumter. Beauregard had asked him to preside over the details of Anderson's surrender. After dictating terms to a clerk, Pryor took a seat on a chair inside Sumter's empty infirmary while he waited for the clerk to write out a fair copy. Thirsty from excitement, dictation, and the growing heat of a South Carolina afternoon, Pryor grabbed the closest bottle, uncorked it, put it to his lips, and drank it down. Only then did he read the label: "Iodine of Potassium."

He cried out for help. The fort's US Army surgeon rushed in, induced vomiting, and saved the rash man's life.

The next day was reserved for ceremony. Having pledged to Major Anderson that he would be accorded full military honors, he gave the man permission to fire a fifty-gun salute to the colors he had lowered. An ember from the fusillade landed on a powder keg, touching off an explosion that injured five men and killed one, Union private Daniel Hough—who thus became the first soldier to die in the Civil War. There would be—well, no one knows precisely just how many more. The most reliable estimate is 620,000, almost equal to the 644,000 total killed in every other conflict in which American military personnel fought.

The Homestead Act Becomes Law (1862)

On May 20, 1862, with the nation consumed in a civil war that, at the time, was not going at all well for the Union, Abraham Lincoln signed into law the Homestead Act of 1862. The first of several homestead laws enacted through the rest of the nineteenth century and into the early twentieth, it authorized any citizen—or foreign immigrant who swore an intention of becoming a citizen—to select any surveyed but unclaimed parcel of public land west of the Mississippi, up to 160 acres, settle it, improve it, and, by living on it for five years, gain title to it.

What were Congress and the president thinking, to create such momentous legislation while the entire nation, heart and soul, was focused on a desperate war for its very existence?

There were at least two motives. One was that Lincoln wanted his fellow Americans to look beyond the present war and into a future in which the *United* States would spread from sea to shining sea. If the war was a struggle over the abolition of slavery and the restoration of the Union here and now, the Homestead Act staked a claim on a national history yet to come. Beyond this symbolic meaning, the president hoped that by accelerating western settlement, he could strengthen what was left of the Union. If the bonds holding North and South were at present broken, here was a means of welding the East to the West.

But the legislation was about more than the war. Up to this point in American history, the management of federal lands had often been botched and corrupted. Land speculators with access to a lot of money often preempted public lands and then retailed the acreage to others at gouger's prices—or they simply bought up large tracts and used them to develop vast ranches and rangelands instead of family-oriented settlements. The Homestead Act was intended to replace abusive exploitation with orderly settlement by ordinary families, who would become the kernels around which prosperous towns would form. In addition, the

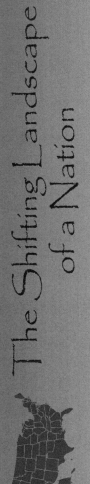

The Shifting Landscape of a Nation

In the 40 year period between 1850 and 1890, the landscape of what is now the United States underwent a dramatic change. Fourteen new states were granted statehood from former territories and republics, and hundreds of thousands of people joined the westward migration. By 1890 the US Census reported that there was no more open land that could be called "frontier."

Many of the homesteaders up to this point had settled east of the 100th Meridian, which first marked the boundary of territory between the Republic of Texas and the vast expanse of the Louisiana Purchase. The 100th meridian – near the present day border of Oklahoma and Texas – marks the general division between the humid and fertile climate of the east and the arid and dry plains states to the west.

Extent of Settled Areas, 1850

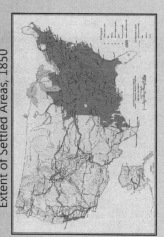

Extent of Settled Areas, 1890

Source: The National Atlas of the United States of America
U.S. Dept. of the Interior, Geological Survey, 1970

The US Bureau of Land Management published this map showing the dramatic effect of the Homestead Acts on the settlement of the American West. BUREAU OF LAND MANAGEMENT prairie lands were potentially fertile. Lincoln and others had visions of creating America's breadbasket, a northern agricultural empire, worked by free labor rather than slaves.

Any family could acquire land by living on it for five years. Alternatively, a homesteader could "preempt" the land after just six months' residence by purchasing it at the bargain price of $1.25 per acre. While the objective was to keep the parcels small enough to be family farms, those homesteaders with sufficient cash could combine preemption with their five-year basic claim, doubling 160 acres to 320.

There was yet another option. A homesteader could add to an original 160-acre grant by staking a "timber claim." The one thing the Great Plains needed was trees. Those who planted ten acres of timber-producing trees on an adjacent available claim were entitled to own an additional 160 acres. Planting them was not easy. The tightly packed, cloddish soil presented a stout barrier to root systems and had to be laboriously broken up. The fact is that technology played a key role in making the Homestead Act possible. Only the development of John Deere's "Grand Detour Plow"—it was named after Deere's hometown, Grand Detour, Illinois—made farming the stubborn prairie soil practical. In 1837, Deere designed and built the first commercially successful cast-steel plow, its share, polished and sharpened to the shape of some slick ship's prow, set into an indestructible wrought-iron frame. Within little more than a decade of its debut, Deere had perfected the design and had begun large-scale manufacture. Equipped with the new plow, the homesteader-farmers of 1862 onward were aptly nicknamed "sodbusters."

While the hard prairie sod made farming difficult, it did offer an abundant and free building material. Building log cabins was all but impossible on the treeless plains, so sodbusters cut the earth into raw bricks. They began by digging a hole in the ground, called a dugout. After laying out a rectangle on the nearest rising slope of earth, they excavated the sod to a depth of six feet and used the slope as one wall. With bricks cut from the sod, settlers raised side and front walls to a height of two or three feet and roofed the entire structure with boards or thatch that was sealed with more sod. The earth-fast house rose barely above ground level, but it provided shelter against the harsh prairie climate. Earth was an excellent insulator—if not particularly clean. As the months and years passed and the family became more settled, they might devote time and energy to building a more comfortable home.

Formulated though it was to prevent fraud and exploitation, the Homestead Act was far from perfect. Ingenious scoundrels found all the loopholes. The legislation stipulated that homesteaders could secure their claim only by constructing a house at least twelve by twelve, with windows. This prompted some unscrupulous speculators to build a house on wheels and then pull it from one claim to another. For the law had specified nothing about the house having to be permanent. Nor did the legislation language go beyond specifying a "twelve-by-twelve" floorplan. "Feet" was intended, but the word was not used, and some speculators set down scale-model miniature houses, twelve by twelve *inches*, complete with tiny windows, in the midst of their 160 acres, protesting that they had satisfied the letter of the law.

Stories of such exploits abounded. They were more amusing than outrageous. Indeed, the true criminals were not the individual con men but the powerful railroads and mining companies, which laid claims by means of "dummy entrymen," individuals hired to file as if they were legitimate homesteaders, only to relinquish their property to the big corporate interests.

Notwithstanding the hardships of prairie life—nightmarish weather, terrible isolation and loneliness, hard labor, and absolute self-reliance—and notwithstanding abuses of the law, the Homestead Act of 1862 and the laws that followed opened the West to thousands, hundreds of thousands, and, ultimately, millions. Sodbusters have often been called a new breed of Westerner. They were families, not the solitary trappers, the bachelor soldiers, and trailblazer-explorers who had come to the West before them. Yet, farmers and farm families had been following frontier adventurers ever since Daniel Boone crossed the Appalachians into Kentucky in the late eighteenth century. What *was* radically new was that the 1862 law made such family settlement and community creation a mission of the federal government. The homestead would serve as the cultural integument of an American national civilization reaching boldly across the entire continent.

Abraham Lincoln Issues the Emancipation Proclamation (1862)

On August 19, 1862, abolitionist editor Horace Greeley published in his *New-York Tribune* "The Prayer of the Twenty Millions," an open letter to Abraham Lincoln demanding the president act to free the slaves. Three days later, Lincoln replied, "My paramount object in this struggle is to save the Union," he explained, "and is not either to save or to destroy slavery. If I could save the Union without freeing any slave I would do it, and if I could save it by freeing all the slaves I would do it; and if I could save it by freeing some and leaving others alone I would also do that."

What Lincoln didn't mention was that he already had a draft of an "Emancipation Proclamation" in his desk drawer. The year before, in August 1861, Lincoln asked Congress to declare slaves in the rebellious states "contraband" property so that they could be seized by the federal government, which could then refuse to return them. In March 1862, Congress passed a law forbidding Union army officers from returning fugitive slaves to their owners. In July 1862, Congress enacted legislation freeing slaves confiscated from owners who were "engaged in rebellion."

Clearly, the Lincoln administration had been steadily edging toward emancipation, but Secretary of State William H. Seward warned the president that an outright proclamation of emancipation would ring hollow in the wake of the Union's mostly miserable performance on the battlefield. On September 17, 1862, the Union's Army of the Potomac, under Major General George B. McClellan, clashed with Robert E. Lee's Army of Northern Virginia near Sharpsburg, Maryland. The resulting Battle of Antietam pitted 75,000 Union troops against 39,000 Confederates, resulting in 12,410 Northern casualties and some 10,246 Southern losses.

It was the single bloodiest day in American history up to that time, and Lincoln was both appalled and heartbroken. Despite enjoying the

President Lincoln used the narrow Union victory at the Battle of Antietam as a platform from which to issue the Emancipation Proclamation. This photograph suggests the awful cost of that Maryland battle. NATIONAL ARCHIVES AND RECORDS ADMINISTRATION

advantage of superior numbers, McClellan had achieved at most a tactical draw. Nevertheless, in driving Lee out of Maryland, he did win a strategic victory.

"I have thought all along that the time for acting on [emancipation] might probably come. I think the time has come now," Lincoln told his Cabinet. "I wish it was a better time. I wish that we were in a better condition. The action of the army against the rebels has not been quite what I should have best liked. But they have been driven out of Maryland, and Pennsylvania is no longer in danger of invasion. . . . I have got you together to hear what I have written down. I do not wish your advice about the main matter—for that I have determined for myself. . . . What I have written is that which my reflections have determined me to say."

What he read aloud—and what he published the next day, September 23, 1862, as the Preliminary Emancipation Proclamation—freed not a single slave. It merely warned slave owners living in states "still in rebellion on January 1, 1863," that their slaves would be declared "forever free." Only after the deadline had passed was the "final" Emancipation Proclamation issued. It proclaimed freedom only for those slaves living in areas of the Confederacy that were *not* under the control of the Union army. Since the United States had no control in these areas, the slaves might be declared free but could not be freed in fact. In the border states (slaveholding states that had not left the Union) as well as in the parts of the South that *were* currently under Union military occupation and control, slavery was simply permitted to continue.

Lincoln trod a razor-thin line. The Constitution implied that he, as commander in chief, had the power to confiscate contraband property in time of war, but it also recognized slavery and certainly did not authorize the president to end slavery. Had Lincoln unilaterally emancipated all slaves everywhere, his action would have been subject after the war to legal challenge, which the Supreme Court would almost certainly have upheld. Lincoln feared that any rash action now would end up later affirming the legality of slavery—forever. He also feared that emancipating slaves in the border states would drive those states into the arms of the Confederacy, and that freeing slaves in Union-occupied secession territory would reinvigorate violent rebellion in these hard-won areas.

Viewed, then, from a twenty-first-century perspective, the Emancipation Proclamation seems both lawyerly and timid. Yet it was sufficient to elevate the Civil War to a higher moral and spiritual plane, transforming it into a crusade against slavery. This not only galvanized the Northern will to fight to a total victory, which included both the restoration of the *United* States and an end to slavery, but it also ended the South's hope of finding allies abroad. No foreign power—including Great Britain and France, which had shown early sympathy to the Confederate cause—was now about to proclaim itself a defender of human oppression.

True, the Emancipation Proclamation was both severely limited and quite impossible to enforce. Yet it created a legal precedent that resulted in Senate passage of the Thirteenth Amendment to the Constitution on April 8, 1864, and, after a close-fought and intensely bitter fight, passage by the House on January 31, 1865. Ratified by the states on December 18,

1865—some eight months after the assassination of Abraham Lincoln and seven months after the end of the Civil War—the amendment contained but one bold substantive sentence: "Neither slavery nor involuntary servitude, except as a punishment for crime whereof the party shall have been duly convicted, shall exist within the United States, or any place subject to their jurisdiction."

The Union Army Prevails in the Battle of Gettysburg (1863)

Smaller in population, poorly industrialized, and economically challenged, the South was not well positioned to prevail in the Civil War. Nevertheless, Confederate commanders had so far often outgeneraled Union officers, and the commitment of the Northern population to continue a horrifically costly war was always in doubt. Robert E. Lee was commander of the Army of Northern Virginia but, effectively, he was also the senior general of Confederate military forces. His original strategy had favored resisting Northern attempts to conquer the South. His objective was to defend Confederate territory so vigorously that the people of the Union would deem the cost of suppressing the rebellion simply too high, and the two sides would make a peace on terms favorable to the Confederacy.

Yet the war ground on, and it became apparent to Lee that the North could sustain a strategy of attrition far longer than the South. The North could lose men and materiel because it had a lot more of both. By the summer of 1863, Lee decided to take the offensive by invading the North. Do this successfully, and the northern will to continue the fight would be severely undermined.

Lee's Army of Northern Virginia consisted of between seventy-one thousand and seventy-five thousand men at the time. On June 15, elements of it crossed the Potomac River into Maryland. Lee's chief of cavalry, Jeb Stuart, skirmished in Virginia between June 17 and June 21. On June 24, he headed east, rode around the rear of the Union's Army of the Potomac, disrupted supply lines, and captured four hundred prisoners. It was a bold operation, but it took much longer than anticipated, depriving Lee of what he needed most: reconnaissance to determine just where the main Union positions were.

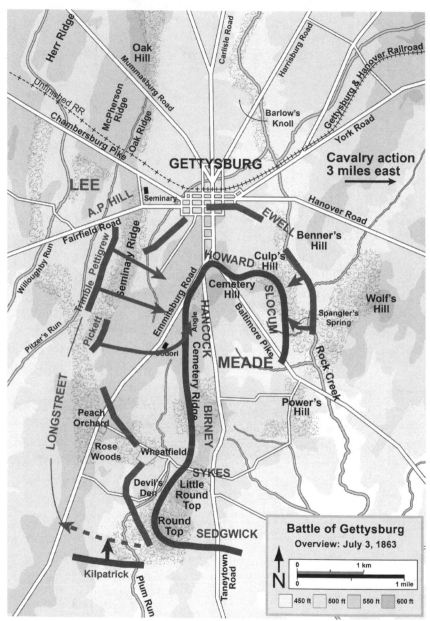

The Battle of Gettysburg spanned July 1–3, 1863. This map shows the Confederate and Union positions on the final day of the battle, in which Robert E. Lee suffered a catastrophic defeat. WIKIMEDIA COMMONS

Lee had not planned to fight the North's principal army in the Pennsylvania crossroads town of Gettysburg, but a Confederate infantry brigade under Brigadier General Richard S. Ewell, foraging for supplies, stumbled into a Union cavalry brigade there. Although he was greatly outnumbered, Union Brigadier General John Buford was determined to prevent Ewell from capturing the high ground on the periphery of central Gettysburg. The Battle of Gettysburg thus began at 9:00 a.m. on July 1, 1863, and by the time Union reinforcements from the main body of the Army of the Potomac arrived, Ewell had been joined by more units from the Army of Northern Virginia. Lee was now on the offensive.

By midday the fighting was chaotic, but, after violent seesaw combat, the Confederates finally drove the Union troops back through the streets of Gettysburg, fighting hand-to-hand before the Northerners withdrew southeast of town along the Baltimore Pike. Because he had no definitive command from Lee, Ewell broke off pursuit. This yielded to Union commanders precious time to take up new positions on the contiguous high ground of East Cemetery Hill, Cemetery Ridge, and Culp's Hill.

On the morning of July 2, the second day of the Battle of Gettysburg, Lee was still out of communication with Stuart and therefore unaware of how large a Union force he was facing. Single-mindedly, however, he was determined to maintain the offensive. His second-in-command, General James Longstreet, protested that, most likely, they were about to face the bulk of the Army of the Potomac, which certainly vastly outnumbered them. He advised withdrawing to the south and maneuvering to attack the enemy from the rear. Lee objected vehemently. To withdraw after achieving a victory on the day before would be demoralizing.

Major General George Gordon Meade, commanding the Army of the Potomac, deployed his forces on high ground that gave them clear fields of view and fire. By day two, nearly ninety thousand Union soldiers opposed something more than seventy thousand Confederates. From a flying bird's perspective, Meade's line would have looked like a giant fishhook. The barb end was just south of Culp's Hill, the hook's curve at Cemetery Hill, the shaft running along Cemetery Ridge, and the tie end of the shaft secured at two hills south of town, Little Round Top and Big Round Top. Lee ordered Longstreet to attack the Union left, the fishhook's shaft and tie end. Ewell was to swing down to smash into the Union's right, the hook and barb at Cemetery Hill and Culp's Hill.

One of Longstreet's subordinate commanders, Major General John Bell Hood, attacked through an area called the Devil's Den and drove Meade's left backward. Realizing that the Confederates were about to seize undefended high ground on the Round Tops, which would put them in a position to roll up the flank of the Union line, Meade's chief engineer, Brigadier General Gouverneur K. Warren, ordered in reinforcements. At the extreme south end of the Union flank was Colonel Joshua Lawrence Chamberlain's Twentieth Maine regiment, which had lost half its strength in the previous day's fighting. Outnumbered by attackers and, what is more, out of ammunition, Chamberlain—a Bowdoin College professor—ordered a desperate downhill bayonet charge into the superior Confederate force. To his amazement, the attackers surrendered. Chamberlain did not win the Battle of Gettysburg on July 2, 1863, but he kept the Army of the Potomac from losing it. It was one of the key tactical tipping points of the Civil War.

As for Lee, he had not won the battle on day 2, as he had hoped. But, come the morning of July 3, he judged that he had sufficiently worn down the enemy to attempt a massive infantry charge across the wide-open field of fire separating his position from the Union line and then fighting that line uphill. Once again, Longstreet objected. Overruled by Lee, he dutifully ordered his commanders to execute the open advance, under heavy fire, of some 12,500 soldiers in what history calls "Pickett's Charge"—although Major General George Pickett commanded only three of the nine brigades involved.

The advance stepped off at 1:45 p.m., in close order, through the withering fire of muskets and artillery, which killed or wounded some 60 percent of those committed to the charge. A handful of Confederate troops did manage to penetrate the Union line but were quickly overwhelmed and cut down. The horrific failure of Pickett's Charge ended the Battle of Gettysburg in Lee's defeat.

The opposing armies held their positions on July 4, but they did not fight, and, that night, Lee began his grim withdrawal back into Virginia. Meade judged that his army was too spent to pursue. Although Abraham

Lincoln was gratified by the defeat of the Confederate invasion, he wrote sternly to Meade, "Your golden opportunity is gone, and I am distressed immeasurably because of it." The Union suffered 23,049 casualties, killed wounded, captured, and missing. Lee lost between twenty-three thousand and twenty-eight thousand killed, wounded, captured, and missing. Months later, on November 19, 1863, President Lincoln would deliver a two-minute speech at the dedication of a military cemetery on the Gettysburg battlefield. In it, he succeeded in defining the significance of the battle and the war: "It is for us the living . . . to be dedicated here to the unfinished work which they who fought here have thus far so nobly advanced," he said. "It is . . . for us to be here dedicated to the great task remaining before us—that from these honored dead we take increased devotion to that cause for which they gave the last full measure of devotion—that we here highly resolve that these dead shall not have died in vain—that this nation, under God, shall have a new birth of freedom—and that government of the people, by the people, for the people shall not perish from the earth."

John Wilkes Booth Assassinates President Lincoln (1865)

The election of Abraham Lincoln—"Black Lincoln," as many Southerners called him—in November 1860 not only broke the nation in two, it also put a target on the person of the American president. Baltimore was the principal city of Maryland, a "border state"—slave-holding but not part of the Confederacy then forming. Here, hardcore Southern sympathizers planned to assassinate the president-elect as he passed through the city on the final leg of his journey from his home in Springfield, Illinois, to inauguration in Washington early in 1861. No less a figure than Allan J. Pinkerton, the man who invented the profession of private investigator, working under contract as head of the government's intelligence service, disrupted the Baltimore plot. Throughout the war, however, security surrounding the president was nearly nonexistent. In those days, the White House was truly the people's house, its halls routinely jammed with seekers after offices and other favors.

Late in 1864, John Wilkes Booth, matinee idol son of America's most celebrated theatrical family, a Marylander who embraced the Confederate cause (albeit short of volunteering to fight), formulated a plot to kidnap Lincoln with the object of trading him for the release of Confederate prisoners of war. He recruited two boyhood Maryland friends, Michael O'Laughlin and Sam Arnold, in addition to George A. Atzerodt, David Herold, and John Surratt. The president was scheduled to attend a performance of a play, *Still Waters Run Deep*, to be given at a military hospital near the Old Soldiers Home outside of Washington. Booth's idea was to waylay Lincoln's carriage en route. He and the others waited, but the president had changed plans and instead attended a reception at Washington's National Hotel—as it turned out, the very hotel in which Booth was staying.

Currier and Ives published this lithograph shortly after the Lincoln assassination. It shows John Wilkes Booth firing the fatal shot, and Mary Todd Lincoln is seen to the president's right, along with the Lincolns' guests Clara Harris and her fiancé, Major Henry Rathbone.
WIKIMEDIA COMMONS

Bitterly disappointed, Booth descended into a black mood that only deepened as the nation's capital celebrated the fall of Richmond on April 3, 1865, and the surrender of Robert E. Lee six days later. The curtain on history's greatest production was coming down, and Booth had yet to play a part.

With the war all but over, kidnapping was pointless. All that remained was revenge. In the two or three days before Good Friday, April 14, the day set for the assassination, Booth began drinking heavily. Of his original conspiratorial band, only Herold and Atzerodt were left, but they were joined by a former Confederate soldier who called himself Lewis Paine and whose given name was Louis Thornton Powell. Booth assigned Atzerodt to kill Vice President Andrew Johnson. Paine and Herold were assigned to murder Secretary of State William H. Seward, an old man convalescing in his home from severe injuries sustained in a carriage accident. Booth claimed the starring role. He himself would kill Lincoln.

Everything was set to go on the evening of the fourteenth. Mostly, it did not go at all well.

Atzerodt got cold feet and never even approached the vice president. While Herold held a horse for him, Paine knocked on the door of the Seward house, claiming to have medicine from Seward's doctor. When Seward's son, Augustus, offered to accept it, Paine knocked him down and dashed into the secretary's bedroom. He bludgeoned and stabbed Seward, clear through the cheek, but the old man, broken bones and all, rolled off and under the bed. In all, Paine attacked and injured Augustus, Seward's daughter Fanny, stabbed a State Department messenger, and slashed a male nurse before running out of the house, screaming "I'm mad! I'm mad."

While these events unspooled, Booth walked into Ford's Theatre, a place the actor knew well. He entered the president's box at about 10 p.m. The lock on its was broken, whether by design or coincidentally has never been determined. Officer John F. Parker, the Washington Metropolitan policeman assigned to guard entry to the box, was absent.

Booth approached. Inches from the president now, he leveled his derringer between Lincoln's left ear and spine. He squeezed the trigger to fire the weapon's single shot. Probably no one among the audience heard it. Even Mary Todd Lincoln, seated next to her husband, and their guests, Major Henry Rathbone and his fiancée, Clara Hamilton Harris, were barely aware of the discharge. The actor-assassin knew well the evening's tremendously popular comedy *Our American Cousin*, and he timed his shot to coincide with the line that always produced the biggest, most protracted laugh.

While the deed was performed with stealth, acrid smoke soon hung heavy in the box. Booth rushed forward to the rail overlooking the stage. Rathbone briefly tangled with him, only to be stabbed in the shoulder just before Booth broke free, mounted the rail, and jumped to the stage below.

"Sic semper tyrannis!"—*Thus ever to tyrants!*—he declaimed. It was the state motto of Virginia. But Booth was not unscathed. As he leapt, he caught his right spur in the Treasury Regiment flag festooning the box. His left foot took all the impact of his leap and broke just above the instep. As a stunned audience looked on, Booth limped into the wings, exited through the rear of the theater and into a byway everyone called Baptist

Alley, mounted a waiting horse, and made his escape from the Capital—so easily, in fact, that a massive conspiracy was instantly suspected.

Booth and Herold retrieved weapons earlier secreted in Surrattsville, Maryland, and rode to the house of Dr. Samuel A. Mudd, who splinted the assassin's broken leg. They crossed the Potomac on April 22 and the Rappahannock on the twenty-fourth, some twenty miles below Fredericksburg, Virginia. By now, the largest manhunt in American history to that time was fanned out across the countryside in search of the conspirators. Colonel Lafayette C. Baker, formerly chief of a band of federal agents calling themselves the National Detective Police, sent a small detachment under the direct command of his cousin Luther Baker to precisely the place where Booth and Herold had taken refuge. How Baker knew where to find them has never been adequately explained.

After midnight on April 26, the manhunters closed in on the Garrett family's Virginia tobacco barn. Herold gave himself up, but Booth refused to leave the barn. The soldiers decided to burn him out. Booth was visible through spaces in the barn boards, a silhouette against the flames. Someone—the soldier who claimed credit was Sergeant Boston Corbett—shot at that silhouette. The round passed through Booth's neck. He was dragged from the blazing structure and laid out on Garrett's porch, paralyzed.

"I thought I did for the best," Booth reportedly said. Asking one of the soldiers to lift his hands for him so that he might see them, he whispered, "Useless, useless." Some say these were his final words.

Booth did not live to see the effect of the murder. Intended as southern vengeance, it instead brought down upon the defeated South the bitter wrath of the victorious North. Under Lincoln's leadership, the government would have doubtless attempted to pursue a policy of reconciliation. Absent Lincoln, Radical Republicans held sway in Congress, commandeered Reconstruction policy, and punished the South economically and politically even as they vigorously pursued the enfranchisement and rights of former slaves. The heavy hand of Reconstruction without Lincoln produced southern white resistance and unleashed a reign of terror against the region's African American population. It is a racial divide yet to be erased.

The Cowboy Becomes an American Icon (1866)

The young men of Texas answered in large numbers the Confederacy's call for volunteers at the outbreak of the Civil War. Those among them who owned livestock turned them loose on what Texas had in plenty: land—"range." The animals fended and foraged for themselves, and they ended up doing astoundingly well. By war's end, millions of head of cattle ranged freely across the state. Good thing, too. For these were now among the precious few money-making resources Texas had to offer. The defeat of the South had visited economic ruin on the former western Confederacy. The men who had survived the war to come marching home found the South a wreck. Texans as well as veterans from other parts of the former Confederacy learned of the strays just waiting to be rounded up, branded, and driven to hungry markets in the victorious, prosperous North. That is how the trail drive cattle business began.

Rarely can the birth of a great industry be traced to a single man. In the case of the trail drive industry, however, Charlie Goodnight is as likely a candidate as any for the title of father. Born on a southern Illinois farm in 1836, Goodnight settled in the Brazos River country of Texas with his family in 1845. Even then, the longhorns ran wild, and ranchers needed skilled horsemen to round up unclaimed beeves, put a brand on them, and lead them to market. Thus, the profession of the cowboy developed.

But Charlie Goodnight had bigger dreams than being a hired hand, even if he liked the way he looked on a horse. Partnering with his step-brother, Goodnight began assembling his own small herd—only to leave the state, like so many others, to fight for the Confederacy. He joined the Texas Rangers early in the war, fought, and then mustered out in 1864, a year before Appomattox. On his return, reunited with his stepbrother, he marveled at his good fortune. When he had ridden off to war, he left a herd of 180 head. Now it numbered more than five thousand. And that was just the beginning. The two men rode the open range, rounding up every stray they spotted, adding each to their multiplied herd.

Money on the hoof is not money in the hand. At mid-century, the ranchers of Texas routinely drove their cattle to the railheads of Kansas, from which they would be shipped to eastern markets. There was no shortage of cattle going into Kansas—so many animals, in fact, that prices per head were chronically depressed as supply nosed closer to demand. Goodnight wanted as much as he could possibly get for his four-footed treasure. So, with Oliver Loving, a cattleman from way back, he decided to drive his herd in a totally different direction. While common sense dictated getting the meat to the most densely populated parts of the country—namely east of the Mississippi—Goodnight knew that postwar mining operations and military outposts were not only peopling the West but also creating a major, underserved demand for beef. He and Loving resolved to pioneer a cattle trail to Colorado, where both mine production and Indian fighting were now big business.

In 1866, the pair set out together with two thousand of their longhorns. They hired eighteen riders to work for them. When all was ready, they rode out, animals and men together, following the stage route of the Southern Overland Mail to the head of the Concho River. Here they paused to give their stock a long, long drink. The desert they faced beyond the Concho was hot, unforgiving, and, mostly, bone dry.

They counted on suffering losses. Before they reached their endpoint in the markets of Colorado, Goodnight and Loving had lost about four hundred head. Three hundred had dropped dead of thirst, and another hundred were trampled to death in a frantic stampede when a waterhole was finally reached. Ordinarily, such "wastage" would have been catastrophic. So great was the surging demand in Colorado, however, that this, the very first drive along the Goodnight-Loving Trail, netted the two men $12,000 in gold.

The Goodnight-Loving Trail became the first of the four principal cattle trails blazed in the years following the Civil War. The Chisholm trail ran from Brownsville, Texas, to the Kansas railheads of Dodge City, Ellsworth, Abilene, and Junction City. The Shawnee Trail left Brownsville and headed into Kansas City, Sedalia, and St. Louis, Missouri. The Western ran from San Antonio, Texas, to Dodge City, and then on to Fort Buford, at the fork of the Missouri and Yellowstone rivers, deep in Dakota Territory.

It was boom times for cattle drivers. But like so much else in the Western economy, boom was followed by bust. During the frigid winter of 1886–1887, the unrelenting assault of nature virtually wiped out the range-cattle business. It was the agricultural version of Napoleon's retreat through the snows of Russia in 1812. Nevertheless, between 1866, when Loving and Goodnight pioneered their trail, and that apocalyptic winter of 1886–1887, nearly one hundred million beeves and ten million horses were driven along the four legendary trails.

Why were these trails the stuff of legend?

They moved more than beef. They created the trail drive cowboy, who was quickly elevated to become the single most cherished and celebrated worker in the nation's history. The Middle Ages produced the mounted knight in Europe. In the American West, the cowboy who came into being at the end of a war that had nearly brought an end to the nation became America's own knight on horseback. He was a colorful figure—his "armor" a high, broad-brimmed hat, a bright bandanna, and elaborately worked high-heeled boots with spurs at his feet—and he was deemed brave, honest, and by nature noble. In a nation embittered by war and peopled, it seemed, by crooked politicians, rapacious plutocrats, corrupt police, and tyrannical bosses, the cowboy was beholden to nothing and to no one except the animals given into his care.

Such, in any case, was the narrative quickly spun about men who were, when you came down to it, among the poorest of the poor. The first generation of cowboys were mostly Confederate veterans bereft of friends, family, and property. Many were misfits, loners who could hold no job but the dirtiest and most dangerous. Very rapidly, new groups were added to the cohort of former Confederates. While popular culture pictures the cowboy as a physically rugged specimen of Anglo-Saxon manhood, many were Indians, African Americans, and Mexicans, people whose ethnicity consigned them to the lowest rungs of white western American society.

The cowboy's work was dirty, dangerous, exhausting, lonely, and poorly compensated. Yet the romance of the cowboy persists and is an indelible feature of American iconography, mythology, and collective identity.

The Transcontinental Railroad Is Completed (1869)

The Lincoln administration committed the nation's resources and focus to fighting the Civil War to absolute victory. Yet the president also took on two other major initiatives. The first was ushering through Congress the Homestead Act of 1862, and the second was the Pacific Railroad Act of 1862, which was variously modified by four additional railroad acts, in 1863, 1864, 1865, and 1866. As with the Homestead initiative, the railroad acts were about strengthening the Union along its East-West axis even as the nation had split apart North from South. Like homesteading as well, western railroading looked to the future, proclaiming the essential faith of both Congress and the president in a Union that was destined to live and prosper as one nation.

The Pacific Railway Act and the legislation that followed granted huge tracts of public land to the Union Pacific, which laid track from east to west, and the Central Pacific, which built eastward from the West Coast. The lands were granted not just for the right of way—the corridor through which the tracks were laid—but also for the two railroads to sell to pay for construction while also populating the countryside adjacent to the rails. As if this were not enough, the government also funded or guaranteed large packages of loans.

Strangely, despite the abundant funding in place, the transcontinental railroad project was slow to get under way. Even after construction finally began on both the eastward-bound Central Pacific and the westward-heading Union Pacific, the pace soon slackened. Legislation enacted in 1864 provided greater incentives to move forward, but when this stimulus fell short, President Lincoln, in 1865, called in a friend, the prominent industrialist Oakes Ames. His original fortune had been built on the manufacture and sale of all manner of shovels and tools for excavation. For this reason, he was popularly known as the Ace of Spades.

In 1887, the US Pacific Railway Commission presented to Congress this "Diagram of the Transcontinental lines of road Showing the Original Central Pacific and Union Pacific And their Competitors." The Union Pacific-Central Pacific route is the thickest line, running from Omaha, Nebraska, to Los Angeles and Sacramento in California. THE COOPER COLLECTION OF US RAILROAD HISTORY, PUBLISHED ON WIKIMEDIA COMMONS

Lincoln asked Ames to "take hold of" the railroad project. With that admonition, the president gave him carte blanche and subjected him to precious little oversight. The Ace of Spades dug in with a passion, vigorously recruiting investors in a corporation conjured up by Union Pacific vice president Thomas Durant. Named after the company that had successfully financed the French railway system a decade earlier, Crédit Mobilier was unlike any previous business proposition. It was, in fact, the mother of all sweetheart deals for investors. It worked like this: Crédit

Mobilier, which was run by the directors of the Union Pacific, was paid by the Union Pacific to build the Union Pacific. Because the directors were also the principal investors, they made a profit on the railroad as well as on the cost of building the railroad. Put most simply, the board members were investing in themselves.

Not surprisingly, the Crédit Mobilier scheme incentivized elaborately padded construction bills and all species of additional corruption, which finally blew up into a spectacular scandal the like of which would not be seen in America again until the Enron fraud of 2002.

Crédit Mobilier might be written off as one of American history's greatest embarrassments were it not for the fact that the thoroughly corrupt company not only got the railroad off the dime, it also got it completed. Under the direction of Major General Grenville Mellon Dodge, a US Army engineer, the Union Pacific began laying prodigious lengths of track—266 miles in 1866 alone. In places, the terrain was extraordinarily challenging, the weather potentially deadly, and the remoteness from sources of supply formidable. In some country, construction crews were menaced by hostile Plains Indians. Yet the Union Pacific and Central Pacific kept laying track. They drew heavily upon immigrants for labor. The westward-moving Union Pacific hired large numbers of recent Irish arrivals. The Central Pacific, progressing from the Pacific Coast, used new Chinese immigrants. Western geography presented the more daunting obstacles, in the form of spectacular mountain ranges, to the Central Pacific. In places roadbed had to be blasted out of the sides of mountains or tunnels blasted through them. The mortality rate, especially among the Chinese, was very high.

While the immigrants supplied the muscle, the railroad tycoons furnished the graft necessary to buy off government officials and others with power or influence. In turn, hopeful western towns, yearning to prosper by becoming stations along the great iron road, lavished bribes on managers, engineers, and tycoons. As for feeding the workers, the railroads—especially the Union Pacific—hired buffalo hunters such as William "Buffalo Bill" Cody to slay the herds of bison that roamed the plains, ensuring a steady supply of red-blood protein to keep the human machines running.

The herds were not merely overhunted, they were hunted nearly to extinction. But this was not the only symptom of government prodigality. Public acreage was given away by the millions of acres. It was pegged to the amount of track laid, an incentive that induced the converging railroads to build past each other for some two hundred miles before they were finally coaxed to meet at Promontory Summit, Utah. On May 10, 1869, the eastbound and westbound rails were joined. Workers and executives alike gathered to witness the moment of continental union, which was symbolized by Central Pacific president Leland Stanford, whose task was to drive a ceremonial Golden Spike into the final tie. Telegraph wires were connected to the spike and the hammer so that each blow would be transmitted nationally.

The ceremonial union was a grand idea. But it did not go at all well. To begin with, a gang of Chinese workmen, having endured the hateful threats and acts of their Caucasian employers and coworkers, gingerly lowered the final length of rail in place when a photographer assigned to commemorate this hollered out, "*Shoot!*" The workers dropped the five hundred-pound rail and ran—they thought—for their lives. Then came Leland Stanford. A powerful member of California's "Big Four" railroad tycoons—the others were Collis Huntington, Mark Hopkins, and Charles Crocker—Stanford raised the sledge to drive the spike, came down hard on it, and missed. Repeatedly. At last, a laborer gave him a hand, and the Golden Spike was finally driven home. Between the earlier expansion of the telegraph and the completion of the transcontinental railroad, the American nation took a step toward the conquest of its single greatest geographical feature: seemingly limitless space, as daunting as it was full of opportunity.

Sitting Bull and Crazy Horse Triumph
in the Battle of the Little Bighorn (1876)

The policy of the US government toward Native Americans swung like a broken pendulum from one extreme to another. At times, it was respectful of Native rights and claims, at others oblivious or even antagonistic to them. Treaties were made in abundance and, in abundance, broken— more often by the government than by the tribes. While some tribes were ordered to confinement on designated reservations, the government also recognized tribal ownership of certain lands. Among them were the Black Hills of the Montana and Wyoming territories. Yet the federal government had little practical power to enforce Indian property rights, and, provoked by frequent white incursions into the Black Hills, the Lakota and Dakota Sioux of the northern Plains responded by almost routinely raiding settlements in Montana, Wyoming, and Nebraska during the 1870s.

A low-level state of war was well under way when, in 1874, Lieutenant Colonel George Armstrong Custer led a military expedition into the Black Hills. His mission was to police the "hostiles," but, along the way, his command discovered gold. Word quickly spread and, within a year, in breach of the 1868 Treaty of Fort Laramie, thousands of prospectors swarmed hills the Sioux considered sacred. Hoping to avert a wider war, the government offered to purchase or even lease the Black Hills from the Indians. The tribes would not, however, compromise their spiritual beliefs. At last, as 1875 ended, the government cut off negotiations and summarily ordered Dakota and Lakota people to report to a reservation by January 31, 1876. Those outside of the reservation after that date would be deemed hostile, pursued, and, if need be, killed.

General Philip Sheridan, justly or unjustly associated with the aphorism "The only good Indian is a dead Indian," launched a winter campaign

Sitting Bull was the Hunkpapa Lakota leader most universally associated with the final stages of the Native American resistance to the Indian policies of the US government. LIBRARY OF CONGRESS

immediately after the deadline. Relentless storms soon brought that to an end, and a new campaign began late in the spring of 1876. Sheridan's plan was for Major General Alfred Terry to lead a force from the east—which included Custer and his 7th Cavalry—while another force, under Colonel John Gibbon, marched from the west. A third contingent, commanded by Major General George Crook, was to advance out of Fort Fetterman (eleven miles northwest of present-day Douglas, Wyoming). The three forces were to converge on the Yellowstone River, toward which, according to the army's scouts, the Sioux were traveling.

On the morning of June 17, Crook, leading more than one thousand troopers, halted to rest at the head of the Rosebud Creek, in what is today South Dakota. His Crow and Shoshoni scouts sighted Sioux and Cheyenne led by Sitting Bull, a Hunkpapa Lakota "chief" recognized widely as a leader of the resistance against US government policies. The scouts' warning averted an outright ambush, but the Indians fell upon Crook's position nevertheless, and a six-hour battle ensued. Crook's column got the worst of the encounter and was forced to retreat. Sitting Bull's warriors set up camp on the ground Crook had vacated.

While the Rosebud fight was under way, Terry's column linked up with Gibbon's at the mouth of the Rosebud. Unaware of Crook's withdrawal, the officers of both commands, Custer included, held a council of war in a cabin aboard the Yellowstone River steamer *Far West*. Here they laid out their strategy for the next phase of the campaign. The men were confident that they would find the "hostiles" encamped on a stream the Indians called the Greasy Grass and the white men called the Little Bighorn. What they lacked was any idea of the size of the camp.

The absence of this intelligence proved fatal. The Sioux village along the Little Bighorn had grown with the arrival of Indians who had left the reservation for the spring and summer. Now some seven thousand were camped on the river, among them many warriors.

The *Far West* plan called for Custer to lead the 7th up the Rosebud, cross to the Little Bighorn, and then march down its valley from the south as Terry and Gibbon marched up the Yellowstone and Bighorn to block the Indians' route of retreat from the north. Sitting Bull, they believed, would be crushed between the pincers of a two-column flanking assault.

The operation stepped off on the morning of June 22. It was assumed that Custer's cavalry would be the first to make contact and thus would begin the fight, driving the Indians against the other column, catching them between Custer and the forces of Gibbon and Terry. To the strains of its regimental marching tune, "Garry Owen," the 7th Cavalry passed in review before Terry and Gibbon. As Custer rode off to join his men, Gibbon called after him: "Now, Custer, don't be greedy, but wait for us."

"No, I will not," Custer called over his shoulder.

In fact, he departed from the *Far West* plan of crossing to the Little Bighorn Valley south of the Indians' position because he concluded that the trail of Sitting Bull's warriors was fresher than had been thought. On June 25, Custer's scouts discovered a Sioux camp as well as warriors near it. The prudent action would have been additional reconnaissance to estimate numbers. But Custer—called the "Boy General" during the Civil War—was anything but prudent. Maximum aggression was the only language he spoke, and his only focus now was to attack before the enemy eluded him. The fact was that most of the effort in the so-called Indian Wars was expended in marching and maneuver. Major battles were few. Indians appeared and then, as quickly, disappeared.

Not this time.

Custer accordingly led his troopers across the divide between the Rosebud and the Little Bighorn. He sent Captain Frederick W. Benteen with three cavalry troops—125 men—to the south to ensure that the Sioux had not moved into the upper valley of the Little Bighorn. As Custer then approached the Little Bighorn, he saw about forty warriors. He sent Major Marcus A. Reno, with another three troops, after them.

But how many warriors were they all going up against? Later estimates range anywhere from 1,500 to 6,000. Custer, however, had no idea at all. His combined strength was six hundred, and this number had been reduced to about four hundred by the detachment of six troops. Three of those, Reno's 112 men, having been sent in pursuit of forty warriors, were quickly overrun by masses of Sioux. Custer led his command into the fight, still unaware of just how badly outnumbered he was.

The Hunkpapa chief Gall led a surge of warriors galloping across the Little Bighorn. They pushed Custer and Reno back. As Gall continued to press from the south, Crazy Horse, venerated leader of the Oglala Lakota, arrived with his warriors from the north. It was now George Armstrong Custer and his 7th Cavalry who were caught in the jaws of a tactical pincers. Within the space of an hour, it was over.

Custer and those immediately under his command at the time lay dead—save for Giovanni Martino, a bugler Custer had sent off to secure reinforcements and ammunition. Benteen managed to tie in with the remainder of Reno's command as it withdrew from the Bighorn Valley. The combined forces of Reno and Benteen, 368 officers and men, dug themselves in along the bluffs and fought off a siege that stretched into the night, only to be renewed the next day, June 26. The warriors finally dispersed at the approach of Terry and Gibbon. The body count among cavalry and scouts was 262 killed. Of the sixty-eight wounded, six later died. The losses among the Lakota, Dakota, Northern Cheyenne, and Arapaho involved in the battle have never been accurately counted. Estimates range from 31 to 300 killed and up to 160 wounded.

After "Custer's Last Stand," Congress authorized an increase in the army's strength and transferred the Sioux Indian agencies and reservations from civilian to military control. Custer's defeat demoralized the army for months but then unleashed a military approach to the Indian Wars that was more aggressive than ever. The Battle of the Little Bighorn was the last major military victory of the Plains Indians.

Thomas Edison Demonstrates His Incandescent Electric Lamp (1879)

Thomas Edison did not invent electric lighting. In 1806, fully four decades before the inventor was born, the distinguished British scientist Sir Humphry Davy demonstrated to the Royal Society an electric arc light. It consisted of two charcoal rods wired to banks of sulfuric acid batteries. When the rods were drawn close to one another, a spark bridged the gap between them, creating a dazzling arc of light.

This may have been the earliest electric light. It failed, however, to be of commercial value. The batteries were unwieldy and dangerous, and the charcoal rods rapidly burned away. Yet, as practical electric generators began to appear in the 1860s and 1870s, several inventors patented their own arc lamps. Even these, however, had a limited market. While their brilliant light made them useful as searchlights and for other outdoor applications, they were useless indoors, where lighting was needed most. Nevertheless, numerous inventors continued to envision a commercial future for electric lighting. Among this modest crowd was Thomas Edison, who, one day in 1878, visited the workshop of William Wallace. A brass and copper founder, by vocation, Wallace was also a part-time inventor. Assisted by an electrical innovator, Moses Farmer, Wallace had been working on an electric arc lamp system. Edison called on Wallace and Farmer not because they had a breakthrough version of the arc lamp—they had no such thing—but because their generator system was capable of powering many such lamps simultaneously.

Indeed, Edison was impressed by what he saw. The generator lit eight lamps. As he explained to a reporter for the *New York Sun* a month later, "I saw for the first time everything in practical operation. It was all before me. I saw the thing had not gone so far but that I had a chance. I saw that what had been done had never been made practically useful. The intense light had not been subdivided so that it could be brought into private houses."

What the Wallace-Farmer system showed Edison was, first, that a generator could power numerous electrical devices. At the same time, he realized, the innovation had only gone so far. Edison still "had a chance" in the marketplace because "what had been done had never been made practically useful." While Wallace and Farmer demonstrated a practical solution to producing electricity, they had failed to get beyond the arc lamp, whose "intense light had not been subdivided so that it could be brought into private houses."

With this insight, Edison started working on a system of subdividing light. It was a bold project for this humble native of Milan, Ohio. Born in 1847 to a working-class family, Edison was a poor student at school and had to be home-schooled by his doting mother. Moreover, a childhood injury and illness left him significantly hard of hearing. Early in his teens, he embarked on his own business, peddling candy and newspapers to railroad passengers. Working on the rail line, he became fascinated by telegraphy and was befriended by a number of telegraphers, who found him a quick study. Young Edison soon became a proficient telegrapher and discovered that these men constituted a grassroots fraternity of tinkerers, who continually cobbled together small electrical gadgets, many of them idiosyncratic improvements on components of the telegraph system.

For Edison, tinkering morphed into invention so that, by the time of his death in 1931, he had more than one thousand patents to his name for inventions that impacted almost every aspect of American life. They included the stock ticker, the phonograph, vast improvements on both the telegraph and telephone, motion pictures, and much more.

His most iconic invention, however, the incandescent electric lamp, cost him many months of frustrating experimentation and failure. He had early on concluded that passing a current through the right material would cause the material to grow hot and glow—producing practical, regulatable light suitable for indoor use. But how to keep the filament from simply burning up? Putting it in a vacuum helped; however, the stumbling block proved to be finding just the right filament material. Edison once famously quipped, "Genius is 1 percent inspiration and

99 percent perspiration." He was a trial-and-error inventor, and he ended up trying some ten thousand substances before he hit on carbonized cotton as his first practical filament. On October 21, 1879, he produced several prototypes of the lamp in his Menlo Park, New Jersey, laboratory. The best of them burned for forty hours, every one of which Edison closely studied. Three months later, on December 31, 1879, he demonstrated the lamp publicly and was awarded a patent the next month.

The lamp itself was a wonder. But its more significant effect was as a reason for people to demand electric power. The first commercial installation of electric lights was made on a steamship, the *Columbia*, belonging to the Oregon Railroad and Navigation Company. But by 1881 Edison built the world's first central electric power plant, the Pearl Street Station in lower Manhattan, and was using it to light streets and buildings, as well as to drive small electric motors. The electric light gave birth to a whole new utility, and Edison invented every part of the system. It transformed America, the world, and civilization itself. Thanks to Edison, the United States was at the core of this great transformation.

The "Battle" of Wounded Knee Ends the Indian Wars (1890)

With the arrest of Geronimo in 1886, the principal period of the post-Civil War "Indian Wars" ended. At this point, nearly a quarter-million Native Americans were living on reservations. Among these were the Hunkpapa Lakota at the Standing Rock Reservation on what is today the border of South and North Dakota. Their chief, Sitting Bull, was the most influential and revered Indian leader of his day, a man famed among Native Americans and non-Indians alike. He lived peacefully at Standing Rock yet quietly declined to cooperate with the local Indian agent, and his counsel to the other Hunkpapa was to avoid contact with the white world altogether. Although this was not an incitement to war, it was an act that defied US Indian policy, which mandated "civilizing" Indians, dismantling tribal structure to assimilate Native Americans into the white mainstream.

By the late 1880s, Wovoka, the son of a Paiute shaman, was becoming influential throughout the western reservations. He preached a hybrid religion compounded of Native and Christian traditions. It promised the dawn of a new day, exclusively Indian, a world in which dead Indians would be resurrected, and in which the bison would again proliferate on the plains. The message inspired a following, who revered Wovoka as their prophet. He called on his faithful to hasten their own deliverance by dancing the Ghost Dance—an homage to ancestral spirits—and by maintaining peaceful relations among themselves and with whites.

Reservation authorities did not believe the message of peace and feared the spread of the Ghost Dance, which they regarded as frenzied and violent. Indeed, among the Teton Sioux, the admonition to peace was suppressed, and the Ghost Dance did become a feature of a frankly militant movement. Teton chiefs Short Bull and Kicking Bear exhorted

The camp of Big Foot three weeks after the "Battle" of Wounded Knee. Four Lakota bodies are wrapped in blankets in the foreground, and US soldiers are seen among the debris in the snow-covered background. PHOTOGRAPH BY TIGER & KUHN, CHADRON, NEBRASKA, PUBLISHED ON WIKIMEDIA COMMONS

their people to a violent uprising, the object of which was white extermination. In response to both perceived and actual unrest, the US Army sent troops to the Pine Ridge and Rosebud reservations on November 20, 1890. Far from intimidating the Indians, the intrusion of the soldiers provoked some three thousand residents of the two reservations to move to a plateau at the northwest corner of Pine Ridge. Authorities called this "the Stronghold."

It is a measure of the ineptitude with which government and military officials conducted relations with the Indians that General Nelson A. Miles, believing he had the means of peacefully ending the Ghost Dance crisis, summoned the internationally famous western showman, William "Buffalo Bill" Cody, to Standing Rock, even over the protest of the reservation's agent, James McLaughlin. Miles was aware that Sitting Bull had once been featured in Cody's Wild West Show, and he believed that the old chief not only trusted Cody but would also do as he said. Miles thought that Buffalo Bill would succeed in persuading Sitting Bull to give himself up. McLaughlin countered that the showman's presence would create a circus liable to explode into a general uprising. Hoping that Miles would rescind his order, McLaughlin intercepted Buffalo Bill and kept him entertained in a saloon, pending revised orders. In fact, those cancelation orders did arrive, on December 15, 1890, and, after packing Buffalo Bill off, McLaughlin dispatched forty-three reservation policemen to arrest Sitting Bull before he slipped out of Standing Rock.

Predictably, the arrest went terribly wrong. It quickly erupted into a melee, during which Sitting Bull was shot in the chest. It is unclear who, if anyone, ordered the chief to be fired on, but, once it happened, a reservation police sergeant, Red Tomahawk, decided to ensure Sitting Bull's death by executing him with a single shot in the back of the head.

Word of the execution spread quickly, giving the Ghost Dance movement a martyr. The uprising McLaughlin had feared became inevitable. Apprised of the explosive situation, General Miles decided to intercept another leading figure in the Ghost Dance movement, Big Foot, chief of the Miniconjou Sioux. Tragically, Miles was unaware that Big Foot had renounced the Ghost Dance religion. The chief believed it not only futile but also likely to hasten the final destruction of the Indians. Miles also did not know that Chief Red Cloud, a Pine Ridge leader friendly to the whites, had asked Big Foot to come to the reservation to persuade the Indians gathered at the Stronghold to surrender. All the general *knew* was that Big Foot was heading for the Stronghold. What the general *assumed* was that his intentions were hostile.

Miles sent troopers to intercept Big Foot and the Miniconjous. A 7th Cavalry squadron located the chief and some 350 followers on December 28, 1890, camped near a stream called Wounded Knee. By the next morning, five hundred cavalrymen commanded by Colonel James W. Forsyth surrounded the camp. They had with them four forty-two-millimeter light mountain cannon called Hotchkiss guns, whose five rotating barrels were capable of firing one round per second. Forsyth trained these weapons on the camp from hills surrounding it. Covered in this way, the colonel planned to disarm the Indians, march them to the railroad, and load them on trains that would take them out of the "zone of military operations."

A disarming operation was always fraught with hazard because it was inherently provocative. The troopers were met with resistance, and, soon, both sides opened fire. As a full-on fight developed, the Miniconjous took flight, whereupon Forsyth, in a bid to contain them, ordered the Hotchkiss guns to open fire. Within less than an hour what the US Army designated as the "Battle of Wounded Knee" was over. Big Foot and 153 other Miniconjous lay dead. Many more limped or crawled away. No one knows the final death toll, but it is estimated that about 300 of the 350 who had been camped at Wounded Knee Creek died. Seventh Cavalry casualties were twenty-five killed and thirty-nine wounded, almost all of them victims of friendly fire, cut down in the Hotchkiss cross fire.

Wounded Knee provoked previously friendly Sioux bands to join the "hostiles" in a general uprising. On December 30, warriors descended upon the 7th Cavalry near the Pine Ridge Agency. Outnumbered, the 7th Cavalry had to be rescued by elements of the 9th Cavalry, a segregated unit of "Buffalo Soldiers," as African American cavalry troopers were called. After his men were withdrawn to safety, General Miles mobilized 3,500 out of a total force of 5,000 troopers in the area. With these, he surrounded a mass of warriors who had gathered fifteen miles north of the Pine Ridge Agency along White Clay Creek. For once, however, the military commander avoided making a bad situation worse. Miles exercised prudent and patient restraint. Having surrounded the "enemy," he ordered the ring of troopers to slowly contract. Sheer numbers convinced the Sioux that continuing to fight was futile. On January 15, 1891, the entire Sioux nation surrendered, and, with that, America's "Indian Wars" came to an end.

William Jennings Bryan Refuses Crucifixion on a "Cross of Gold" (1896)

Rural America during the 1880s and early 1890s was an unhappy place. Farmers' lives, always hard, had become harder than ever. After the Civil War, industrialists increasingly seized from agricultural America the political clout they had once enjoyed. Pressed by the big financiers and tycoons, Congress lifted what little regulation kept railroads and mills in check. Farmers were held hostage to high freight costs and high storage and processing costs levied by grain elevator owners, who were in the railroad tycoon's pockets.

Industry gave farmers a wealth of new machinery—everything from sulky plows with wheels and a driver's seat, mechanized corn planters, end-gate seeders, spring-tooth rakes, automated binders, and highly efficient threshing machines, hay balers, hoisting forks, and corn shellers, all of which increased productivity and even helped the South recover from the devastation of the war. But the boost in output took farming away from mere self-sufficiency. Now the farmer had to produce for the market. His increased yields, combined with a revolution in communications and transportation, ended his rural isolation. Many farmers saw this as a wonderful thing—until they found themselves suddenly thrust into a global market, competing not just with neighbors but people halfway around the world. Worse, the farmers enjoyed no government protection. They were at the mercy of business and price cycles they little understood and over which they had no control. All most farmers knew is that while their expensive investment in machinery had greatly boosted production, the prices they commanded had dropped and continued to decline. A farmer might not understand the market, but he knew injustice when he saw it. The bigger his farm grew, the more he produced, and the less he earned. He was land rich and dirt poor.

As the gap between income and expenses relentlessly widened, farmers began mortgaging their land to cover debts. Thomas E. Watson of Georgia, who would become head of the Populist Party, spoke for agricultural America toward the end of the nineteenth century. Farmers felt "like victims of some horrid nightmare."

They fought back by forming unions, alliances, and political parties under a variety of names, starting with the old People's Party created by the Grange—the first national association of farmers—in 1874. From 1876 to 1878, many farmers joined the Greenback Party and then the Greenback Labor Party, which ran slates of candidates in 1880, 1882, and 1884. In 1888, it was the Union Labor Party, followed by the Farmers' and Laborers' Union in 1890. Regardless of the name, these organizations proposed some of the most radical economic and political changes of the late nineteenth century. They wanted government ownership of the railroads and utilities, a graduated income tax pegged to income, the secret ballot, women's suffrage, and Prohibition. Most of all, they demanded looser credit and a freer money supply by supplementing the gold standard with a silver standard—the so-called "the free coinage of silver." Along with this, the agricultural interests demanded that the government act to regulate and rein in industry and finance. The captains of industry had to be coerced into behaving responsibly to promote the social well-being of Americans.

On February 22, 1892, at a massive meeting of the Congress of Industrial Organizations (CIO) in St. Louis, the National Farmers Alliance seized control of the floor over delegates from assorted labor reform groups—the Knights of Labor, the Nationalists, Single-Taxers, Greenbackers, Prohibitionists, and a dozen others—and declared the formation of a new political party, the People's Party, which became better known as the Populist Party. The most radical third party in American history, the Populists called for a national political convention to nominate a candidate for president in 1892.

On July 4, 1892, in Omaha, the Populist Party nominated James B. Weaver, member of the House of Representatives from Iowa's 6th District. He lost, and he served as a spoiler that caused the loss of the Republicans to the Democratic nominee, Grover Cleveland. This bothered the Republican establishment more than it did the members of the new party, who believed they were ushering in a much-need era of reform. The Populist Party served to bridge the gaps between the Republican Party and the Democratic Party, neither of which served large swaths of America—rural areas, African Americans, and the working class. The Populists revived the pre–Civil War agrarian alliance between the South and the West, and it added a never-before-seen alliance between farmers and labor.

Feeling empowered, the Populist Party wrested, in 1896, the Democratic nomination away from Cleveland and gave it to William Jennings Bryan, already known as the "Great Commoner" and the "Boy Orator of the Platte." Running against the backdrop of an intractable financial panic named for the year in which it had begun, 1893, Bryan was able to champion radical ideas and make radical demands that, amid bank failures and stock market crashes, sounded not only rational but also urgently needed. A graduated tax on income? Yes. Votes for women? By all means. So, with the Populist Party growing rapidly, the Democrats invited Bryan to speak at their 1896 convention. He electrified the audience with an address that became known as the "Cross of Gold" speech, advocating bimetallism—the introduction of free silver coinage—decrying the tyranny of the gold standard with his defiant concluding words: "you shall not crucify mankind on a cross of gold." The speech won Bryan the Democratic presidential nomination over incumbent Grover Cleveland, who was tossed out with the party's entire "Bourbon" (conservative, pro-business) faction.

Fronting a joint Populist-Democratic ticket, William Jennings Bryan tested the limits of the American electorate—and was soundly defeated by Republican William McKinley, whose highly popular 1898 war with Spain and his determination to elevate the United States into a world power fired the American imagination and brought Populism to an early end.

Or so it seemed. In 1901, the assassination of McKinley propelled his vice president, Theodore Roosevelt, into office. Under his administration, Populism was clothed in the tonier middle-class garb of Progressive reform, and a new American era, one with more staying power, commenced.

To Hell with Spain (1898)

Just ninety miles off the Florida coast, Cuba by the end of the nineteenth century was a rebellious Spanish colony in which American businesses, especially sugar plantations, had huge investments. The revolutionary unrest posed a threat to business, whereas a successful revolution, if properly managed by the United States, could create a nominally independent Cuban government friendly to US enterprise. Perhaps Cuba might even become a new American territory.

But how to move the American people and their government to aid Cuba?

In February 1896, Spain sent General Valeriano Weyler to bring order to the island. One of his first acts was to build "reconcentration camps" in which rebels and Cubans suspected of sympathizing with them were confined. US presidents Grover Cleveland and his successor William McKinley resisted intervention, but the popular American press, led by the rival New York papers of Joseph Pulitzer and William Randolph Hearst, whipped up public outrage with stories of atrocities committed both inside and outside of the camps. On February 9, 1898, Hearst published a leaked private letter in which the Spanish minister to the United States insulted President McKinley. America's war fever spiked.

President McKinley had already dispatched the battleship USS *Maine* to Havana harbor to protect "American interests" in Cuba. On February 15, an explosion tore through the *Maine*, killing 266 crewmen and sinking the vessel. Resisting immediate calls to war, the president ordered a naval court of inquiry, which concluded that the ship had struck a mine—but it drew no conclusion as to whether the mine had been placed by the Spanish or by the rebels. (Modern analysts believe that the *Maine*'s capacious powder magazine ignited through spontaneous combustion.)

The American lithography firm of Kurz & Allison published this depiction of the "Destruction of the U.S. battleship *Maine* in Havana Harbor" shortly after the February 15, 1898, event. LIBRARY OF CONGRESS

As far as Hearst and Pulitzer were concerned, the issue was clear. Spain had committed a heinous act of war, and Americans raised the cry of "Remember the *Maine* . . . to hell with Spain!" It echoed the iconic battle cry of Texas independence: "Remember the Alamo!" For its part, the Spanish government moved to avert war. It had already agreed to withdraw from Cuba, and now it accelerated the process. McKinley stalled throughout the early spring but at last gave in to popular pressure. He requested Congress to authorize an invasion of Cuba. In response, the lawmakers voted up a resolution to recognize Cuban independence. This brought a Spanish declaration of war against the United States on April 24, 1898.

The temperature of American war fever far exceeded its preparedness to fight a "foreign" battle even across a mere ninety miles of open sea. True, the navy had benefitted from a program of expansion, but the post–Civil War regular army was diminutive: 26,000 enlisted troops commanded by 2,100 officers, supplemented by a National Guard of about 100,000. Worse, the army had no mobilization plan for an overseas campaign. As for the Guard, it was highly doubtful that it could be sent outside of the United States—legally. Congress hurriedly passed a Mobilization Act on April 22, 1898, which authorized the use of National Guard units and provided for the recruitment of 125,000 volunteers, to which an additional 75,000 were soon added. A unique ten-thousand-man force, called "the Immunes," was formed from those who possessed "immunity from diseases incident to tropical climates." The authorized strength of the regular army was raised to sixty-five thousand so that by the end of what turned out to be a ten-week war, in August 1898, the regular US Army numbered 59,000, and the volunteer forces, 216,000.

Assembling manpower was just part of the problem, and enthusiastic young men volunteered in ample numbers. Initial strategy, however, did not call for committing these eager ground troops to combat—at least not before October, which marked the end of the sickly rainy season. Instead, the navy was to establish a blockade of Cuba, which would persuade the Spanish to abandon the island. At that point, American ground forces could sail in and set up a military government. Under the circumstances, it was not a bad idea, but the American people demanded swift and glorious action. Again, the president complied, and Secretary of War Russell M. Alger ordered regular infantry regiments to be transported to New Orleans, Tampa, and Mobile, ports from which they could be immediately dispatched to Cuba. The trouble was that the army lacked the needed logistical infrastructure for an expeditionary operation: no troop ships, insufficient clothing, inadequate sanitation for large encampments, and insufficient food supplies. Corrupt victualers supplied improperly canned meat, which poisoned a significant number of soldiers even before they left the States.

While the army dithered, unable to depart American shores, the US Navy took action not against Spain in Cuba but in the Spanish-occupied Philippine Islands. US Rear Admiral George Dewey, learning of the declaration of war, sailed his Asiatic Squadron from Hong Kong to Manila

Bay. On May 1, 1898, he fired on the Spanish fleet riding at anchor there, destroying all ten ships in the bay. President McKinley sent eleven thousand troops to the Philippines, and that force, along with Filipino irregulars commanded by Philippine independence fighter Emilio Aguinaldo, defeated all Spanish forces in Manila on August 13.

In the meantime, beginning on May 29, a US Navy blockade bottled up the Spanish fleet at Santiago Harbor on the eastern end of Cuba. In June, seventeen thousand American troops finally landed at Daiquiri and advanced toward Santiago. The Americans, including Lieutenant Colonel Theodore Roosevelt's volunteer Rough Riders, stormed and captured San Juan Hill (and adjacent Kettle Hill) on July 1. This was the key Spanish land position. On the water, Spanish Admiral Pascual Cervera came under artillery fire from the American troops who had taken the high ground on and around San Juan Hill. Desperate, Cervera decided to run the naval blockade. In a four-hour engagement, the US fleet devastated the Spanish fleet, which lost 343 sailors killed, 151 wounded, and 1,889 captured—a third of its strength. On August 12, Spain agreed to withdraw from Cuba and to cede to the United States Puerto Rico and Guam, a Pacific island of the Marianas archipelago. Subsequent peace negotiations in Paris resulted in Spain's selling the Philippine Islands to the United States for $20 million—although Filipino nationalist guerillas waged a war against the American occupiers from 1899 to 1902.

The United States quickly established a territorial government in Puerto Rico but, by May 1902, abandoned plans to annex Cuba. Instead, Cuban leaders were permitted to draft a new constitution for an independent Cuba, provided that clauses were included allowing the establishment of US military bases on the island and explicitly authorizing American intervention in Cuban affairs to "preserve" the island's independence. For most Americans, this was a triumph sufficient. In fact, US secretary of state John Hay famously dubbed the conflict a "splendid little war" because it instantly elevated the United States to preeminence in the hemisphere and set it on course to become a formidable world power.

The victory emboldened Theodore Roosevelt—who was vice president at the start of McKinley's second term and assumed office following his assassination in September 1901—to establish a frankly imperialist policy toward the Caribbean islands and Latin America after he was elected president in his own right in 1904. In that year, Roosevelt articulated what became known as the Roosevelt Corollary to the Monroe Doctrine, a policy that explicitly called for the United States to serve as an international regional police force. No longer would the nation embrace the isolationism that had guided it since George Washington in his Farewell Address of 1796 cautioned against becoming entangled in foreign affairs.

Edwin S. Porter Directs *The Great Train Robbery* (1903)

Photography was invented in 1816, when the Frenchman Nicéphore Niépce used a camera to make negative images on paper that had been coated with light-sensitive silver chloride. By 1839, Louis Daguerre's daguerreotype process made photography practical. From this point on, experimenters began to look for ways to record more than still images. But how to capture motion? The American Eadweard Muybridge used multiple cameras to make sequences of still photographs that could be assembled not merely to study motion but also to reproduce it. His 1878 "Sallie Gardner at a Gallop" is a series of twenty-four still photographs of a galloping mare shot in rapid succession. When exhibited using a mechanical device that Muybridge created—the zoopraxiscope, through which images were arranged on a rotating disk—continuous motion was convincingly recreated.

The next technological breakthrough came at the end of the 1880s, when American photography pioneer George Eastman invented flexible, transparent celluloid photographic film. This material inspired Thomas Edison and his employee William Kennedy Laurie Dickson to invent the Kinetograph, the first practical motion-picture camera, which emerged in several iterations between 1889 and 1892. In 1891, Edison demonstrated the Kinetoscope, the exhibition counterpart of the motion-picture camera. With this, the peephole movie viewer was born. Edison and his workshop employees continued working on the Kinetoscope, and on January 9, 1894, released a five-second film, "Fred Ott's Sneeze," which became the first motion picture to receive a US copyright.

During the 1890s, Edison and others began experimenting with ways to exhibit motion pictures more dramatically and profitably than with peep-show viewers. In 1896, Edison worked with other inventors

Movie audiences had never seen an image like this on film. The gun pointed squarely at them sent some running from the theater in terror. *The Great Train Robbery* marked the beginning of the modern movie entertainment industry.
LIBRARY OF CONGRESS

to develop projection systems. In the meantime, in France, a magician named Georges Méliès purchased from the Lumière brothers a cinematograph projector and began making motion pictures for exhibition. His most famous and spectacular production, *Le Voyage dans la Lune* (*A Trip to the Moon*), inspired by the science fiction novels of Jules Verne, was produced in 1902. Spanning eighteen minutes (at a jittery twelve frames per second [fps]) or nine minutes at a more realistic twenty-four fps speed, it told a story—at least of sorts—and captured the popular imagination.

By this time, Edison was convinced that motion pictures could make money as vehicles for entertainment and education. In 1899, Edison had hired Edwin S. Porter, an early electrical engineer who had become involved in motion picture technology in 1896. Edison put him in charge of the motion picture production studio he had established in New York as a division of the Edison Manufacturing Company. The earliest Edison films told no real stories, so Porter looked for ways to use the technology of moviemaking to create narrative. His *Jack and the Beanstalk* (1902) and *Life of an American Fireman* (1903) not only imitated the techniques of Méliès and other early pioneers but also elaborated on them. Porter developed narrative transitions, including fades and dissolves, which mimicked the physiology and psychology of human perception. He also pioneered editing techniques, by which it became possible to establish different points of view and even to manipulate time itself.

He put this new technical vocabulary of cinematography into *The Great Train Robbery*, a twelve-minute "Western" filmed in Milltown, New Jersey, in 1903 and inspired by a sensational train robbery committed just three years earlier by Butch Cassidy. The movie—that is what it should be called—combined many of the foundational elements of modern cinema: composite editing, shooting on location instead of exclusively in a studio, camera movement, close-ups, and cross-cutting (to show simultaneous action occurring in different locations).

The Great Train Robbery established the "one-reeler," a cinematic form that took up precisely the same amount of time as the traditional live turn on the vaudeville stage of the era. It also created the Western, one of the most durable movie genres in film history. But, most of all, it opened up the possibilities for telling stories in a brand-new medium, and it created the movie industry, of which the United States became the capital.

Nickelodeons, as early movie theaters were called, sprang up in virtually every neighborhood in the nation. Studios and distributors rented movies to exhibitors nationwide and then worldwide. By 1908, at least eight thousand nickelodeons were active in the United States, delighting mostly urban working-class audiences, people who might not be able to afford an evening at the live theater but who could watch the "flicker pictures" all day for a nickel. Movies became a genuine popular art form, the first mass medium since Gutenberg invented movable type in the fifteenth century. A powerful industry, moviemaking shaped perceptions, ideas, and ideals on a mass and massive scale. America became the epicenter of movie production and has continued to be the nexus of popular media.

The Jungle Aims for America's Heart but Hits It in the Stomach (1906)

Upton Sinclair was a socialist by political orientation and a novelist by vocation. In 1904, he combined the two when he decided to write a novel about the meatpacking industry centered in Chicago. For seven weeks, he applied, in disguise, for a job in one of the big meatpacking plants and for seven weeks worked undercover as a laborer in the plant. In 1906, he published *The Jungle*, which told the harrowing story of Jurgis Rudkus, a Lithuanian immigrant who worked in a meatpacking plant.

The Jungle focused on two themes: the first was the plight of the poor American immigrant, a figure routinely oppressed and forced to take the jobs no citizen wanted; the second was the reckless rapacity of the captains of industry in an environment devoid of government regulation. In some ways, the two themes got in each other's way. Readers sympathized less with Rudkus, the exploited immigrant, than they were outraged and disgusted by the grossly unsanitary practices of the meatpacking industry. As Sinclair—for whom the novel made a fortune—later remarked, "I aimed at the public's heart, and by accident I hit it in the stomach."

Although Sinclair used Rudkus and his other immigrant characters to delineate the hard lot of millions of immigrants, who were heartlessly exploited by employers, policemen, politicians, and anyone with any authority at all, it was the exuberance of the meticulously nauseating detail with which the novelist evoked the horrors of the meatpacking business that made for truly effective fiction. Sinclair wrote of the large-scale use of condemned meat, of tubercular beef, and of nearly rotten meat to make sausage and tinned meats of various sorts. He described a policy in which everything was loaded into the great industrial meatgrinders, rats, insects, and, when an exhausted worker fell into the machinery, human beings. The public indignation was overwhelming. People wrote to their congressmen, senators, and the president, Theodore Roosevelt, demanding action against an industry whose arrogant disregard for minimum standards of health and cleanliness was breathtaking. The demand was for the federal government to take seriously the constitutional duty of promoting "the general welfare." The president endorsed these pleas, and a mere six months after the novel's publication, Congress passed the Pure Food and Drug Act as well as a Meat Inspection Act.

This was indeed a turning point. At the early height of an age of Progressive reform, the US federal government claimed the right to regulate certain key practices of private industry. Not only was pure food a priority but also the regulation of pharmaceuticals to ensure that were made to high standards and were shown to be effective and not harmful. The United States was a great consumer of patent medicines, many of which made outrageous curative claims. The new legislation took aim. Capitalism in America had been founded on the principle of *caveat emptor*—let the buyer beware. Now the government was putting more of the responsibility on the makers of products.

Sinclair was representative of a new American literary tradition. Realism had already been established both in European and American literature. At the start of the twentieth century in America, however, realism took a new turn into what President Theodore Roosevelt called "muckraking." It was a word he appropriated from *Pilgrim's Progress*, by the seventeenth-century English Puritan writer John Bunyan. This Christian allegory—of the faithful believer's progress "from this world to that which is to come"—remained popular in Roosevelt's day. In one episode of the allegory, Bunyan portrays a man armed with a "muck-rake," who sweeps up the filth around him while remaining quite unaware of the celestial glory above his head. President Roosevelt admired Sinclair and the other modern critics of society—but he had come to believe that they reveled in the corruption—the "muck"—and failed to acknowledge the nation's higher aspirations and achievements.

Literary muckraking was the convergence aesthetic realism, the newly developing profession of investigative journalism, and the Progressive movement. Sinclair, Ida Tarbell (who exposed the abuses of the great Standard Oil monopoly), Lincoln Steffens (whose *The Shame of the Cities* revealed the criminal corruption of big city political machines), and others worked as earnest, dispassionate, yet committed observers of the American scene. The muckrakers exposed the dark side of capitalism, targeting for exposure business and political corruption, child labor, slum life, race discrimination, prostitution, sweatshop labor, insurance fraud, and illegal stock and financial manipulations. A host of popular magazines, such as *McClure's*, *the Atlantic Monthly*, and *Collier's*, built huge readerships publishing muckraking exposes. It was *McClure's* that serialized Ida Tarbell's *History of Standard Oil* in 1902 and Steffens's *The Shame of the Cities* (1904). Part of the appeal of their work was sensationalism, yet it also created genuine and needed change in American society, galvanizing a diverse cadre of progressive-minded individuals into a national social and political movement. Their influence can be felt today in the investigative journalism of media venues ranging from small independent publications and websites to some of the largest corporate broadcast media organizations.

The Triangle Shirtwaist Factory Fire Kills 146 Immigrant Workers (1911)

Americans have long felt ambivalence toward immigrants. In some periods, they welcomed them, especially when the economy was booming and business had need of cheap and plentiful labor. At other times, however, a nativist tendency dominated, and immigrants were feared or shunned. The period between 1880 and 1920 was a boom time for immigration, as industrialization and urbanization drew some twenty million newcomers. Journalists such as Jacob Riis and novelists such as Upton Sinclair portrayed the hard lives of the urban immigrants, who were crowded into slum districts, consigned there to miserable human warehouses called tenements, and felt themselves lucky to find steady work in urban sweatshops. The middle-class urban establishment largely turned a blind eye to these people—until March 25, 1911.

Toward the end of that workday, one of the five hundred employees of the Triangle Shirtwaist Company, which occupied the top three floors of the ten-story Asch Building at 23–29 Washington Place in Manhattan's Greenwich Village, saw a fire in a rag bin under a cutter's table on the eighth floor. No sooner did she see it than the flames suddenly leaped up. That was bad, because the overcrowded building was a fire trap.

Shirtwaists, a popular style of blouse made especially fashionable by its appearance in Charles Dana Gibson's illustrations of the iconic "Gibson girl," were in high demand from the end of the nineteenth century through the first two decades of the twentieth. Sweatshops like Triangle produced them in seemingly limitless quantity. Immigrant labor, mostly young women, was cheap and plentiful. Recently, however, labor organizations such as the Women's Trade Union League were organizing strikes and agitating for eight-hour days and livable wages. Max Blanck and Isaac Harris, the owners of Triangle, led the opposition to the unions and received the

Open coffins mark the high cost of dangerous working conditions for immigrants. The victims, mostly young women, had leaped to their deaths in a frenzied effort to escape the flames of the Triangle Shirtwaist fire. WIKIMEDIA COMMONS

backing of Tammany Hall boss Charles F. Murphy. Murphy, in turn, sent police to break up demonstrations and even hired thugs to further intimidate organizers. Focused on hours and wages and the relentless opposition of management, no one working at Triangle complained about the way cloth scraps accumulated on the floor, even as the cutters—almost exclusively male tailors—flicked their cigar ashes on them, often igniting small blazes. No one protested that, seeking to keep workers from sneaking unauthorized breaks or pilfering merchandise, fire exits were closed and locked in violation of city fire regulations. Exploited economically, the immigrant labor at Triangle Shirtwaist was also endangered physically.

As soon as the fire was discovered, workers tried to put it out, but it spread from fabric pile to fabric pile much too quickly. Sam Bernstein, manager of the factory, directed his male employees to unroll the fire hose, which was connected to a standpipe in the wall. They quickly discovered that the canvas hose had been allowed to rot. It fell apart as soon as it was unrolled.

The only alternative was escape. Three means presented themselves: the freight elevators, the fire escape, and the stairways. For many, the first impulse was to rush to the fire escape, which descended from the tenth floor to the second. A ladder was supposed to lower onto a small courtyard. The spindly structure was too narrow for the volume of workers who crowded onto it. Some fell from one landing to the next, and one employee tumbled to his death from the eighth floor to the courtyard.

As for the stairways, the eighth-floor workers quickly discovered the door to the stairway on one side of the building was locked. They ran to the other stairway, which was now jammed with workers in desperate flight from the ninth and tenth floors. This left the freight elevators as the only viable means of escape from the eighth floor. Several heroic cutters risked their lives to take turns operating the elevator, carrying one load of workers to safety and then taking the elevator back to get another, and another.

The seventy employees who worked on the tenth floor used the staircases or climbed onto the roof. Students at New York University, whose principal building was located across the street from the Asch Building, stretched ladders across to the roof. Those employees who had gathered there gingerly crawled across these improvised bridges.

It was the 260 workers on the ninth floor who were in the most difficult position. The warning telephone call that had gone out from the eighth-floor workers never reached them. By the time they discovered the fire, every avenue of escape was either blocked or jammed. Some intrepid souls leaped to the freight elevator cables and climbed down them. Others forced their way into the stream of humanity descending the narrow staircase. Others made their way to the fire escape. By that time, however, it was vastly overloaded. Under the added weight, the structure began to tear away from its moorings in the masonry wall, finally falling away altogether, carrying many people with it as the structure disintegrated.

Fire in tall buildings often forces victims to a hard choice: burn alive or leap to almost certain death. Those ninth-floor employees who could find no other escape climbed out onto the window ledges. A hundred feet below, firemen stretched a net. Workers began jumping off the ledge. Some of the young women sought to lessen their terror by holding hands and jumping in pairs. The first few jumpers were lucky, but, soon, the repeated impacts and the combined weight of paired leapers was too much for the fabric, which split as bodies ripped through it.

The New York Fire Department sent everything they could muster, thirty-five pieces of equipment in all, including a hook and ladder. Young women on the ninth-floor ledge looked on in horror as the ladder, fully extended, got only as far as floor six. Others down below—who had never before given immigrant laborers a second thought—were moved to act in desperately inventive ways. An ambulance driver ran his vehicle up over the curb and onto the sidewalk, hoping that jumpers could hit his roof and somehow save their lives. Draymen yanked the tarpaulin from their delivery wagon and stretched it out between them as an improvised net. The very first body that hit it tore the cloth from their bleeding hands.

"The first ten [to hit the sidewalk] shocked me," reporter William Gunn Shepherd dashed off in his notebook. Then he looked up and saw people raining down from the sky.

The firefighters were not helpless. In fact, they and their equipment arrived very quickly, and the men fought the blaze aggressively, knocking down the eighth-floor conflagration within a quarter-hour of its start. But the ninth-floor blaze had become hopeless. The whole level was engulfed. Later, after the blaze had burned itself out for want of fuel, bodies were found piled in a twelve-foot heap in the loft area. Another badly charred group was discovered, pressed up against the Greene Street exit.

The last body fell at 4:57 in the afternoon. There were 146 broken bodies, many of them laid out on the street, 123 women—almost all of them very young, aged fourteen to twenty-three—and 23 men. Most were recent immigrants, either Jews or Italians. The police took them to a temporary morgue on 26th Street, where, over the next several days, benumbed troupes of survivors filed through to identify their coworkers. In the end, all but six were given names.

District Attorney Charles Seymour Whitman acted swiftly to obtain a grand jury indictment against Blanck and Harris for negligent homicide because they had locked the stairway doors. A Tammany Hall legal gun for hire, Max D. Steuer, who had once been a garment worker himself, defended the partners—successfully.

Nevertheless, the public called for laws to prevent the repetition of such a tragedy. A New York Factory Investigating Commission was assembled to tour and inspect factories throughout the entire state. The commission put two-and-a-half years of research into a comprehensive report that moved the state legislature and the city government to change existing laws and even write new ones. The Triangle fire made a deep impact on politicians of the era, from established progressives like Theodore Roosevelt to rising figures such as Franklin Delano Roosevelt and others. It would move the new generation of leaders to carry government more deeply into American lives.

Ford's Moving Assembly Line Begins Operation in Highland Park, Michigan (1913)

Most famous as the inventor of the cotton gin, Eli Whitney was also a gun manufacturer, who pioneered the use of interchangeable parts in 1798. During the nineteenth century, the innovation of machine tools, especially screw-cutting lathes and milling machines, made the mass production of interchangeable parts a reality. When a variety of fixtures and jigs were used to control the working path of the machine tools, thereby partially automating their operation, interchangeable parts technology took a further leap.

Before the nineteenth century ended, steam and electric power were being applied to conveyor systems. At first, the conveyors were used strictly for loading and unloading cargo ships, but as early as 1867 Chicago meatpackers began using them to transport animal carcasses through meat processing plants so that they could be "disassembled"—butchered by a series of workers at fixed stations, each worker responsible for making a specific cut in the disassembly process. Thus, the precursor of and inspiration for the twentieth-century assembly line was a nineteenth-century *disassembly* line.

Ransom Olds used a version of an assembly line in 1901 to build his Oldsmobile Curved Dash, which may be regarded as the first mass-produced automobile. But it was one of Henry Ford's factory managers, William "Pa" Klann, who connected the technology of Swift & Company's slaughterhouse—its highly developed disassembly line—with Ford's much bigger automotive operation. Klann was impressed by the efficiency of production achieved when each worker was assigned a specific operation, removing the same piece of meat over and over as each carcass passed by. Klann described this process to Peter E. Martin, who was on the verge of promotion to lead Ford production. Martin was skeptical but not closed-minded. He gave his blessing for Klann to propose the idea of a moving conveyor assembly line to Henry Ford. The idea struck a chord in Ford's imagination, because, about 1906, he had toured the extensively automated main mail-order facility of Sears, Roebuck, a vast complex spread over some forty acres in Chicago.

Martin and others at Ford began experimenting with conveyor assembly as early as 1908, but the company's first fully developed moving assembly line, dedicated to the production of Model T automobiles, did not begin operation until October 7, 1913, at Ford's Highland Park Plant. Martin and other Ford engineers continually observed and refined the design and operation of the assembly line, using cutting-edge time and motion studies. Soon, Ford engineers had reduced Model T production time to ninety-three minutes per vehicle. This was a pace faster than the paint on the vehicle bodies could dry. When his employees reported to him that only japan black paint dried fast enough to keep up with the pace of production, Henry Ford began producing black cars exclusively. He did not add other colors until the following year, 1914.

Most historians of technology credit the Highland Park facility as the first fully developed moving line ever installed. The idea was to move the work-in-progress from one worker to another until it emerged as a complete subassembly. These units would then be continuously moved in synchronized fashion to a moving final assembly line, from which the finished automobile came. Lack of individual customization was part of the cost of assembly line mass production. So was the death of individual craftsmanship as workers were subordinated to the relentless pace of the moving line. Yet, dramatically decreased costs of production brought the price of a Model T to within the range of the working class. In 1908, Ford had turned out 10,607 cars. In 1916, 730,041, priced at $360 each. By 1927, the last year the Model T was made, Ford had produced fifteen million of them. Mass assembly line production transformed America into a consumer society, but it profoundly altered the relation of labor and management by changing the very nature of industrial work.

The Zimmermann Telegram Is
Revealed (1917)

World War I—the Great War, as it was known at the time, except in the United States, where it was usually called "the European War"—was triggered by the assassination of the Austrian imperial heir apparent Archduke Franz Ferdinand and his wife, Grand Duchess Sophie, in Sarajevo, the capital of Bosnia-Herzegovina, on June 28, 1914. The Austro-Hungarian government blamed Serbia for the assassination and slapped the small country with an ultimatum in July. Serbia refused just one provision of the ultimatum because it fatally undermined the nation's sovereignty. The refusal set off a chain reaction in a complex of international treaty obligations that brought most of Europe into the war. The nations fought either alongside the Allies (whose leading members were France, Britain, Russia, and, later, Italy) or the Central Powers (mainly Germany, Austria-Hungary, and Turkey).

President Woodrow Wilson proclaimed the United States neutral in the conflict and continued doing business with the European powers. Since freedom of the seas was essential to America's rights as a neutral, Germany's policy of unrestricted submarine warfare was of great concern to the Wilson government. On May 7, 1915, a German U-boat, without warning, torpedoed and sank the British liner *Lusitania*, with the loss of 1,198 lives, including 124 Americans. Anxious to maintain neutrality, Wilson did no more than issue a stern note of diplomatic protest to the Germans. Hawkish political figures, such as Theodore Roosevelt, condemned the note as weak, whereas pacifists, most prominently Wilson's own secretary of state, Williams Jennings Bryan, thought it provocative. After Wilson issued a second note, Bryan resigned in protest. In August, another passenger ship, the *Arabic*, was sunk. But, anxious at last

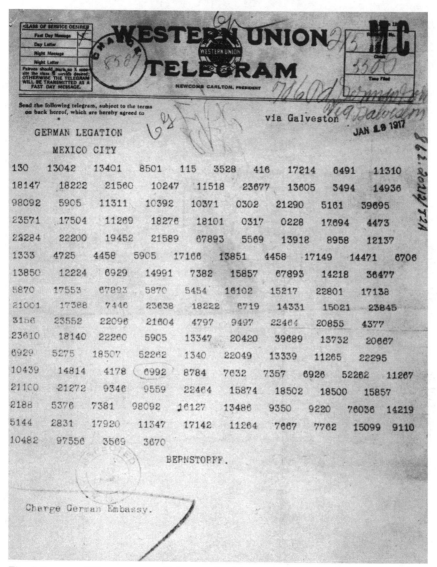

The infamous "Zimmermann Telegram," which precipitated US entry into World War I, was transmitted in a diplomatic cipher cracked by the British intelligence service and shared with US president Woodrow Wilson. NATIONAL ARCHIVES AND RECORDS ADMINISTRATION

to avert US entry into the war, Germany's Kaiser Wilhelm II ordered an end to unrestricted submarine warfare.

Acting on the Kaiser's concession, Wilson dispatched his chief personal adviser, Texas politician Edward M. House, to London and Paris to offer American mediation between the belligerents. House botched the assignment, concluding with British foreign secretary Sir Edward Grey the so-called House-Grey Memorandum of February 22, 1916, which specified Grey's understanding that the United States might enter the war if Germany rejected Wilson's mediation, even as it reserved to the British government the right to initiate that mediation. In short, Grey implied that Wilson was contemplating entering the war on the side of Britain. This alienated Germany and the other Central Powers. When Germany resumed unrestricted submarine warfare at the start of 1917, President Wilson severed diplomatic relations, bringing the nation to the brink of entry into the "European War."

By this time, Britain and France were reeling under relentless German offensives on the Western Front and were desperate for America to pitch in. In February 1917, British intelligence authorities turned over a telegram they had intercepted between German foreign minister Alfred Zimmermann and the German ambassador to Mexico. Transmitted on January 16, 1917, the *Zimmermann Telegram*, as it was called, authorized the ambassador to propose a German-Mexican alliance to Mexican president Venustiano Carranza. In return for a declaration of war against the United States, Mexico would receive German support in a military campaign to recover its "lost territory in New Mexico, Texas, and Arizona." It was a hare-brained idea, which Zimmermann made even more outrageous by asking Carranza to invite Japan to join the anti-American alliance.

The revelation of the message was explosive. There is no evidence to suggest that Carranza seriously considered the proposed German-Mexican alliance, but President Wilson made the Zimmermann Telegram public on March 1. As he knew it would, the document stirred patriotic outrage and a tsunami of anti-German popular sentiment. Feeling that he had a mandate, the president asked Congress for a declaration of war on April 2, 1917. Congress gave it to him on April 6.

The United States was not directly threatened by the war in Europe, but Wilson had reached the conclusion that America stood to gain political, ideological, and moral advantages as a true world power if it fought in the Great War. The Zimmerman Telegram gave him the leverage he needed to recruit popular support for a decision that was political and ideological rather than existential. Entry into the Great War was thus more a matter of choice than necessity. Still, Wilson's war message was filled with high-minded idealism: "There is one choice we can not make, we are incapable of making: we will not choose the path of submission and suffer the most sacred rights of our nation and our people to be ignored or violated." Most memorably, he spoke of fighting a war "for the ultimate peace of the world and the liberation of its peoples, the German peoples included." It would be, he proclaimed, a war to make the "world . . . safe for democracy." Woodrow Wilson had nominated the nation he led to be the savior of the world's freedom. It would become an enduring aspect of American self-identity.

A Worldwide Influenza Pandemic Begins
in the United States (1918)

It was called the *Spanish* Flu, but nobody knows where it originated. Over the years, researchers have suggested various points of origin, although all agree that the conditions created by World War I—masses of people together in armies, widespread malnutrition and privation, the mass movement of refugees—contributed to the pandemic's virulence and global spread.

In the United States, most recent authorities give credence to historian Alfred W. Crosby's theory that the so-called Spanish Flu originated in Kansas at the start of 1918 and was especially widespread in military camps there and elsewhere in the heartland. Thus, it is possible that US soldiers carried the flu to Europe, where it rapidly spread. American soldiers, having contracted the disease while serving abroad, furthered its spread when they returned home.

The first evidence of the 1918 outbreak in the United States was in Haskell County, Kansas, in January 1918. On March 4, a US Army cook, Albert Gitchell, went on sick call at Fort Riley, Kansas, and became the first officially recorded victim. In short order, 522 Fort Riley soldiers fell ill, and by March 11, flu was diagnosed in Queens, New York. During the summer, what had been described as a more virulent influenza strain was diagnosed in the port city of Brest, France; in Freetown, Sierra Leone; and in Boston, Massachusetts.

Americans sent some two million soldiers to Europe during 1917–1918—out of a total of 4.7 million Americans in uniform. Of this number 116,516 died, 53,402 in combat and even more, 63,114, from disease, mainly influenza. American families worried about their sons, but most civilians felt themselves insulated from the war. The scope and lethality of the pandemic brought unexpected anxiety and even panic to a continent-spanning nation accustomed to feeling blissfully protected between the Atlantic and Pacific oceans. Worldwide, it is now believed that between fifty and one hundred million persons died during the pandemic from 1918 to 1919. Estimates are that 10 to 20 percent of those infected perished. Worldwide, about a third of the population came down with the flu. Thus, between 3 and 6 percent of the people on this planet succumbed. It is believed that the pandemic claimed more victims than the infamous Black Death—the Plague—of the European middle ages. No corner of the globe was immune.

In the United States, 28 percent of the population fell ill, and between 500,000 and 675,000 died. Native American and Inuit communities were especially devastated, and urban neighborhoods were hard hit. Even among those who recovered, the symptoms of the 1918 flu were so severe that the disease, at least early in the outbreak, was often misdiagnosed as cholera or typhoid. In especially dire cases, fevers became hemorrhagic, with uncontrollable bleeding from the nose, stomach, intestine, ears, skin, and even the eyes. Death was most often the result of secondary infection by bacterial pneumonia. The 20 percent overall mortality rate was unprecedented, since influenza, even when it is epidemic, typically kills only 0.1 percent of those infected.

The pandemic came in two major waves, the second of which—uncharacteristically of the flu—swept France, Sierra Leone, and the United States in the late summer, beginning in August. Whereas the first wave was fatal mostly to the infirm and the elderly, the second wave hit all age groups, including the young American men who were winning victories in France. This seemed especially cruel, but, then, so did every aspect of the pandemic. Americans had watched the first three years of the "European War" from afar. They felt blessed in their splendid American isolation. President Wilson's decision to enter the war in April 1917 staked a claim on American world power but at the sacrifice of American innocence. Then, even as US intervention in the world war was bringing victory to the Allies, the nation came to share in what had hitherto been considered a European catastrophe: deadly epidemic disease. As America approached the end of the twentieth century's second decade, it had never before been so powerful or so vulnerable.

Prohibition Becomes a Federal Case (1919)

The framers of the US Constitution wanted to create a living document. Revolutionaries that they were, they recognized that times and circumstances change, and so they included an amendment process for changing the Constitution. At the same time, they wanted to make the process deliberate and demanding, if not downright difficult. Amendments could be proposed by Congress, with a two-thirds vote in both chambers, or by a convention of the states, provided that two-thirds of state legislatures voted the proposed amendment up. In either case, whether approved by a supermajority of Congress or of a convention of the states, either three-quarters of the state legislatures or three-quarters of the states meeting in convention had to ratify the proposed amendment before it could become part of the Constitution.

Since colonial times, substantial numbers of Americans objected to alcoholic beverages and desired their prohibition. But, also since the colonial era, even more Americans wanted to drink. The Constitution did not guarantee the right to make, buy, and consume alcoholic beverages, and so, individual states, counties, towns, and other jurisdiction were free to prohibit or regulate liquor, beer, and wine as they wished. The fact remained that most Americans wanted access to alcohol. The thing is, amending the Constitution is not a matter of popular referendum or plebiscite. It is a legislative issue, and in 1919, thanks to a coalition of religious and social reformers and wives and mothers tired of being variously abused by drunk men or left dependent on men too drunk to hold down a job, enough representatives and senators voted up the Eighteenth Amendment and enough state legislatures—mostly of rural states, which detractors called the "hayseed coalition"—voted ratification to make Prohibition the law of the land.

As written, the amendment went into effect one year after ratification, whereupon the manufacture, transport, and sale of alcoholic beverages anywhere in the United States were prohibited. Pursuant to ratification, the Volstead Act was passed to provide for enforcement of the prohibition. Although the amendment did not represent the popular will of the people—especially those who lived in urban areas, including most of the nation's immigrant population—its ratification nevertheless marked the triumph of a fundamentalism that had taken root in rural America beginning well before the Civil War. This had given rise to a Temperance Movement, which was linked not only to religious belief but also the crusade for women's rights. By 1855, thirteen of thirty-one states outlawed the manufacture and sale of alcoholic beverages. The Civil War—1861–1865—temporarily broke the momentum of Temperance, and post-Civil War Reconstruction drew the attention of reformers elsewhere. During this lull, the dominant Republican Party was reluctant to take a stance favoring prohibition, fearing that this would meet with popular resistance and diminish its hold on government at both the state and federal levels.

By the 1870s, groups of activist women began reclaiming the lost momentum of the movement and formed the Woman's Christian Temperance Union (WCTU) in 1873. To the WCTU was added, in 1895, the efforts of the newly founded Anti-Saloon League, which focused on influencing state and local elections to bring "dry" candidates in office. Through relentless but methodical activism, the WCTU, Anti-Saloon League, and other organizations managed to gain majorities in twenty-one state legislatures by 1916. These bodies outlawed saloons in their states, and voters that year sent a "dry" majority to Congress.

The new Congress moved fast, securing passage of the Eighteenth Amendment in the House and the Senate. With a dry wind now at their backs, they wasted no time in submitting the amendment to the states for ratification in December 1917. Although President Woodrow Wilson was opposed to Prohibition, arguing presciently that it would transform the United States into a nation of lawbreakers, it was, in part, his expression of high moral motives in taking America to war that helped propel to ratification what future US president Herbert Hoover called "the Noble Experiment." Indeed, drink was widely seen as far more than a harmless refreshment and relaxation. It was regarded as a force that destroyed families, endangered women and children, and weakened the American economy by crippling productivity.

But enforcing Prohibition did not rely on moral rectitude. A whole new branch of federal law enforcement was created by the Volstead Act. With between 1,500 and 3,000 agents, the Prohibition Bureau was tasked with identifying and bringing to trial all those who engaged in the illegal liquor trade. Almost immediately, the "Prohees," as the Prohibition agents were called, made corrupt bargains with the majority of Americans who did not want to stop drinking. As President Wilson predicted, the United States became a nation of lawbreakers—not just among the "lower orders" but through the middle and upper classes as well. The same big city ethnic neighborhoods that had blocked earlier attempts at prohibition on the local level now started brewing beer and distilling bootleg bathtub gin and moonshine, typically with the encouragement and participation of their friends and neighbors. The neighborhood bootleggers made bargains with local grocers, who supplied the necessary raw materials, and with former saloon keepers as well as current restaurateurs and the operators of ice cream parlors and soda fountains to serve and distribute their products. Pharmacists, who were legally permitted to sell "medicinal spirits" on presentation of a doctor's prescription, didn't necessarily examine too closely whatever scrip a paying customer presented to them.

As for the neighborhood cops, they mostly looked the other way—especially if given a sample of the product or a few dollars. Neighborhood networks warned one another about impending raids. Early in Prohibition, the laws were honored far more in the breach than the observance, but there were risks. Actual raids did occur, and people were punished. Immigrants, in some cases, lost their citizenship.

As the risks began to outweigh the rewards for otherwise law-abiding citizens, gangsters moved in, and bootlegging became a big, brutal illicit business, ranging from the domestic manufacture of rotgut to the illegal and covert importation of spirits from nearby Canada and Mexico and far-off Europe. Mobsters began terrorizing the illegal traffic in liquor, extorting protection money and punishing the uncooperative. Gangs battled each other for control, and the background music to the Roaring

Twenties became a mixture of early jazz and the tattoo of the Thompson submachine gun. The mix of criminality and consumer business produced increasingly sophisticated levels of "organized crime." By the time the "noble experiment" was ended in December 1933 by ratification of the Twenty-first Amendment, which repealed the Eighteenth, organized crime had become an American institution. With liquor once again legalized, the new breed of criminal turned to a variety of racketeering enterprises, ranging from extorting control of labor unions, engaging in illegal gambling operations, prostitution, and, within a decade or two, all manner of illegal narcotics. The American "underworld" was here to stay.

Congress Rejects the League
of Nations (1919)

Woodrow Wilson took the United States into World War I not as a matter of necessity—we were not attacked—but as a matter of choice. He saw an opportunity to win a place at the head of the table of world nations not only for the United States but also for himself. He believed—sincerely—that he, alone among world leaders, was capable of imposing on the family of nations a regime of peace. He assured his fellow Americans that they were sending their sons and brothers and fathers to fight in a "war to end all wars" and to "make the world safe for democracy."

Indeed, Europe greeted Woodrow Wilson as a savior when he arrived in Paris in January 1919 for the conference tasked with hammering out the terms of peace for the Great War. He brought with him the broad peace plan he had presented in a speech to Congress in January 1918, "Fourteen Points," which included the creation of a "league" of nations that would mutually guarantee the political independence and territorial boundaries of all the world's countries and that would serve as a forum to resolve international disputes without resort to war. Hope was in the air.

Although all the nations that had allied against Germany, nations great and small, were invited to the Paris conference, the power to craft the treaty was concentrated in the "Big Four"—England, the United States, France, and, to a significantly lesser extent, Italy. As for Germany and the other Central Powers, they were given no voice in the peace conference and were told that they would have to accept whatever terms were given them or face renewed warfare.

Despite the welcome he received, Wilson soon discovered that the Allies had very different motives from his. Where Wilson wanted to rearchitect an international order that promoted peace, Prime Minister Georges Clemenceau of France wanted nothing less than the punishment of Germany and its reduction to a preindustrial state; Prime Minister David Lloyd George of Britain was less vengeful in spirit than Clemenceau, but he was determined to protect and expand the interests of the British Empire, a motive that clashed with Wilson's pledge to promote self-determination for all nations. Vittorio Emanuele Orlando, prime minister of Italy, wanted the territorial compensation Italy had been promised when it agreed to join the Allied cause. Little wonder, then, that the terms the Big Four negotiated were far from likely to ensure a lasting world peace. Gravely disappointed, Wilson comforted himself with the fact that the Treaty of Versailles did incorporate the establishment of the League of Nations. So, although the treaty failed to guarantee freedom of the seas, promote disarmament, and call for reduction of tariffs—all key to his Fourteen Points—and although it punished and emasculated Germany, Wilson forced himself to believe that the League of Nations, once in operation, would correct all these grave deficiencies.

By leading the United States to victory and a place of influence in the world, Woodrow Wilson earned a good deal of political capital—which he proceeded to squander. For one thing, he excluded virtually everyone from consultation on the Treaty of Versailles. He turned his back most forcefully on the Republicans in Congress, who now enjoyed a majority. When he returned home to present the Versailles treaty and the League of Nations to the Senate and the American public, he believed that the nation was with him. Never mind that he had been in Europe for months and had lost touch with the postwar temper of America, which was basically a desire to be left alone.

It was probably true that most Americans favored joining the League of Nations, but the members of the Senate, whose constitutional duty was to advise and consent on treaties, presented a very different picture. Thirty-seven senators had voiced their opposition to the League as early as March 1919. Others, both Republican and Democratic, were outraged that the president had high-handedly excluded them from any role in drafting the treaty. A powerful Republican cadre argued forcefully that the United States would sacrifice its sovereignty by joining a body that had the authority to arbitrate international conflicts. They probably even more opposed the League because they could no longer stand the imperious Wilson.

The president needed a two-thirds supermajority to achieve Senate ratification of the treaty and the League. What is more, signing on to the treaty obligated membership in the League. While Wilson had the support of most Democrats, he needed the support of many Republicans as well. Leading that party's opposition to the treaty and the League was Senator Henry Cabot Lodge of Massachusetts, who insisted on protecting American sovereignty. He drafted the so-called Lodge Reservations, which held that Congress, based on its constitutional treaty-making authority, should also have the authority to decide when to abide and when not to abide by any decision made by the League. In addition, he stipulated that Congress had the voting authority to ignore the League's commitment to the political independence and territorial integrity of any of the signatories. Lodge successfully campaigned to gather Republican support for the reservations. As insistent as these were, there was still room for negotiation—but Wilson, who despised Lodge and who was suffering from the stress of dangerously failing health, dug in his heels. He refused any compromise concerning the League. His proposition to the Republicans and to the American people was all or nothing, take it or leave it.

Wilson believed that by appealing directly to the American people, he could persuade them to so pressure the Senate that a two-thirds majority would be created. Accordingly, he embarked on a 9,500-mile whistle-stop tour across America, beginning on September 4, 1919. It proved too much for the exhausted, ailing man. On September 25, after speaking at Pueblo, Colorado, Woodrow Wilson collapsed. The speaking tour was cut short, and his train raced back to Washington and the White House. There, on October 2, 1919, he suffered a stroke. It was not his first, but it was his worst. Partially paralyzed, profoundly fatigued, and generally incapacitated, Wilson, from his sickbed, continued to demand that his followers settle for nothing less than unconditional acceptance of the treaty and the League. The inevitable result came on November 19, 1919, when the Senate vote of 55 to 39 fell short of the required two-thirds majority. The

Treaty of Versailles and membership in the League of Nations failed of ratification.

Congressional debate dragged on until July 2, 1921. On that date, Congress did resolve that war with Germany and the other Central Powers was indeed at an end, but the Senate made final its refusal to ratify the Treaty of Versailles and the League. Far too sick to run for an unprecedented third term (there was no constitutional two-term limit in 1921), Wilson demanded that the Democratic Party make full acceptance of the League part of its platform. When the Republicans nominated Warren G. Harding as their presidential candidate, he ran on a campaign slogan that promised a "return to normalcy." This, it was understood, included rejection of League membership, and after Harding trounced Democrat James M. Cox and went on to inauguration, he declared in his inaugural address that "we seek no part in directing the destinies of the world." Later, to Congress, he flatly stated that the League "is not for us."

Without the United States, the League of Nations was indeed doomed to impotence. It was, of course, powerless to avert the outbreak of World War II, which came just short of twenty years after the end of World War I.

Americans Ratify the Nineteenth Amendment, Giving Women the Vote (1920)

"We hold these truths to be self-evident, that all men are created equal," the second paragraph of the Preamble to the Declaration of Independence begins. Generations of Americans have since decried the bitter hypocrisy of this clause as a moral justification for a revolution that proclaimed equality even while preserving slavery. There was no hypocrisy, however, concerning the founders' position on the condition of American women in 1776. The phrase "All men" made no pretense of including women, either grammatically, morally, politically, or legally.

The fact is that the American Revolution, while fought to secure political rights, never claimed the intention of securing them for women. They joined slaves, indentured servants, men without property, and—in many states—free blacks as a group denied the ballot. During the revolution, just one state, New Jersey, permitted women to vote. This, however, was the result of carelessly drafted voting legislation, worded to allow all individuals worth fifty pounds or more to vote. In 1777, women who met that cash criterion went to the polls. State legislators quickly plugged the loophole thereafter.

It was 1848 before the issue of female suffrage was seriously reconsidered when 240 women and men met at the Seneca Falls (New York) Convention and founded a movement to secure the vote for American women. They knew they were in for a fight, but they surely had no idea of how long it would take. Organized by Elizabeth Cady Stanton and Lucretia Mott—like most American suffragists also passionate abolitionists—the Seneca Falls Convention was so successful that it was reconvened annually prior to the Civil War. The run-up to that conflict caused many women to direct their activism toward abolition, which even they considered more urgent than women's suffrage. After the war, however, the suffrage movement resumed with renewed momentum—only to be divided over the question of whether to tie the campaign for women's rights to the campaign to enfranchise former slaves. Stanton and Susan B. Anthony fought for constitutional amendments to enfranchise both African Americans and women, and Mott was elected to chair the Equal Rights Association, which represented the union of the two causes. But when the Fourteenth Amendment (guaranteeing citizenship and equal protection of the law, regardless of race) and the Fifteenth Amendment (prohibiting states from denying the vote on account of "race, color, or previous condition of servitude") extended the vote to black men but made no mention of women, Mott did not object. Stanton and Anthony broke with her and the Equal Rights Association to form the National Woman Suffrage Association, which opposed the Fifteenth Amendment and accepted only women as members. Another splinter group, the American Woman Suffrage Association, believed the Fifteenth Amendment was a step toward liberalizing voting rights and therefore supported it.

Even divided, the women's movement attracted the sponsorship of various local women's clubs and federations of them. Some, like the Woman's Christian Temperance Union (WCTU), had other interests—prohibition, in the case of the WCTU—but signed on to the crusade for women's suffrage just the same. In 1890, the two main rival women's rights organizations, the National Woman Suffrage Association and the American Woman Suffrage Association, reconciled and merged under the leadership of Anna Howard Shaw and Carrie Chapman Catt, emerging as the National American Woman Suffrage Association. It was this organization that carried the cause of women's suffrage over the goal line. From 1900 to 1920, it spearheaded an unrelenting national campaign and managed to unify the movement—except for one maverick organization, the Congressional Union's National Woman's Party. Founded by Alice Paul, the Congressional Union was aggressively militant. Its members staged pickets, hunger strikes, and other acts of civil disobedience. Their goal was not merely to gain the vote but also to move passage of a new constitutional amendment that granted women equal rights with men in all areas.

It was, however, the less militant majority that prevailed. In 1919, Congress and President Woodrow Wilson—despite his lack of enthusiasm for women's suffrage—approved the straightforward wording of the proposed Nineteenth Amendment. It did no more and no less than give women the vote. It was ratified by the states on August 18, 1920, when Tennessee, after a hard-fought battle, became the thirty-sixth state to approve the amendment. Alice Paul and her followers were not done, however, and her Congressional Union suffrage reformers formed the National Woman's Party, which, in 1923, began a national campaign for an Equal Rights Amendment. Ratification has proved a rocky road, and the ERA remains unratified as of 2018.

Congress Cracks Down
on Immigration (1924)

The American national "brand" is the Nation of Immigrants. With respect to the "Old" World of Europe, Asia, and Africa, the Americas are the "New" World, a pair of continents whose modern population was imported from abroad. The United States has traditionally advertised itself as a haven for those whose native places were either oppressive or offered little opportunity. The Statue of Liberty, designed by the French sculptor Frédéric Auguste Bartholdi and built by the French engineer Gustave Eiffel, was presented to the people of the United States as a gift from the people of France, but the funds to erect it in New York Harbor were raised privately in America, mostly from contributions of less than a dollar. Among those who contributed to the fund drive was the American poet Emma Lazarus (1849–1887), who donated the manuscript of her 1883 sonnet "The New Colossus," celebrating the statue, to an auction. Lazarus portrayed the still-to-be-erected statue, which she called "Mother of Exiles," as an invitation to immigrants:

> *"Keep, ancient lands, your storied pomp!" cries she*
> *With silent lips. "Give me your tired, your poor,*
> *Your huddled masses yearning to breathe free,*
> *The wretched refuse of your teeming shore.*
> *Send these, the homeless, tempest-tost to me,*
> *I lift my lamp beside the golden door!"*

In some periods of American history, the "world-wide welcome" glowing from Liberty's "beacon-hand" has shone more brightly than in others.

The early 1920s began an especially dim period. Several laws were enacted to reduce what had been a heavy influx of immigrants from Europe,

Ireland, and Asia, a tide welcomed by American industrialists in need of labor, a flow that transformed America's major cities in the years leading up to the Civil War. The pace of immigration continued through the early twentieth century. But, as the United States emerged from participation in World War I—the "Great War" that many persisted in calling the "European War"—a wall of xenophobia rose up. Many Americans feared that millions of new immigrants would take jobs from the native-born. The very American capitalists who had previously clamored for immigrant labor now blamed immigrant labor for obstreperous unions and the rise of radical dissent. With the Russian Revolution and Russian Civil War constantly in American headlines during the late teens and twenties, the middle-class Americans who put President Warren G. Harding in office because he promised a "return to normalcy" were ready to interpret the newest wave of American unrest as the work of immigrant communists. And it is true, the various Communist parties that came into being immediately after World War I collectively boasted about one hundred thousand members in America. They were highly visible.

In late April 1919, some thirty-six dynamite bombs were mailed to prominent Americans, including newspaper editors and businessmen. Capitalist mogul John D. Rockefeller, Supreme Court justice Oliver Wendell Holmes Jr., and US attorney general A. Mitchell Palmer were among those targeted. A few bombs detonated and caused injury, but several were never delivered because they bore insufficient postage. On June 2 that year, eight bombs exploded in eight cities. The intended targets, prominent government officials, escaped harm, but one bomb took the life of a New York night watchman, William Boehner. All of the devices were traced to immigrant anarchists, and the bombs of 1919 were quite sufficient to unleash a fear of terrorist immigrants.

The first major manifestation of the new xenophobia was the Red Scare of 1919, in which Attorney General Palmer launched a series of raids to round up suspected radical leftists and deport them. The Palmer Raids of 1919 and 1920 amassed sixty thousand names, cast a wide net (in New York City, 650 were arrested), but in the end deported just forty-three people.

The next xenophobic manifestation was more lasting and consequential, however. In 1920, Congress passed the Immigration Act. For the first time in American history, immigrant quotas based on country of origin were set. Gone instantly were the pre–World War I days of what amounted to unlimited admission. In 1924, the Immigration Act was superseded by the Johnson-Reed Act, which restricted immigration more drastically. The act admitted a mere 150,000 immigrants annually, divided by quotas so that almost 90 percent of even that small number had to come from northwestern Europe. The character of America's urban ethnic neighborhoods changed as "new immigrants" from southern and eastern Europe were largely denied entry into the country.

From 1924 on, a nativist strain entered American political and social life, sometimes emerging more powerfully than others and belying the American immigrant "brand." Following the terrorist attacks on New York and Washington on September 11, 2001, nativism emerged quite powerfully, propelling in 2016 the candidacy of Donald J. Trump, who promised to "build a wall" on the nation's southern border and called for a ban on Muslim entry into the United States. He became the nation's forty-fifth president.

Sacco and Vanzetti Are Executed (1927)

One was a shoemaker and night watchman, the other a fishmonger. They were the kind of immigrants Americans were learning to fear in the 1920s. Nicola Sacco, the shoemaker-night watchman, had been born on April 22, 1891, in Puglia, Italy, and had entered the United States when he was seventeen. The fishmonger Vanzetti was born on June 11, 1888, in Villafalletto, Piedmont. He came to America at twenty. Both arrived in 1908 but did not meet until 1917 when they participated in a strike. They were leftists and self-proclaimed anarchists, believed to be followers of Luigi Galleani, a radical Italian anarchist who openly advocated bombing and assassination and published a periodical called *Cronaca Sovversiva* (*Subversive Chronicle*). Ever since the Red Scare of 1919–1920, Italian anarchists, especially Galleanists, topped the US government's lists of subversive organizations.

On April 15, 1920, two men were robbed and murdered while transporting the payroll of the Slater-Morrill Shoe Company factory in Braintree, Massachusetts. Alessandro Berardelli, a security guard, was shot four times, and paymaster Frederick Parmenter was shot twice—the second shot in the back, as he was trying to flee. After grabbing the payroll boxes, the robbers escaped in a stolen dark-blue Buick, which witnesses said was carrying several men.

Sacco and Vanzetti were arrested for the murders. A witness made an identification that put the two men at the scene of the crime, but Sacco and several corroborating witnesses testified that he was at the Italian consulate in Boston on the day of the murder. On clearly flawed testimony, Sacco and Vanzetti were nevertheless convicted by a jury on July 14, 1921, and sentenced to death.

Several organizations, including the International Workers of the World (IWW), backed appeals based on recanted testimony and contradictory ballistics evidence as well as a confession by an alleged participant in the robbery. Despite this strong basis, each appeal was denied. Soon, the case became an international cause that provoked protests in virtually every major American city as well as cities elsewhere in North America and Europe and as far away as Tokyo, Sydney, Buenos Aires, Johannesburg, and Auckland. An international who's who of literary, artistic, academic, and political figures, including heads of state, supported the appeals and then pleaded for clemency to the governor of Massachusetts. Even the Pope added his plea. Felix Frankfurter, a Harvard law professor who would go on to be a Supreme Court justice, published an *Atlantic Monthly* article brilliantly arguing their innocence.

It was all to no avail. The only thing that mattered was Sacco and Vanzetti's association with anarchism—and the fact that they were immigrants of Italy, a country especially out of favor among American immigration policymakers. The two were executed on August 23, 1927, in the electric chair. Riots broke out in American cities as well as in Paris and London.

Rampant American xenophobia killed the two Italians. Radicals argued that they were also victims of a nation whose legal system served the monied classes and whose middle classes were thoroughly conditioned to fear anything resembling radical politics. Few truly thoughtful people ever thought Sacco and Vanzetti were guilty, and in the 1970s an underworld informant revealed that the crime had been committed by the Morelli gang, five brothers, members of the Italian Mafia, who were notorious in the 1920s. In 1977, Massachusetts governor Michael Dukakis commissioned a review of the fifty-year-old case and on August 23, 1977, the anniversary of the execution, he proclaimed "Nicola Sacco and Bartolomeo Vanzetti Memorial Day," asserting that they had been unfairly tried and unjustly executed. Some in the state senate voted to censure Dukakis for the proclamation, but the censure was voted down 23 to 12.

The Stock Market Crashes (1929)

The presidential elections of Republicans Warren G. Harding, Calvin Coolidge, and Herbert Hoover were aspects of a popular revolt against Democrat Woodrow Wilson, advocate of internationalism, big government, and the Progressive government regulation of big business. The Republican presidents created a business-friendly environment with loose rules that made credit abundant. In response, post–World War I America speculated on Wall Street in record numbers. Americans became avid consumers as well, pouring their salaries and savings into stocks and goods. At the beginning of 1929, the market was climbing steadily higher and higher. Come September, however, there were signs of trouble. The market wavered wildly up—the Dow Industrials reaching a high of 386—and down, with the average prices decreasing. On October 24, a selling spree put almost thirteen million shares up for sale. Five days later, the market plunged and stocks lost an average of forty points, more than 10 percent of its value in a single day.

They called it Black Tuesday, a day in which many big-time investors joined ordinary middle-class Americans in losing practically everything they had. Yet the crash was not the cause of the Great Depression that followed it. It was a symptom, and, like many symptoms, it was the herald of worse to come. In July 1932, the Dow Jones average would tumble to a low of 40.56 points, a decline of 89 percent from the September 1929 high.

The causes of the Great Depression are many and complex, but at their root is the rapid industrialization of America in the late nineteenth and early twentieth centuries. As the country industrialized, its wealth became concentrated in the hands of a few. Technology advanced and production soared. Investors poured gasoline on the fire by ladling in money. Yet the markets for all the new goods did not keep pace with the increasing volume and tempo of production. Arguably, demand was

The initial impact of the Stock Market Crash of 1929 was felt mostly by corporate shareholders, but the Great Depression soon reached into every corner of the nation. This 1936 photograph by Dorothea Lange, *Migrant Mother*, emerged as the most iconic image of the period. NATIONAL ARCHIVES AND RECORDS ADMINISTRATION even shrinking as inventories swelled. American consumers simply did not have enough cash to buy all the products industry made, and a vicious cycle began. Workers were laid off as industry cut back. Industry could not hire workers because there was no market for their goods. There was no market for their goods because the workers had no money. The workers had no money because industries could not hire them. It was a black dog chasing its black tail.

Failure cascaded through the American economy. Industries shut plants and workers lost their jobs. They withdrew their bank deposits, and banks across the country failed. In 1930, the first full year of the depression, 1,300 banks were shuttered, and over the next two years another 3,700 followed suit. As the banks failed, people were denied access to funds. This in turn prevented the public from pumping money into the economy.

Eight months in office when the bottom fell out in 1929, President Herbert Hoover took much of the blame—not for causing the Crash and the Depression but for being helpless to curb their effects. Many historians persist in criticizing Hoover as clueless, but he was, in fact, far from oblivious to the crisis. Hoover introduced a program of federally financed public works projects in the hope of creating employment and stimulating the economy. The Hoover Dam, often cited as one of the crowning achievements of Franklin Roosevelt's New Deal, was begun by Hoover, who also called for the reduction of taxes on low-income Americans (Congress did not respond) and the closure of some tax loopholes that favored the wealthy (this was mostly accomplished). He even advocated government-funded $50-per-month pensions for those over sixty-five (Congress failed to act).

Yet he stood firm on refusing to allow the federal government to directly dole out money to citizens. He encouraged the states to do this—alas, their coffers were empty—but he argued that *federal* handouts would forever demoralize the people, transforming the democratic, free-market culture of the United States into a culture of perpetual dependency and entitlement.

Not that Hoover altogether failed to intervene. It's just that his interventions made everything worse. The Smoot-Hawley Tariff of March 13, 1930, was supposed to protect domestic industries. Instead, it crippled international trade with Europe and China. This, along with retaliatory tariffs enacted by several US trading partners, deepened the Depression—profoundly. Hoover obtained stratospheric increases in the top personal income tax bracket, from 25 percent to 63 percent, and increases in corporate taxes. He managed to produce a balanced budget in 1933, but the cost was the discouragement of both consumer buying and investor finance of new businesses. The Depression deepened yet further. No sector of the economy escaped. Farmers, who had been struggling under depressed prices since the end of World War I, suffered even more as jobless Americans reduced their family food budgets. People, as well as markets, simply starved without money.

President Hoover struggled to tamp down panic with unconvincing claims that prosperity was "just around the corner." He felt that his hands were tied. Americans now stood in bread lines for what little public and private relief was available. When they lost their homes, they moved to slums, and when they could no longer afford even slum rents, they huddled in "houses" constructed of packing crates and sheet metal erected in empty lots and roadsides. They were called "Hoovervilles."

In the summer of 1932, twenty thousand out-of-work veterans marched to Washington to demand early payment of bonuses promised in the World War Adjusted Compensation Act of 1924. But the promised payout date was 1945, and Congress refused to make it earlier. Nearly two thousand protesters lingered in the capital after Congress rebuffed their pleas. Living in a Hooverville at Anacostia Flats, in the shadow of the Capitol, the "Bonus Army" decided to wait out Congress. Hoover sent in federal troops under no less a figure than General Douglas MacArthur to clear them away. A fire broke out in the Hooverville. People were injured, a woman miscarried, and one man died of enteritis, which some blamed on the army's use of tear gas. The vision of the US Army pursuing unarmed Americans, coupled with the dire economic and social conditions, put an end to the Republicans' hopes for victory in the presidential election of 1932 in which an ebullient Franklin Delano Roosevelt promised that, if they sent him to the White House, Americans would get a "New Deal." Edging toward revolution in a world in which "great dictators"—Hitler and Mussolini chief among them—were in the ascendant, the American democracy was about to become a welfare state.

Franklin D. Roosevelt Announces a "New Deal" (1933)

Probably any Democrat would have defeated Herbert Hoover when he ran for reelection in 1932, but the huge margin of Franklin Delano Roosevelt's (FDR's) electoral vote victory—472 to 59—gave this Democrat an overwhelming popular mandate to do whatever he deemed necessary to pull the nation out of the economic quagmire of the Great Depression.

The "New Deal" FDR promised in his speech accepting his party's 1932 nomination for the presidency turned out to be a set of initiatives aimed less at strategic long-term recovery than immediate relief. Even responding to an economic emergency with emergency measures, however, required FDR to radically redefine the role of government as expressed in the Declaration of Independence and the Constitution. The president proposed that the job of modern government was to defend economic welfare as an "unalienable right" on a par with life, liberty, and the pursuit of happiness. In contrast to his predecessor, Herbert Hoover, who cited the American tradition of self-reliance as a reason not to use federal resources to directly assist individuals, Roosevelt argued that, in the life-and-death crisis of the Great Depression, rugged individualism had to yield to the common good. Yes, people would have to make individual sacrifices, but the government would, in return, provide *direct* help and support.

Roosevelt embarked on the transformation of the United States into a *welfare state*. To achieve this, he assumed unprecedented executive power. Much, like his fifth cousin, Theodore Roosevelt, FDR regarded the president as the tribune of the people, nothing less than the principal agent of democratic government over and above both the Legislative and Judicial branches. Immediately after his inauguration on March 4, 1933, the president's promised New Deal took shape in a torrent of executive orders. Bypassing Congress, FDR issued an order proclaiming a Bank Holiday intended to halt a rash of runs and bank failures. During the first "Hundred Days" of the Roosevelt administration, the president also goaded Congress to create the Federal Deposit Insurance Corporation (FDIC) to guarantee bank deposits, to expand the powers of the Federal Reserve Board, to establish the Home Owners' Loan Corporation, and to pass a Federal Securities Act, requiring companies to fully disclose financial information on new stock issues. To combat unemployment, Roosevelt successfully urged Congress to appropriate $500 million for relief programs and to create job programs, the most famous of which was the Civilian Conservation Corps (CCC). To stimulate industry, the president asked Congress to pass the National Industrial Recovery Act (NIRA). NIRA established the Public Works Administration (PWA) and compelled industrial leaders to enact codes of fair practices, allowing them in turn to set prices without fear of antitrust prosecution. In effect, NIRA institutionalized the essence of crony capitalism. Through NIRA, the federal government set minimum wages and maximum work hours. Workers were also given the right to bargain collectively. In addition, NIRA established the National Recovery Administration (NRA), which drafted business codes and labor regulations. At the same time, labor unions used the NRA to accumulate more clout and attract more members.

The Great Depression had hit the agricultural sector first and hardest, and Roosevelt prevailed on Congress to create the Agricultural Adjustment Administration (AAA) in May 1933, which imposed production limits and provided federal subsidies to raise agricultural prices to "parity" with the prices farmers had enjoyed when agriculture was in its best years. This was (and, for many economists, remains) among the most problematic, even egregious, of the New Deal measures. With the outbreak of World War I in 1914, American agricultural output came into great demand by the European nations. The demand increased tremendously when the United States entered the war in 1917 and was sustained after the war, when America became the breadbasket of a war-ravaged Europe. From the farmer's perspective, the "best years" of American agriculture were a boom period created not by normal demand but by wartime scarcity. The severity of the depression in the agricultural sector, coupled with a massive natural disaster—a drought that transformed much of the lower Midwest and parts of the West into a "Dust Bowl"—dramatically retarded economic recovery in farming states. Nevertheless, the aim of the agricultural price and production controls and subsidies was to restore the agricultural sector not merely to viability but also to an artificially prosperous level. Farmers came to rely on federal support long after the Great Depression came to an end. The legacy of the AAA is a culture of agricultural subsidies that persists to this day.

The Hundred Days also witnessed the birth of the Tennessee Valley Authority (TVA), an agency responsible for broad social and public works programs within the Tennessee River Valley region. Hydroelectric plants, nitrate manufacturing for fertilizers, soil conservation, flood control, and reforestation were all aspects of a program covering parts of seven states.

Without question, the New Deal made people feel better. Some of its programs may well have saved lives and families. Quite possibly, it even prevented a political upheaval at least verging on revolution in an era in which much of the world was falling into the grip of dictators such as Hitler, Mussolini, and Stalin. Yet, as a long-term strategy, the New Deal was not very effective. In 1934, despite the New Deal measures, nine million people were still out of work. The most memorable of the initiative's employment programs, the Works Progress Administration (WPA), left its most lasting mark on America in the cultural and social sphere, with its Federal Theater Project, Federal Writers' Program, and Federal Art Project, rather than creating an enduring economic stimulus. In short, despite the volume of cash injected into the economy by the federal government, the Great Depression continued little abated. That Roosevelt was elected to a second term (1936) and an unprecedented third term (1940) may well be evidence that, by 1936, the New Deal was thickly shrouded in a popular mythology. Nevertheless, the welfare state became the dominant model of American government through the administration of Lyndon Baines Johnson in the 1960s and was not seriously challenged until the election of Ronald Reagan in 1980.

The Great Strike Wave Sweeps the Nation (1934–1937)

The Great Depression was bad for people and bad for business. But the one thing big business counted on was being able to lowball wages and extract maximum hours from a workforce grateful to have a job. Big business was wrong. Between 1933 and 1937, the United States was swept by a tidal wave of labor strikes, almost all of them tinged by left-wing politics and, as many saw it, portending the possibility of revolution. The state of the American republic had not seemed so precarious since the era of the Civil War.

The strikes of the 1930s were not simple labor disputes but bloody class conflicts. On the labor end was the failure of the New Deal's National Recovery Administration (NRA) to make good its key guarantee of the right of workers to form unions. By the end of 1934, disgruntled workers were complaining that "NRA" stood for the "National Run-Around." On the political end of the spectrum, incited local radicals—Marxists of all stripes—were inspired to seize on the discontents of labor as the beginning of the fulfilment of what Karl Marx had both predicted and called for: a class war that would replace allegiance to nations with allegiance to class.

In some ways, though, both the labor unions and the political activists were less influential during this period than the workers themselves. Outrage and despair were at the grassroots, and workers everywhere began to wield a new weapon in the art of the strike: the sitdown.

It started in Akron, Ohio, in 1934, the epicenter of the US rubber industry, home to Goodyear, Firestone, and Goodrich along with more than twenty plants operated by smaller firms. At its peak, Akron's rubber industry employed forty-thousand workers. By 1933 one-third to one-half of Akron's workers were unemployed, and Firestone along with six smaller companies closed down their plants. Goodyear was down to a two-day week. On June 19, 1934, tire builders at the General Tire and Rubber Co. walked out when wage changes were announced. The local union's executive committee recommended accepting a wage increase the company offered, but it was part of a production speedup, and the workers refused and set up their own strike organization and left the union in droves, membership dropping from forty thousand to five thousand in days. In response to assembly line speedup, the Akron workers developed, spontaneously, the sitdown. It was a direct response to the tyranny of the accelerated assembly line.

The workers soon realized that no more than a dozen workers deciding to sit would stop all production. From 1934 to 1936, sitdown strikes were a feature of life in Akron, and the tactic spread through industries and factories nationwide, always in response to companies attempting to use the Great Depression as means of extorting more and faster work from hourly employees. The appeal of the tactic was that sitdowns became social affairs. Workers conversed with another and got to know each other.

At Goodyear, managers tried to break one sitdown by force. After securing a court injunction against mass picketing, which the workers simply ignored, management called in the sheriff, who assembled 150 deputies to open the plant that the sitdown strikers had occupied and shut down. Ten thousand workers of all trades from all over Akron gathered around the Goodyear plant, wielding lead pipes and baseball bats. The sheriff's forces retreated.

Next came a "Law and Order League," a gang of 5,200 vigilantes organized by a former mayor who was financed by Goodyear. When word of a planned attack leaked, the Summit County Central Labor Council announced that it would call a general strike against all plants and industries if there was a violent attack at Goodyear. The vigilantes were checkmated. For three years, through 1936, hardly a week went by in Akron without a sitdown strike, and hardly a day went by nationally without some major labor walkout.

The NRA Division of Research and Planning launched a study of the national wave of strikes in 1934, focusing on the auto industry. The chief finding was that "the grievance mentioned . . . uppermost in the minds of those who testified is the stretch-out. Everywhere workers indicated that they were being forced to work harder and harder, to put out more and more products in the same amount of time and with less workers doing the job." The authors of the study called the resulting labor disruption and unrest a "conflagration." A later study of the General Motors strike of 1936–1937 concluded that the stretch-out was resented less for the absolute rate of production than for the loss of freedom. Workers felt oppressed because they were not permitted "to set the pace of [their] work and to determine the manner in which it was to be performed." As one Buick worker complained, "You have to run to the toilet and run back. If you had to . . . take a crap, if there wasn't anybody there to relieve you, you had to run away and tie the line up, and if you tied the line up you got hell for it." Wives complained that their husbands were "so tired like they was dead, and irritable. . . . And then at night in bed he shakes, his whole body, he shakes." Another woman commented, "They're not men any more if you know what I mean. They're not men. My husband is only 30, but to look at him you'd think he was 50 and all played out."

In the end, the sitdown tactic—the nonviolent occupation of plants and idling of production—combined with the unions vowing to call general sympathy strikes if violence were applied brought management to the bargaining table. The tactic was so successful that the Bureau of Labor Statistics recorded sitdowns involving nearly four hundred thousand workers in 1937 alone.

Nor was the sitdown restricted to private enterprise. In Amsterdam, New York, for instance, municipal garbage men sat down on their trucks in the city Department of Public Works garage when their demands for a wage increase were refused. A similar strike occurred in Bridgeport, Connecticut. In New York City, seventy maintenance workers, half white, half black, barricaded themselves in the kitchen and laundry of the Hospital for Joint Diseases. Forty grave-diggers and helpers prevented burials in a North Arlington, New Jersey, cemetery by sitting down in the toolhouse to secure a raise for the helpers. Seventeen blind workers sat down to demand a minimum wage at a workshop run by the New York Guild for the Jewish Blind and were supported by a sympathy sitdown of eighty-three blind workers at a workshop of the New York Association for the Blind. In Brooklyn, draftsmen and engineers sat down against a wage cut in the Park Department.

Political leaders condemned the wave of sitdowns as the work of left-wing radicals. They portrayed the actions as challenges to the government, to patriotism, and to the rule of law. In fact, the sitdown was more a challenge to management decisions in which the workers were given no voice. Soon, the sitdowns were being used to challenge more than low wages and production speedups. They were launched against a wide range of social grievances. In Detroit, for instance, thirty-five women occupied a welfare office demanding that the supervisor be removed and that a committee meet with a new supervisor to jointly determine the qualifications of families for relief. In New York, representatives of fifteen families who lost their homes and belongings in a tenement fire sat down at the Emergency Relief Bureau demanding complete medical care for those injured in the fire and sufficient money for rehabilitation, instead of token payments the Bureau had offered. In Columbus, Ohio, thirty unemployed men and women sat down in the governor's office demanding $50 million for poor relief. In St. Paul, Minnesota, two hundred sat down in the State Senate chamber, demanding action on a $17 million relief bill. Prisoners sat down in the state prison in Joliet, Illinois, to protest working in the prison yard on Saturday afternoon, a designated time of rest. Pittsburgh children sat down in a movie theater when the manager ordered them to leave before the feature film began. At Mineville, New York, 150 high school students staged a sitdown because the contracts of the principal and two teachers had not been renewed.

The strikes were empowering. As one striker remarked, "Now we know our labor is more important than the money of the stockholders, than the gambling in Wall Street, than the doings of the managers and foremen." Indeed, by 1937, as the country was just beginning to feel the effects of war preparedness, many employers began dealing with unions voluntarily, and by the entry of the United States into World War II, unions were in virtually all large industrial companies. It made sense for corporations to engage in collective bargaining with a union rather than try to face a mass of individual disgruntled employees. As the production demands of war returned the United States to full employment, unions were instrumental in creating an industrial workplace without speedups and with shorter hours and higher wages, as well as generally improved working conditions and such perks as vacations with pay, seniority, and reasonable job security. Labor leader John L. Lewis called it "industrial democracy," and it was a turning point in American worker–industrial relations.

The Japanese Bomb Pearl Harbor (1941)

Japan's victory over Russia in Russo-Japanese War of 1904–1905 was a wake-up call for the Western nations. Long thought of as quaint and backward, Japan was suddenly revealed as an industrial and military powerhouse. By the 1930s, it was busily engaged in expanding its empire, determined to gain control of Asian nations rich in natural resources and to create concentric defensive rings moving outward from the Japanese home islands by setting up military outposts in the islands of the south and central Pacific. Beginning in 1937, Japan engaged in a brutal war of invasion and conquest against China. In the summer of 1941, Japanese diplomats negotiated with the American government over its demands that Japan withdraw from China. The emperor's representatives stalled, not wanting to provoke the United States, its chief supplier of oil, steel, and other strategic materials.

As Japan drifted closer to an alliance with Nazi Germany and fascist Italy in the late 1930s, President Franklin D. Roosevelt, believing that trade pressure was a peaceful economic alternative to war as a means bringing Japan to heel, imposed an embargo on all strategic exports. In fact, this step provoked Japan into secretly planning for an attack on the United States. When World War II began in Europe with the German invasion of Poland on September 1, 1939, and France fell in the summer of 1940, Japan attacked French Indo-China (Vietnam). US secretary of state Cordell Hull protested. Turning a deaf ear, Japan signed the Tripartite Treaty with Germany and Italy, creating the Axis in September 1940.

As the threat of Japan loomed, US rearmament accelerated and trade with Japan was further limited. By the winter of 1940–1941, US shipments to Japan of strategic commodities had completely stopped. On July 26, 1941, FDR issued an executive order freezing Japanese assets in the United States.

Japan had no wish to fight a long war with the United States. What was needed was a hard strike that would keep America out of the world war, securing peace on terms favorable to Japan. Japan's top admiral, Isoruko Yamamoto, believed that a devastating strike against the US Navy's Pacific Fleet at Pearl Harbor, Hawaii Territory, would be unrecoverable, especially if (as he assumed) the United States would be drawn into an Atlantic war against Hitler and Mussolini. Destroy the US Pacific Fleet, and a two-front war would become impossible. Combine the attack on the Pacific Fleet with overwhelming assaults on other US and Allied possessions in the Pacific and Asia—including the Philippines, Guam, Wake Island (all US-held) and British-held Singapore and Hong Kong, the Dutch East Indies, and Australia—and America would have to come to terms.

The key thing was that the Pearl Harbor attack had to be total, the fleet annihilated, not just crippled. If the United States saw a way to recover, Yamamoto warned, it would retaliate and defeat Japan in the fullness of time. Yamamoto based this conclusion on his experience in the United States, where he had studied at Harvard University from 1919 to 1921 and where he served from 1925 to 1928 as Japanese naval attaché in Washington, D.C. He knew the American character and had seen the magnitude of American industry. Japan's rising class of militarists ignored Yamamoto's warnings even as they approved his plan.

The first imperative was total surprise. The attack was to be launched before a formal declaration of war was made, but the declaration was to be made before the bombers reached their target. Yamamoto cautioned that bombing before a declaration was delivered would so anger the American people that, no matter how devastating the attack, they would never allow a negotiated peace.

The second imperative was to resolve a tactical problem. Pearl Harbor's waters were too shallow for torpedoes dropped from torpedo bombers. The torpedoes would bottom out before they reached their targets. Yamamoto learned that Japanese naval observers had witnessed the British air raid at the Battle of Taranto on November 11, 1940. British torpedo bombers successfully attacked the Italian fleet anchored at the Taranto naval base in southern Italy using torpedoes modified to function in shallow water and pilots trained in a bombing technique that reduced the depth to which the launched torpedoes descended below the surface of the water. The Japanese emulated the British tactics, and they added wooden fins to the torpedoes to reduce their tendency to plunge. American naval planners were blissfully ignorant of all this, believing that the shallow waters of Pearl Harbor made the base immune to airborne torpedo attack.

It is a myth that America was "completely" unprepared for war in late 1941. The nation's first peacetime draft had begun in 1940, and military spending was at unprecedented levels. This said, American planners were confident that Pearl Harbor was safe from torpedo assault, that no great Japanese fleet could approach undetected, and that the first Japanese attack, if it came, would be against the Philippines or perhaps against US military outposts at Wake or Midway islands. For this reason, General Walter Short, commander of the army facilities adjacent to Pearl Harbor, transferred many of his P-40 fighters to Wake and Midway. Also, fearing that the real danger in Hawaii was from saboteurs—the island was home to many recent Japanese immigrants, whose loyalty to the United States was in doubt—Short ordered that all aircraft on the US Army Air Forces fields adjacent to Pearl to be clustered close together, wingtip to wingtip, so that they could be more effectively guarded by sentries on the ground.

On November 27, 1941, US Army Chief of Staff George C. Marshall issued to all commanders a "war warning," a message indicating that, based on the continued failure of negotiations, war with Japan was imminent. Again, assuming that sabotage was the only real danger, Admiral Husband E. Kimmel, commander of the Pearl Harbor naval base, moored the ships of the fleet close together. Only every fourth machine gun aboard those vessels was manned; all ammunition was securely locked away to keep it out of the hands of saboteurs. Kimmel also decided not to squander personnel to continuously man antiaircraft batteries. Nor did he order any special air reconnaissance. In fact, on December 7, 1941, only one out of three of the fleet's captains were even aboard their ships. The rest were on shore leave, along with most of their officers.

Bad as the poor preparation was, even worse was the failure of Kimmel and Short, officers in "rival" service arms, to regularly share intelligence and other information with one another. But then, the nation's civilian leaders likewise failed to share information with the military high command in Washington or Hawaii. Incredibly, US cryptanalysts had broken key Japanese diplomatic and military codes and routinely intercepted messages, but a bureaucratic breakdown prevented the vital intelligence from being sent to the commanders in Hawaii.

On November 22, the Japanese task force rallied in the Kurile Islands and then sailed on November 26 toward Pearl Harbor. Vice Admiral Chuichi Nagumo was in charge of the elite force. With great skill, he used a weather front, which moved at about the same speed as the fleet, to mask the movement of his six aircraft carriers—the *Akagi* (Nagumo's flagship) and the *Hiryū, Kaga, Shōkaku, Sōryū*, and *Zuikaku*. With these were two battleships, two heavy cruisers, a light cruiser, nine destroyers, and three fleet submarines. On board the carriers were 423 aircraft, including Mitsubishi Type 0 ("Zero") fighters, Nakajima Type 97 ("Kate") torpedo bombers, and Aichi Type 99 ("Val") dive bombers. Ahead of this striking force was an Advanced Expeditionary Force, which included twenty fleet submarines and five two-man Kohyoteki-class "midget" submarines. The subs' mission was to gather last-minute intelligence and to sink any American ships that might flee the attack.

Nagumo advanced under absolute radio silence—no chatter—and reached his attack station 275 miles north of Hawaii without being detected. At 6 a.m. local time, on Sunday morning, December 7, 1941, he launched his first wave: forty-nine bombers, forty torpedo bombers, fifty-one dive-bombers, and forty-three fighters. This was followed by a second wave, consisting of fifty-four bombers, seventy-eight dive-bombers, and thirty-six fighters.

In Washington, where it was already afternoon, the staff of the Japanese embassy laboriously decrypted and transcribed instructions from Tokyo to the ambassador. In the end, the declaration of war was not delivered to the ambassador until well after the attack was under way. This was precisely what Yamamoto had warned against. On December 8, when he asked Congress to declare war on Japan, President Roosevelt would call December 7 a "date that will in infamy." America's will to fight had been instantly galvanized by an infamous "sneak attack."

The attack on Pearl Harbor achieved total surprise and was a tactical triumph that nevertheless sealed Japan's strategic doom. Roused to war, the United States mounted a total effort. But not before suffering a humiliating defeat in Hawaii. The Japanese aircraft homed in on Pearl Harbor by following the signal of commercial radio broadcasts from Honolulu. The pilots adhered to a bombing grid drawn up by the Japanese consul general stationed in Honolulu. Anchored in the harbor were seventy warships, including eight battleships and twenty-four major auxiliary vessels. Not present in port were the heavy cruisers and fleet carriers, which were at sea on maneuvers. These vital ships were thus saved from destruction.

The first wave of aircraft attacked from 7:55 to 8:25. At 9:15, the dive bombers of the second wave attacked, withdrawing at 9:45. About 360 of Nagumo's aircraft participated and took a terrible toll: the battleship *Arizona* was destroyed, and the battleship *Oklahoma* capsized; the battleships *California, Nevada*, and *West Virginia* sank in shallow water. In addition, three cruisers, three destroyers, and four other vessels were either damaged or sunk. On the airfields, 164 aircraft were destroyed on the ground and another 128 were badly damaged. The human toll was 2,403 army and navy personnel and civilians killed and 1,178 wounded. Japanese losses were a mere twenty-nine aircraft and six submarines.

Initial reports thrilled Nagumo. But he was a cautious commander and fatefully decided not to launch a planned third wave, fearing a counterattack by US submarines. This attack was to have focused on the base's repair facilities and fuel installations. Had the third wave struck, Pearl Harbor would likely have been knocked out of the war for a very long time. As it was, the facility was quickly repaired and back in service almost immediately. Moreover, Nagumo failed to appreciate the consequences of the survival of the aircraft carriers and heavy cruisers. They would serve as the core of a resurrected and greatly enlarged US Pacific Fleet. Indeed, even the severe losses of that Sunday morning were not total. The *Arizona* was a total loss, but the other damaged battleships were quickly repaired. Even those that had sunk in shallow water were refloated. Six of the eight battleships hit at Pearl Harbor returned to service before the end of the war, as did all but one of the other ships bombed that day. Japan had drawn into combat the only Pacific power capable of defeating it.

Executive Order 9066 Authorizes the "Internment" of Japanese Americans (1942)

When Pearl Harbor was attacked on December 7, 1941, some 120,000 persons of immediate Japanese descent were living in the United States. Of these, about eighty thousand had been born here and were birthright citizens. Within four days after the Pearl Harbor attack, the FBI arrested and detained 1,370 American citizens of Japanese descent as "dangerous enemy aliens," even though they were, in fact, citizens. On December 22, the Agriculture Committee of the Los Angeles Chamber of Commerce issued the first public call to put all Japanese Americans "under federal control."

Consider the source. For years, Japanese American farmers had been enormously successful farming in California, Oregon, and Washington state, making themselves formidable competitors to their Anglo neighbors. Without doubt, the "infamy" of a "sneak attack" against US territory gave Americans reason to fear that those of Japanese descent would align themselves with their country of origin or ancestry, would be disloyal, and would even commit sabotage. Without doubt as well, Pearl Harbor and the war that followed made a convenient excuse for bringing years of agricultural competition to an end.

On January 5, 1942, US draft boards summarily classified all Japanese American selective service registrants as enemy aliens. Many Japanese Americans already serving were discharged or restricted to menial labor duties. On January 6, 1942, Leland Ford, Congressman from the district encompassing Los Angeles, asked Secretary of State Cordell Hull to remove all Japanese Americans from the West Coast. "I do not believe that we could be any too strict in our consideration of the Japanese in the face of the treacherous way in which they do things," Ford wrote to the secretary. Before the end of the month, the California State Personnel Board barred from state civil service positions all "descendants of natives with whom the United States [is] at war." In principle, this included descendants of Germans and Italians. In practice, it was enforced only against Japanese Americans.

On January 29, US Attorney General Francis Biddle established "prohibited zones" forbidden to all enemy aliens. Japanese aliens (not citizens) and German and Italian aliens were ordered to leave San Francisco waterfront areas. The very next day, California attorney general Earl Warren—who would in the 1950s become the iconic civil libertarian chief justice of the Supreme Court—called for preemptive action to prevent repeating Pearl Harbor. In response, the US Army designated twelve "restricted areas" in which enemy aliens were to be subject to a curfew from 9 p.m. to 6 a.m. and in which they were permitted to travel only to and from work. They were restricted to travel within no more than five miles from their homes.

On February 6, 1942, a Portland, Oregon, American Legion post publicly demanded "removal" of what it called "enemy aliens." A week later, the entire West Coast congressional delegation appealed to President Franklin D. Roosevelt to order the removal "all persons of Japanese lineage . . . aliens and citizens alike, from the strategic areas of California, Oregon and Washington." On February 16, the California Joint Immigration Committee urged that all Japanese Americans be removed from the Pacific Coast and other vital areas. Three days later, the FBI was holding 2,192 Japanese Americans, and President Roosevelt signed Executive Order 9066, authorizing the secretary of war to define military areas "from which any or all persons may be excluded as deemed necessary or desirable."

As Secretary of War Henry Stimson interpreted the executive order, this meant that Japanese Americans, citizens and noncitizens alike, Nisei (those born in the United States or Canada whose parents came from Japan) and Issei (Japanese immigrants), living within two hundred miles of the Pacific Coast were to be "evacuated." More than one hundred thousand persons were moved to internment camps quickly erected in

California, Idaho, Utah, Arizona, Wyoming, Colorado, and Arkansas. Postwar comparisons of these facilities to Nazi concentration camps were hyperbolic and unfounded. The camps were spartan, but livable. Nevertheless, many internees suffered significant financial hardship and loss. Quaker activists and the American Civil Liberties Union (ACLU) brought suits before the Supreme Court, alleging a violation of due process of law and other constitutional guarantees. All, most notably *Hirabayashi v. United States* and *Korematsu v. United States,* failed as the high court upheld the constitutionality of the executive order in a war-time emergency.

While "interned," some 1,200 young Japanese men secured release by enlisting in the US Army. They were segregated in the 442nd Regimental Combat Team, which also consisted of about ten thousand Japanese-Hawaiian volunteers. (Japanese-Hawaiians had not been subject to the removal order.) The 442nd was sent to Europe and fought valiantly in Italy, France, and Germany, emerging from the war as the most highly decorated unit of its size and length of service in American military history.

Internment ended on December 17, 1944, when Major General Henry C. Pratt issued Public Proclamation No. 21, which, effective January 2, 1945, permitted "evacuees" to return to their homes. To a degree, Congress acknowledged the injustice of the internment policy by passing the Japanese American Evacuation Claims Act in 1948. It paid out some $31 million in claims, which was a small fraction of financial losses internees incurred. After this, however, all court cases seeking federal compensation failed until 1968, when a new congressional act reimbursed some who had lost property because of their relocation. After another twenty years, in 1988, Congress appropriated more funds to pay a lump sum of $20,000 to each of the sixty thousand surviving Japanese American internees. Although the internment has had numerous apologists—some of whom argue that segregation actually amounted to protective custody—most Americans, regardless of political orientation, regard it as a stain on US law and democracy.

The US Navy Prevails in the Battle of Midway (1942)

Japanese admiral Isoroku Yamamoto's rationale for the December 7, 1941, attack on Pearl Harbor was nothing less than the total destruction of the US Pacific Fleet, which was supposed to bring about a nonaggression agreement with the United States. Destructive as the attack was, it fell far short of total destruction. Not only were the fleet's carriers and heavy cruisers at sea during the raid—and therefore escaped the attack—the raid's third wave was canceled, leaving much of Pearl Harbor's infrastructure intact. Instead of offering terms to Japan, the United States declared total war against the nation. Seeking to regain momentum, Yamamoto devised an ambitious plan to lure the US fleet into a single decisive sea battle that would complete the unfinished the work of Pearl Harbor by destroying the American fleet or at least crippling it so severely that a negotiated peace in the Pacific theater would be the only choice left to the United States.

Midway Island, a thousand miles west of Hawaii, was strategically located real estate from which either side could launch major attacks against the other. Yamamoto believed that he could ambush the American Pacific fleet there and administer a coup de grâce. He began the operation by sending a diversionary force to the Aleutian Islands, part of the US territory of Alaska in the northern Pacific. He knew that the Americans would have to divert resources here to defend any Japanese attack or landing. In the meantime, Admiral Chuichi Nagumo, the force commander who had led the Pearl Harbor attack, sailed a four-aircraft carrier striking force toward Midway, followed by a full invasion fleet. The total complement of his forces was about eighty-eight ships.

Thanks to ULTRA intelligence—the top secret Allied decryption of Japanese naval and diplomatic codes—US Navy Pacific commander,

Admiral Chester A. Nimitz, shrewdly anticipated Yamamoto's moves and motives. Instead of avoiding a possible trap at Midway, Nimitz decided to oblige the Japanese commander by giving him the decisive battle he wanted. However, the American's plan was to produce a very different outcome—a decisive US Navy victory.

Admiral Nimitz rushed to assemble two task forces east of Midway: TF 16, under Admiral Raymond Spruance, and TF 18, commanded by Admiral Frank Fletcher. In addition to the aircraft launched from the fleet carriers *Enterprise*, *Hornet*, and *Yorktown*, land-based planes would operate from US-held Midway itself. Indeed, these aircraft were the first to engage the Japanese fleet, attacking a portion of it when it was still more than five hundred miles west of Midway, on June 3, 1942. Unfortunately, the daring attack failed to do significant damage, and US aircraft losses were heavy. This opening did not bode well, and on the next morning, June 4, Nagumo seized the initiative, sending 108 planes against Midway Island, causing heavy damage, including the loss on the ground of fifteen of the twenty-five Marine Corps fighter planes tasked with defending the US base there.

At the same time, American torpedo bombers made a second air attack against the Japanese fleet. Results were again disheartening. The bombers hit no ships and seven of the aircraft were lost. In a second strike on this day, eight of twenty-seven Marine Corps dive bombers were shot down, again without having inflicted damage. The Americans then hurled against the Japanese 15 US Army Air Forces heavy B-17 bombers, flying out of Midway. Incredibly, the Japanese carriers escaped unscathed.

Undaunted, Nimitz launched torpedo bombers from all three of his fleet's carriers. Yet again they inflicted little damage, and, this time, losses were, on the face of it, catastrophic. Thirty-five of the forty-one torpedo bombers engaged were shot down. Yet these terrible tactical losses gained a key strategic advantage. The attack, failure though it was, forced the Japanese carriers to launch all their aircraft in defense. This left these ships vulnerable to a follow-up American attack. As the Japanese crews rushed to land, refuel, and rearm their returning aircraft, fifty-four American dive bombers from the *Enterprise* and *Yorktown* (the *Hornet*'s planes failed to find their targets) suddenly descended on three of the great Japanese carriers—*Akagi*, *Kaga*, and *Soryu*. At the time, all were loaded with just-recovered aircraft, which, however, were not yet ready to take off. In a mere four minutes, the dive bombers sent all three ships to the bottom, along with crews, aircraft, and pilots. Nagumo's fourth carrier, *Hiryu*, was sunk in a second attack later that afternoon—although not before the *Hiryu*'s planes savaged the *Yorktown*, forcing its abandonment. (An attempt was made to salvage the ship, but it was sent to the bottom by a Japanese submarine on June 7.)

The Battle of Midway was costly for American pilots and sailors: The *Yorktown* was lost, a destroyer sunk, and some 150 aircraft shot out of the sky. Three hundred seven men were killed. The fight was, however, fatal to the Japanese. Losing four aircraft carriers, 248 aircraft, one heavy cruiser badly damaged, along with 3,057 sailors and airmen—including the core of the Japanese navy's most experiences fliers—Nagumo withdrew from the Battle of Midway on June 5. US Navy forces were themselves too battered to give chase—although on June 6 they caught up with the heavy cruiser *Mikuma* and sunk it. For Japan, it was an unmitigated strategic defeat, and the Battle of Midway stands as the turning point of the Pacific war. Before Midway, Japan was on the offensive, a juggernaut. After Midway, it fought only a defensive war in the Pacific, steadily retreating toward the empire's home islands. Although World War II would continue until the summer of 1945, militarily—strategically—the war ended on June 4, 1943.

The American Crusade in Europe Begins on the Shores of Normandy (1944)

Propelled into World War II by the surprise Japanese attack against Pearl Harbor on December 7, 1941, the United States and its allies—chief among which were the United Kingdom and the USSR—went from defeat to defeat early in the conflict. Quickly mobilizing both its military and industrial might, however, America clawed its way from a desperate defensive posture to an increasingly successful offensive strategy. By the late spring of 1944, the United States, Great Britain, and Canada joined together in the ultimate offensive, the biggest amphibious invasion in the history of the world.

Launched on June 6, 1944, it was an invasion of German-occupied France via Normandy. Officially, it was the implementation of Operation Overlord and, more specifically, the initial amphibious assault of Overlord designated Operation Neptune. Although these operations were the products of some two years of planning, training, and build-up of personnel, equipment, and supplies, success or failure came down to a single day, the day of commencement, called in operational parlance "D-Day."

By May 1944, forty-seven divisions—about eight hundred thousand combat troops—had been assembled at embarkation points in England, poised to cross the English Channel to designated Norman beaches. Overlord was under the executive command of US general Dwight David Eisenhower, Supreme Allied Commander, Europe. Serving directly under him was British general Bernard Law Montgomery, assigned as field commander of all Allied ground forces.

The designated landing beaches were laid out along a fifty-mile expanse of Norman coast, from Caen west to the base of the Cotentin Peninsula. For purposes of the operation, this area was divided into five beaches, code-named, from east to west, Sword (to be assaulted by the

Chief Photographer's Mate Robert F. Sargent captured this image of an LCVP (Landing Craft, Vehicle, Personnel) disembarking troops of Company E, 16th Infantry, 1st Infantry Division (the Big Red One) onto Omaha Beach in Normandy on the morning of June 6, 1944. Before the day ended, two-thirds of Company E were dead or wounded. NATIONAL ARCHIVES AND RECORDS ADMINISTRATION

British 3rd Division), Juno (Canadian 3rd Division), Gold (British 50th Division), Omaha (US 1st Division and part of the 29th), and Utah (US 4th Division). The initial landings on June 6 were made by about 156,000 troops.

Their objective was beyond formidable. Adolf Hitler renamed the European continent, which he largely occupied, *Festung Europa* ("Fortress Europe"), and its coastal defenses, thickly fortified, were collectively called the "Atlantic Wall." They consisted of mammoth hardened forts and gun emplacements in addition to all manner of beach and sea obstacles as well as explosive mines. Positioned behind the Atlantic Wall were the German Seventh Army (commanded by Friedrich Dollmann) and a portion of Army Group B, commanded by the legendary Field Marshal Erwin Rommel. One of the armies of Rommel's group, the Fifteenth, commanded by Hans von Salmuth, was stationed north of the Seine River. German forces in Western Europe were under the highly capable Field Marshal Gerd von Rundstedt. Available at or near the coast were a total of thirty-six infantry and six Panzer (armored) divisions—well over six hundred thousand men.

The Allies were acutely aware that the success of the initial assault depended on surprise—not easily maintained when a large force was involved. Geography dictated that the obvious place for the initial landings was at the Pas de Calais, which was not only at the shortest distance between the English and French coasts but which also provided a direct line of advance inland. For these very reasons, the Allies rejected the idea of landing there. It was too obvious. They chose Normandy instead, and, in the months preceding the operation, staged an audacious campaign of deception, called Operation Mincemeat, which included disinformation disseminated through double agents, phony radio traffic, and elaborate decoys, all designed to dupe the Germans into believing the obvious: that the landings would be made at the Pas de Calais.

The deception was spectacularly successful. German high command deployed most of its forces directly opposite the Pas de Calais, leaving Normandy relatively lightly defended. German forces could, when needed, be rapidly moved, but the deception was so thorough that, even after the initial Allied breakout from the Norman beachheads, German high command wrote off the Normandy landings as a mere feint. The generals persisted in believing that much larger forces were about to assault Pas de Calais. For this reason, the entire Fifteenth German Army was kept at its original position, north of the Seine. It did not participate in resisting the initial Allied breakout.

The success of the treacherous cross-Channel invasion depended, first and foremost, on the right combination of tidal conditions, moonlight, and weather. Timing was critical. A severe storm forced a one-day delay in the launch, but a narrow window of marginally acceptable weather permitted the invasion to proceed on June 6. These landings were preceded the night before by an airborne assault by paratroops from the US 82nd and 101st Airborne divisions behind Utah Beach. Their mission was to capture exits into the Cotentin Peninsula. At the same time, the British 6th Airborne parachuted onto the eastern margin of Sword Beach to take bridges over the Orne River and the Caen Canal, which would be vital to the protection of the invasion's left flank. The air component of the invasion also included operations by 4,900 fighter planes and 5,800 bombers, all under British air chief marshal Trafford Leigh-Mallory. During the first twenty-four hours of the operation, these aircraft flew some 14,600 sorties against German coastal defenses.

The landings began at dawn on the sixth and were supported by a massive naval bombardment and close air support. By the evening of the first day, four of the five beachheads had been completely secured. These included, on the left (the east end of the assault, Gold, Juno, and Sword beaches), the Second British Army (Miles Dempsey) and the Canadian 3rd Infantry Division and 2nd Armoured Division. On the right, elements of the First US Army (Omar Bradley) advanced five miles inland at Utah Beach on D-Day, but at Omaha Beach, by far the most heavily defended of the five, the US 1st Division ended June 6, 1944, having gained only the most precarious hold on its beachhead and had suffered some two thousand casualties (compared to 197 at Utah Beach). The planners of D-Day anticipated horrific casualties. They were relieved that, in the first twenty-four hours, "just" 8,500 men had been wounded and 2,500 killed—a heavy toll, to be sure, but far less than had been anticipated. German casualties on D-Day have been estimated at between four thousand and nine thousand.

In the first six days following the initial landings, the Allied liberators consolidated their five beachheads into an eighty-mile-broad "lodgment," with an average occupied depth of ten miles. During this period, eight additional combat divisions were landed so that there was virtually no chance that the invasion would be driven back into the sea. Still, the "breakout" into the French inland would not be easy. On the left flank of the invasion, Panzers (armored troops) kept the British Second Army out of strategically vital Caen for weeks after the landings. On the right, three corps of the First US Army defended the perimeter from Caumont to Carentan. North of Carentan, the US VII Corps attacked to the west across the base of the Cotentin Peninsula. Progress was greatly impeded by the *bocage*, or hedgerows, of the Norman coastal farmlands. On June 18, the Americans were able to turn north, and, on June 20, the 9th, 79th, and 4th Infantry divisions reached the outer defenses of Cherbourg. From June 22 to June 27, the Americans battered Cherbourg's defenses. This port, once secured, became a major gateway of supply for the growing forces of the invasion.

Elsewhere, the battle of Normandy developed with great violence. The Allies raced to build up forces behind their lodgment preparatory to a major breakout. For their part, the Germans poured in reinforcements, struggling to contain the breakout. On June 28, however, Seventh German Army commander Dollman was killed. Hitler panicked, relieving the highly capable Rundstedt on July 3 and replacing him with Field Marshal Gunther von Kluge, who was transferred from the Eastern Front, where Hitler's forces were being mauled by Russia's Red Army.

On July 3, the First US Army attacked to the south but made excruciatingly slow progress. In the meantime, on the left flank of the invasion, the Second British Army at long last took at least part of Caen (west of the Orne River) on July 8, but it was not until July 20 that a second attack succeeded in taking the rest of the town. Although the landing phase of the Normandy invasion had gone remarkably well, by July 20 the invading forces held little more than 20 percent of the area that had been assigned to them. Nevertheless, by July 24, the forces were poised for a major breakthrough in a new operation, codenamed Cobra, which would be spearheaded on the right flank by the Third US Army under the Allies' greatest field commander, Lieutenant General George S. Patton. Europe was on the verge of liberation. As for America, it would end the war in Europe and Asia as the planet's preeminent superpower.

Congress Enacts the "GI Bill" (1944)

Only the Civil War (1861–1865) presented the United States with a graver and more urgent existential crisis than World War II. Both wars required Americans and their government to focus maximum effort and resources on the struggle. Yet, during the Civil War, Congress and the Lincoln administration acted to encourage Western settlement with the Homestead Act and legislation funding construction of a transcontinental railroad, both passed in 1862. These measures not only extended the reach of the Union westward, they also asserted confidence in an American future. On June 22, 1944, just sixteen days after Allied forces landed at Normandy on D-Day, President Franklin D. Roosevelt signed into law the Servicemen's Readjustment Act. Better known as the "GI Bill of Rights" or, more simply, the "GI Bill," it was an extensive package of benefits for returning World War II veterans and would prove instrumental in triggering a postwar boom in housing, education, employment, and babies. When it was signed, the outcome of the war was far from decided. Americans still faced formidable enemies across both oceans, and yet it was the government's expression of gratitude for the service of American soldiers, sailors, and airmen as well as a pledge of absolute faith in a future that would be heralded by military triumph and consummated in better lives for young men returning from war to start families or reunite with them.

The legislation established a system of veterans' hospitals, provided for the vocational rehabilitation of those wounded in war, furnished low-interest mortgages for returning GIs, and provided stipends covering tuition and living expenses for veterans attending college or trade schools. World War I, which Woodrow Wilson promised would be the "war to end all wars," did result in victory but a peace that was little more than a turbulent twenty-year truce, marked by severe economic depression. The generation of World War II was determined that it would not repeat the mistake of winning the war only to lose the peace. And, so, the GI Bill was an attempt to begin making a new and better postwar America.

It succeeded remarkably well. Although World War II was followed by a Cold War, which put the entire planet under threat of nuclear and thermonuclear Armageddon, government financing to promote the healing, housing, and education of returning veterans contributed to a booming consumer economy characterized by innovation in leisure and entertainment as well as industry. Instead of the recession or depression that often followed a major war, the end of World War II introduced the longest curve of sustained economic growth the nation had ever enjoyed. Postwar Americans saw the largest real estate boom in history. It was driven by the very American imperative that promoted the "pursuit of happiness." Veterans quite rightly felt they had done great things in defeating the forces of fascism and Nazism. President Warren G. Harding promised soldiers coming back from World War I a "return to normalcy." Those returning from World War II wanted more—not just a *return* to the old normal but also to a new "good life" they themselves would create. This futuristic world required new skills, new knowledge, and new training. The government was willing to finance it all.

And so, the army and navy and air corps that had won the greatest war in history now traded their uniforms for work clothes and began filling classrooms, buying new tract homes, and creating a nation of burgeoning aerospace, automobile, communications, plastics, and steel industries as well as new category of service industries. In the process, they fell in love, they married, and they went about the passionate business of creating a baby boom that became the generation that would identify the cohort of their parents as the "Greatest Generation."

The *Enola Gay* Drops an "Atomic Bomb" on Hiroshima (1945)

At 8:15 (local time) on the morning of August 6, 1945, an unprecedented type of munition was dropped from a US Army Air Forces Boeing B-29 Superfortress bomber, which the pilot, Colonel Paul Tibbets, named after his mother, *Enola Gay*. Deployed by parachute, the bomb, called Little Boy, was detonated (by design) at 1,885 feet above ground to achieve the maximum effect of the blast. Its target was Hiroshima, a Japanese city and manufacturing center of some 350,000 people about five hundred miles from Tokyo. It had been carefully selected by a special US target committee because it had not yet been attacked by US Army Air Forces. The city's pristine condition would not only allow the Allies to assess the effects of the bomb, it would also dramatically demonstrate them to the Japanese.

Little Boy was the product of the vast and ultrasecret Manhattan Project, the origin of which may be traced to 1939, when a group of American scientists, including recent refugees from European fascist and Nazi regimes, grew alarmed by what they knew to be research ongoing in Hitler's Germany dedicated to nuclear fission, a process by which the energy of the binding force within the nucleus of a uranium or plutonium atom might be liberated to produce an explosion of unprecedented magnitude. The scientists prevailed on Albert Einstein, himself a recent refugee from Nazi Germany, to write a letter on August 2, 1939, to President Franklin D. Roosevelt, urging him to authorize atomic research in the United States.

The precursor of the project began in February 1940. By the middle of 1942, project researchers had concluded that a fission bomb was feasible but would require construction of many large and complex facilities, including laboratories and industrial plants, and the efforts of a cadre

Colonel Paul Tibbets flew the *Enola Gay*—the B-29 he named after his mother—to Hiroshima on August 6, 1945, and dropped the world's first "atomic bomb." He is seen here, center, with his crew. US ARMY AIR FORCES PHOTOGRAPH, NATIONAL ARCHIVES AND RECORDS ADMINISTRATION

of the nation's leading physicists and chemists, among others. Because most of the early research was conducted at Columbia University, in Manhattan, the War Department assigned responsibility to Army Corps of Engineers' Manhattan Engineer District in June 1942. In September 1942, Brigadier General Leslie R. Groves, the army engineer who had directed design and construction of the brand-new Pentagon outside of Washington, was put in charge of all military and engineering aspects of what was dubbed the Manhattan Project. Groves chose a brilliant and charismatic physicist, J. Robert Oppenheimer, to lead the scientific aspects of the project.

It was a unique, super-accelerated program of scientific, military, and industrial collaboration and coordination on a vast scale. An entirely new and hitherto theoretical field had to be researched, the research rapidly transformed into practical demonstrations, and those demonstrations quickly prototyped into a workable fission weapon. The unknowns were staggering, and success was far from assured. Moreover, because of the necessity for speed, various research programs had to be conducted simultaneously in the full knowledge that some might prove costly dead ends. Even before research was completed, design and construction of critical production plants would have to get under way.

The first problem that had to be solved was how to separate Uranium 235, the fissionable material that would be the heart of the bomb, from its companion isotope, Uranium 238. A massive plant for obtaining sufficient fissionable material was constructed at Oak Ridge, a seventy-square-mile tract near Knoxville, Tennessee. To complicate matters further, there was another candidate element suitable for fission, Plutonium 239. Groves authorized construction of large-scale production reactors to produce the plutonium isotope. The plant was built on a remote one thousand-square-mile tract along the Columbia River north of Pasco, Washington, and dubbed the Hanford Engineer Works.

While the work of creating fissionable materials was under way, a central laboratory capable of translating bomb theory into a working bomb was established under Oppenheimer on a remote mesa at Los Alamos, New Mexico, north of Santa Fe. The task at Los Alamos was to invent methods of reducing the fissionable materials that emerged from the production plants to pure metal that could be fabricated into the precisely machined shapes that would enable and facilitate an explosive chain reaction. The goal was to bring together very rapidly sufficient amounts of fissionable material to achieve a supercritical mass, which would result in an explosion. This exquisitely difficult feat of materials engineering had to be carried out within a device that could be carried in a bomber, dropped over a target, and detonated at precisely the proper moment above the target.

By the summer of 1945, when enough Pu-239 had emerged from Hanford to produce a nuclear explosion, the Los Alamos scientists had created a weapon they believed was ready to field test. The scientists assembled observation and monitoring equipment to ensure that they would have accurate data on the performance—or failure—of the bomb.

At Alamogordo, 120 miles south of Albuquerque, a special tower was constructed, from which the test bomb—the scientists dubbed it "the gadget"—was suspended. Although the site was remote from population centers, the scientists were far from certain as to the "yield" (the force and extent) of the explosion that would be produced. There was even a chance, some believed, that the detonation of the bomb could set off a chain reaction in the atoms of the air itself, perhaps destroying a vast area. Theoretically, it was even possible that the blast would ignite the very atmosphere of the earth.

The test bomb was detonated at 5:30 a.m. on July 16, 1945. Scientists and a handful of VIPs observed from bunkers and trenches ten thousand yards distant. All who witnessed the explosion were awed. A blinding flash was followed by a heat wave and, finally (since sound travels much more slowly than radiated energy), by a roar and shock wave. The blast produced a great fireball, followed by the mushroom-shaped cloud (rising to an altitude of forty thousand feet), which would become a dreaded emblem of the "atomic age." This first bomb was calculated to have produced an explosion equivalent in energy to fifteen to twenty tons of TNT.

In August, two more bombs, one using U-235 and the other using Pu-239, were ready to be used against Japan.

The U-235 device, Little Boy, was delivered to an airfield on the captured Pacific island of Tinian by the cruiser *Indianapolis*. The bomb was loaded aboard the *Enola Gay*. The bomb's explosive yield was calculated at 12.5 kilotons—the equivalent of 12.5 kilotons of conventional TNT. Of course, the explosive force was only one aspect of the lethality of the weapon. The bomb would produce tremendous heat and radioactivity, including lethal radioactive contamination in the form of fallout.

On detonation, Little Boy destroyed all wooden buildings in Hiroshima within a 1.2-mile radius. Reinforced concrete structures were destroyed within 1,625 feet of the hypocenter of the explosion. A total area of five square miles was incinerated, and 62.9 percent of the city's seventy-six thousand buildings were annihilated by blast or fire. A mere 8 percent escaped substantial damage.

The immediate death rate among those located within three-quarters of a mile of the hypocenter was 50 percent. The one-year death rate—through August 10, 1946—from the Hiroshima blast was 118,661 human beings. Another 30,524 persons were considered severely injured, and 48,606 were considered slightly injured. Nearly four thousand citizens of Hiroshima went missing and have never been accounted for. Of the approximately 350,000 persons believed to have been in Hiroshima at the time, only 118,613 were confirmed uninjured through August 10, 1946. In addition to the civilian deaths, it is believed that about twenty thousand military personnel died as a direct result of the bombing. The longer-term effects of radiation exposure included elevated rates of genetic and chromosome damage and birth defects (including especially stunted growth and mental retardation) of some children born to parents who survived the blast.

Stunningly, the bombing of Hiroshima did not elicit an immediate offer of surrender from the Japanese. On August 9, 1945, at 11:02 a.m. local time, a second B-29, *Bock's Car*, dropped a second bomb, this one a Pu-239 device called Fat Man. Approximately 2.6 square miles of Nagasaki were razed. Of the 270,000 people in the city that morning, at least 73,884 were killed and 74,909 injured. Within days of the bombing, on August 14, 1945, Emperor Hirohito broadcast his surrender message to the Japanese people and the world. World War II would be formally ended by the signing of a treaty on board the USS *Missouri*, riding at anchor in Tokyo Bay on September 2.

Jackie Robinson Signs a Contract with the Brooklyn Dodgers (1947)

Born in 1881 in Ohio, Branch Rickey started playing professional baseball while he was still a student at Ohio Wesleyan University and went on to a pair of seasons during 1906–1907 in the American League as a catcher. After he graduated from Ohio Wesleyan, he went on to the University of Michigan Law School, financing his law education by coaching the university baseball team. In 1910, while he was on the road with the team, he encountered a hotel manager in South Bend, Indiana, home of Notre Dame, who steadfastly refused to provide a room for Rickey's one black player, Charley Thomas. Rickey pleaded and cajoled, finally wearing down the manager, who agreed to let Thomas *share* a room—with Rickey.

Years later, Rickey recalled how Charley Thomas rubbed and rubbed his hands, as if he were trying to wash the color out of them. In the hotel room, Rickey pointed to the man's hands and made him a promise: "Charley, the day will come when they won't have to be white."

After graduating from law school in 1911, Rickey dodged the courtroom and returned instead to the diamond. He took a job as field manager of the American League's St. Louis Browns from 1913 to 1915, then joined the National League's St. Louis Cardinals, serving as club president from 1917 to 1919, field manager from 1919 to 1925, and general manager from 1925 to 1942. He left the Cards to become president and general manager of the Brooklyn Dodgers in 1943 and later became part owner of the team.

From the beginning of his Dodgers leadership, Rickey was determined to "cross the color line" by signing up a black ballplayer. He had two reasons for doing this. First was Charley Thomas. Rickey believed that Jim Crow segregation, in baseball or anything else, was just plain wrong—and maybe he could do something about getting it out of baseball.

Jackie Robinson, ready to swing for the Brooklyn Dodgers in 1954. LIBRARY OF CONGRESS

Second, Rickey was keenly aware that the all-black Negro Leagues had a lot of extraordinary players in its ranks. He could not stand to see them go to waste outside of the major leagues—and, more important, outside of the Dodgers.

Rickey sensed that the times were becoming favorable for an attempt to cross the color line. Toward the end of 1943, baseball commissioner Kennesaw Mountain Landis brought together members of the Black Publishers Association; African American social activist, singer, and actor Paul Robeson; and all sixteen major league baseball team owners as well as the presidents of both leagues. Landis turned the meeting over to Robeson.

"Because baseball is a national game," Robeson said, "it is up to baseball to see that discrimination does not become an American pattern."

Moved by what he heard, Rickey began to push Landis—who, however, continued publicly to oppose the integration of baseball.

But then, in 1944, Landis died. He was succeeded as commissioner by Albert B. "Happy" Chandler, former governor of Kentucky. Rickey told him that he planned to bring a black player on board the Dodgers.

At the time, World War II was approaching its final act. Chandler replied, "If they can fight and die on Okinawa [and] Guadalcanal . . . they can play ball in America."

And there was more. The New York state legislature had just passed the Quinn-Ives Act, barring racial discrimination in hiring, and New York City mayor Fiorello LaGuardia's had just formed an End Jim Crow in Baseball Committee. Rickey petitioned his fellow team owners to allow him to integrate the National League. They voted 15 to 1—against.

Rickey was determined to proceed, but he now had an inkling of how ugly the fight would be. He decided to make a bold strategic retreat. In the spring of 1945, he created the US League as a new "Negro League." Social activists accused Rickey of turning against the cause of integration by creating a new segregated league. In fact, the US League never played a single game. It was nothing more than a front that gave Rickey cover for openly scouting black ballplayers. Out a hundred players, he found Jackie Robinson and asked him to a meeting on August 28, 1945.

Born Jack Roosevelt Robinson in Cairo, Georgia, Jackie Robinson was raised in Pasadena, California, and showed himself to be an exceptional athlete at Pasadena Junior College and the University of California at Los Angeles. In addition to baseball, he played college football and basketball, and he ran track. During his third year at UCLA, Robinson withdrew to help support his family. He joined the army during World War II, in 1942, was enrolled in officer candidate school, and commissioned a second lieutenant in 1943. In 1944, he and the great African American boxer Joe Louis faced court-martial for refusing to follow an order to sit in the back of a military bus. The charges were dismissed and, at the end of the war, Robinson was honorably discharged in 1945. He played professional minor-league football in Hawaii and baseball with the Kansas City Monarchs of the segregated Negro National League.

Rickey began his meeting with Robinson by explaining that he wanted to start him on the Dodgers' minor league farm team in Montreal, Canada, where Jim Crow did not exist. This would prove Robinson's chops as a player and would ease his transition into US major league play. Make it in Montreal, and he would come to Brooklyn.

The meeting stretched into three hours, during which Rickey bore down hard.

"Do you think you can do it? Make good in organized baseball?" he asked

"If I got the chance," Robinson replied.

Rickey told him that he would face insults, slurs, and threats from fans, opposing players, and even some of his own teammates. Rickey even playacted, "Suppose I collide with you at second base. When I get up, I yell, 'You dirty, black son of a— . . . What do you do?"

"Mr. Rickey, do you want a ballplayer who's afraid to fight back?" Robinson quietly demanded.

"I want a ballplayer with guts enough not to fight back! You've got to do this job with base hits and stolen bases and fielding ground balls, Jackie. Nothing else!"

Robinson understood, the men shook hands, and Branch Rickey signed him to a $600-a-month contract with a $3,500 signing bonus to play with the Montreal Royals, then moved him up to the Brooklyn Dodgers at the start of the 1947 season.

Robinson was a great baseball player. That was the first thing. With the Dodgers, he was an immediate and spectacular success. He led the National League in stolen bases and earned the title of Rookie of the Year. In 1949, he won the batting championship with a .342 average and was voted league MVP. His lifetime batting average was .311, and he led Brooklyn to a total of six league championships and one World Series victory.

Robinson also exhibited the strength of character Rickey had hoped for. He endured abuse and threats. Fans threw bottles and insults at him. Some opposing pitchers shot for his head and base runners came in spikes first. In the Jim Crow South, hotels refused to accommodate him and restaurants would not feed him.

"Plenty of times," Robinson admitted later, "I wanted to haul off . . . but I had to hold to myself. I knew I was kind of an experiment. The whole thing was bigger than me."

The racial integration of Major League Baseball quickly followed the introduction of Jackie Robinson. He had an extraordinary decade-long MLB career. He was the winner of the first MLB Rookie of the Year Award in 1947, an All-Star from 1949 through 1954, and claimed the National League MVP Award in 1949. He played in six World Series. As Rickey had hoped, the combination of his performance and his character changed America, contributing materially to the Civil Rights movement that developed in the mid-1950s through the 1960s. After he retired from baseball in 1957, he became the first black MLB commentator on television and was recruited as the first black vice president of a major American corporation, Chock full o' Nuts. He went on to help create the Freedom National Bank, an African American–owned financial institution in Harlem, New York. His health declined in middle age. He suffered from diabetes and heart disease, but his wife believed that the emotional stress of his baseball career had taken a toll. After his death in 1972, at the age of fifty-three, he was posthumously awarded the Congressional Gold Medal and Presidential Medal of Freedom.

The Marshall Plan Goes into Effect, Putting the United States at the Center of Postwar European Recovery (1948)

President Woodrow Wilson took the United States into World War I in 1917 by telling the American people that it would be the "war to end all wars." In fact, it created conditions that made European soil fertile for the rise of Stalin, Mussolini, and Hitler. Two decades after World War I ended in 1918, World War II began in 1939. Little wonder that Americans, verging toward victory in 1945 during that second war, began asking how "to win the war without losing the peace" this time.

The second world war was far more destructive than the first. Entire cities were wiped out, industry was all but destroyed, millions were left homeless, and economies were annihilated. Two needs were most pressing at war's end. Food was in short supply and coal, needed for heating, was unavailable. Observing that the German daily diet in 1946–1947 was under 1,800 calories, US state department official William Clayton pointed out that "millions of people are slowly starving." More quickly, they were freezing.

Whereas the victors in World War I sought to punish Germany and its allies, the United States after World War II began sending relief to Europe, even before the war ended. By 1947, this amounted to some $9 billion. The hope was that Britain and France would soon be able to pitch in, but the fundamentals of the European economy and infrastructure were so disrupted that the cycle of European trade was frozen and needed a massive infusion of capital to thaw. Several plans were on the table at war's end, and one high official, Secretary of the Treasury Henry Morgenthau Jr. had proposed in 1944 the "Morgenthau Plan," by which Germany would be compelled to pay for most of the rebuilding of Europe through massive war reparations, which (by design) would also prevent Germany from ever rebuilding as an industrial power. President Roosevelt liked the idea, but after FDR's death, President Truman saw in it nothing but a disastrous repetition of the Treaty of Versailles, which imposed punitive reparations that created in Germany the universal despair, anger, and desperation that contributed to the eruption of World War II. He rejected Morgenthau's plan, and Morgenthau resigned from office.

In January 1947, George Catlett Marshall, who, as US Army chief of staff during the war, had been one of the architects of the Allied military victory, became Truman's secretary of state. Not only did he agree with Truman about not repeating earlier tragic mistakes, he also pointed out that, because Germany had been the most powerful industrial force in Europe before World War II, its devastated condition was actually holding back the economic recovery of all Europe. He believed that if Europe was to recover, the German economy and infrastructure would have to be restored—along with those of the other nations. To do this, Europe would have to be induced to act with a degree of unity it had never known before.

In the short term, however, there was an acute humanitarian crisis. Marshall understood that the Soviet Union, hailed as a heroic ally of the West during the war, was now determined to exploit the prevailing want, misery, and chaos to expand Soviet communism into Eastern and Western Europe. In February 1946, American diplomat George F. Kennan predicted this Soviet policy of aggressive expansion and advised that the United States respond with a policy of "containment," confronting the Soviets wherever and whenever they attempted to interfere in the affairs of another nation. This had to be done without igniting a nuclear World War III, so Kennan advised using economic aid to keep European nations aligned with the democratic West.

Marshall agreed with Kennan's analysis and proposed an American-financed plan of aid as the key means of containing Soviet influence. He even dared hope that the Soviets themselves might cooperate with the plan. That hope was quickly dashed when the Soviet Union rejected all US overtures. Clearly, Soviet leaders believed that the disintegration of European economies and governments created a vacuum that Soviet influence could fill.

Marshall's disillusionment motivated him to work with President Truman to create, propose, and promote an unprecedented US-funded program of European aid. Marshall decided that the plan would be a wholly American initiative, but that once the American offer was made, it was essential that all Europe take responsibility for proposing just how the funds would be used. Marshall proposed that the European nations get together and formulate collaboratively a single plan to apply to all the nations that wanted to receive aid. The funds would be conditioned on such a unified plan.

The final hurdle was gaining acceptance of the plan from the American people. Marshall decided that the plan had to be spring "with explosive force" to preempt any prolonged political debate. He presented it in a speech at Harvard, when he accepted an honorary degree, on June 5, 1947. He announced there that the "US proposal was aimed at hunger, poverty, and chaos and not against any group" or ideology, and he pointedly left out both the logistical details and the amount of the funding. At once vague, the announcement was also bold. Marshall called on Europeans to meet and to create their own plan for European recovery, which the United States would fund.

Truman and Marshall believed that the aid plan would be unpopular among many, maybe even most, Americans. The president decided that Marshall, as one of the architects of World War II victory, was more popular with the American people than he, and so Truman did all he could to associate the plan with his secretary of state. When Truman's young aide Clark Clifford suggested that the European Recovery Plan be dubbed the "Truman Plan," the president snapped back, "Are you crazy? If we sent it up to that Republican Congress with my name on it, they'd tear it apart. We're going to call it the Marshall Plan."

In the end, Marshall succeeded in selling the plan both to Europe and America. Britain's prime minister Winston Churchill called it "the most unsordid political act in history." Without question, the Marshall Plan saved countless lives, made possible the economic recovery of Europe, and did prove to be the single most effective "weapon" in the Cold War between the forces of Western democracy and Soviet communism. It also laid the foundation for a postwar world with the United States at its very center.

President Truman Authorizes the Berlin Airlift (1948)

After the surrender of Germany in May 1945, the nation was divided among the Allies into four main zones of occupation: the British in the northwest, the French in the southwest border area, and the United States in the south and southeastern border area. The Soviets occupied the eastern portion. Deep within the Soviet zone was the German capital city of Berlin, which was divided between a western sector (subdivided into French, US, and British zones) and a Soviet-occupied eastern sector.

In late March 1948, as alliances among the Western democracies strengthened and as these nations expressed their commitment to establishing a permanent capitalist state of West Germany separate from Soviet-occupied eastern Germany, the Soviets began detaining troop trains bound for West Berlin. On June 7, the Western nations officially announced their intention to create West Germany, and little more than two weeks later, the Soviets blockaded West Berlin, arguing that Berlin, located deep within Soviet-occupied East Germany, could not serve as the capital of a foreign country. This violated an agreement of the Allied Control Council (ACC), the four-power administrative body for occupied Germany, which had established a permanent twenty-mile-wide air corridor from the western zones of Germany through the air space of the Soviet zone to Berlin. It also specified rail and highway traffic be permitted through the Soviet zone as necessary to supply the western zones of Berlin. On June 24, Soviet authorities suspended traffic on the Berlin-Helmstedt railway and stopped all barge traffic into and out of Berlin. West Berlin was now cut off from the rest of the world, save for what passed in and out by air.

C-47 aircraft of the newly independent US Air Force is loaded during the
Berlin Airlift of 1948–1949. NATIONAL MUSEUM OF THE US AIR FORCE

At this point, the US departments of state and defense outlined for
President Truman three possible US policies regarding West Berlin. The
United States could withdraw from the city, it could remain in West
Berlin at all costs, or it could stand firm for now, postponing a decision on
withdrawal until it became necessary to make one. The president rejected
the first alternative as the same mistake British prime minister Neville
Chamberlain had made in "appeasing" Hitler in 1938. Instead of averting
war, appeasement had ensured war. But neither was Truman prepared to
stay in Berlin at the cost of a new world war. Instead, he would stand firm
for now, exploiting the propaganda advantage of exposing to the world
the Soviets as hostage takers.

But the people of West Berlin needed food and, come winter, they
would need fuel as well. Truman tasked the newly independent US Air
Force to do its utmost to supply Berlin. On June 25, 1948, General Lucius
Clay, in command at Berlin, telephoned Lieutenant General Curtis
E. LeMay, at the time commanding United States Air Forces-Europe

(USAFE). He asked LeMay—the general whose fliers had dropped the atomic bombs on Japan in 1945—if he could transport coal by air. "Sir, the Air Force can deliver anything," LeMay replied, and, on the very next day, he began gathering the entire air force inventory of transport aircraft from every corner of the world. The military called the result Operation Vittles. The rest of the world referred to as the Berlin Airlift.

The first thirty-two C-47 Skytrains (military versions of the DC-3 passenger plane) took off for Berlin on June 26, carrying a total of eighty tons of cargo, which included milk, flour, and vital medicines. Two days later, the British Royal Air Force (RAF) made its first flight in the operation. It was anticipated that the airlift would have to be sustained no more than three weeks, and General Joseph Smith, in charge of operations, meant to have 65 percent of available aircraft in the air every day, regardless of the weather. The schedule allowed barely enough time for ground crews to fuel, let alone fully service the aircraft, virtually all of which were veterans of hard service during World War II. No matter; Smith ordered each plane to make three round trips to Berlin daily.

Smith created what he called a "block system," grouping aircraft together into a disciplined convoy system, which aided air traffic control. Indeed, Smith set up an Air Traffic Control Center at Frankfurt am Main dedicated exclusively to the airlift. Soon, days became weeks, and there was no sign of either side giving in. On July 23, 1948, the airlift became the "permanent" responsibility of the Military Air Transport Service (MATS), and Major General William H. Tunner replaced Smith as commander. He orchestrated flight and ground operations according to what he described as a "steady rhythm, constant as the jungle drums." It was like an assembly line. Tunner calculated that there were 1,440 minutes in a day and set as his target the landing of an aircraft every minute. On average, he managed to achieve one landing every three minutes.

Tunner created a system of intensive efficiency. He issued orders forbidding any aircrew member from leaving the side of his aircraft at Berlin's Tempelhof and Gatow airports. Each plane that touched down was instantly met on the field by an operations officer and a weather officer, who drove up in separate jeeps to brief the pilot while another jeep rolled up with hot coffee, hot dogs, and doughnuts. Tunner hired civilian industrial time-motion consultants to analyze loading and unloading operations to minimize the number of steps and movements. Tunner's men perfected a system by which twelve men loaded ten tons of bagged coal into a C-54 Skymaster cargo aircraft in six minutes. Unloading crews were able to cut what had been a seventeen-minute process to five minutes. Refueling personnel reduced refueling times from thirty-three minutes to eight. By the height of operations, Tunner turned each aircraft around within no more than thirty minutes—loading, unloading, refueling.

Still, flying continuous missions so close together 24/7 and in every kind of weather (which in Germany was often miserable) was as hazardous as combat flying. Both air and ground crews were pushed to the very margins of endurance. Remarkably, accidents were few, and no Berliner starved or froze. The machine-like pace of operations in the Berlin airlift was not sustained, not for the planned three weeks but for almost a year. On May 12, 1949, it was Soviet endurance that gave way. On this day, Soviet authorities lifted the blockade.

The airlift continued, albeit at a reduced volume, for another five more months to make up the shortfall of food and fuel that had been created by the blockade. The last flight was completed on September 30, 1949, the US Air Force having made 189,963 flights over Soviet-held territory and Royal Air Force another 87,606. Air Force planes transported 1,783,572.7 tons of food, coal, and other cargo; the RAF, 541,936.9. The quintessential Cold War battle that was the Berlin Airlift was won without bullets. In the end, a gallant people survived, and the world was brought back from the brink of nuclear war.

The North Atlantic Treaty Is Signed, Creating NATO (1949)

The Marshall Plan may have saved Western Europe, but it also hardened the division between the Soviets and the other Allies of World War II. Joseph Stalin denounced the Marshall plan as a capitalist plot to compromise the sovereignty of European nations—even as Stain himself worked to overthrow the fragile new republics of eastern Europe and to permanently partition Germany with the objective of creating a buffer zone of puppet states between the Soviet Union and the rest of Europe.

When the Western European states and the United States responded to the Soviet-backed March 1948 Communist coup in Czechoslovakia by proceeding with the unification of the West German zones of occupation and the establishment of a separate West German currency and government, the Soviets left the Allied Control Council, which jointly administered occupied Germany. Three months later, the Soviets blockaded Berlin. President Truman responded with the Berlin Airlift to supply Western Berlin, and he espoused the policy of containing the expansion of Soviet influence. Instead of intimidating the West into withdrawing from Berlin and Germany and far from driving Americans into their prewar isolationism, the blockade galvanized the resolve of the Western nations.

On April 4, 1949, the foreign policy heads of the United States, Great Britain, France, Italy, the Netherlands, Belgium, Luxemburg, Portugal, Denmark, Iceland, Norway, and Canada met in Washington to create the North Atlantic Treaty Organization, NATO, which emerged as the most important Cold War multinational mutual alliance.

NATO was created by the North Atlantic Treaty, the Preamble to which declared the purpose of the signatories:

The Parties to this Treaty reaffirm their faith in the purposes and principles of the Charter of the United Nations and their desire to live in peace with all peoples and all governments.

They are determined to safeguard the freedom, common heritage and civilization of their peoples, founded on the principles of democracy, individual liberty and the rule of law.

They seek to promote stability and well-being in the North Atlantic area.

They are resolved to unite their efforts for collective defence and for the preservation of peace and security.

The heart of the North Atlantic Treaty is Article 5:

The Parties agree that an armed attack against one or more of them in Europe or North America shall be considered an attack against them all, and consequently they agree that, if such an armed attack occurs, each of them, in exercise of the right of individual or collective self-defence recognized by Article 51 of the Charter of the United Nations, will assist the Party or Parties so attacked by taking forthwith, individually, and in concert with the other Parties, such action as it deems necessary, including the use of armed force, to restore and maintain the security of the North Atlantic area.

Thus far, Article 5 has been invoked only once, when, in the aftermath of the September 11, 2001, terrorist attacks on the United States, the NATO nations mobilized to defend their American ally.

Although the impetus for NATO was the increasing intensity of the Cold War, the organization came into being without any set military structure. Only with the outbreak of the Korean War in June 1950 was a formal NATO military force established. Even then, it was not a standing army, but a permanent command, Allied Command Europe, headquartered in Brussels, Belgium. General policy was made by the North Atlantic Council, which originally met in Paris until France withdrew from military participation in NATO in 1967. In that year, the Council moved to Brussels.

When the Cold War ended with the collapse of the Soviet Union in 1991 and the dissolution of the Warsaw Pact that same year, some European leaders called for replacing NATO with an organization less exclusively focused on military alliance. Later in the 1990s, even the United States reduced its NATO presence by substituting for its large forces dedicated to NATO smaller "rapid deployment forces" available to respond to contingencies. Nevertheless, the alliance continues, reflecting America's commitment to play a role in the ongoing defense of Europe.

Senator Joseph McCarthy Claims Communist Infiltration of US Department of State (1950)

Born in 1908, Joseph McCarthy grew up on a Wisconsin farm, became a lawyer, and subsequently the youngest circuit judge in the history of the state. He joined the Marine Corps early in World War II and served in the Pacific Theater as an intelligence briefing officer for USMC aviators. He volunteered to fly a dozen combat missions as a gunner-observer on Marine Corps dive bombers and picked up—or perhaps bestowed on himself—the nickname "Tail-Gunner Joe." The combination of his judicial and war records made him a shoo-in candidate for the US Senate in 1946, but that is where the rocket-like trajectory of his career finally flattened. He proved to be an undistinguished backbencher for his first three years in office.

Then came February 9, 1950, when he was tapped to address the Women's Republican Club in Wheeling, West Virginia. He pulled from his jacket pocket a piece of paper and announced to his audience that he was holding in his hand a list of 205 communists currently employed in the US Department of State. The ladies were electrified, and a speech in an obscure venue by a lackluster senator was accorded unexpected national coverage.

McCarthy himself was stunned—so much so that he proved unable to repeat, let alone nail down, that 205 figure he mentioned in Wheeling. Speaking in Salt Lake City, Utah, days later, he mentioned fifty-seven communists. On the floor of the Senate on February 20, it was eighty-one. Nobody ever actually saw the figure in the Wheeling speech, and it was widely believed that the paper he pulled out of his pocket was blank—an improvised prop.

Never mind. Not long after Wheeling, the Tydings Committee—the Subcommittee on the Investigation of Loyalty of State Department Employees—was formed within the Senate Foreign Relations Committee, and McCarthy found himself leading what would later be condemned as a "witch hunt" in search of covert communists in the federal government. He was obscure no longer.

Over the next four years, McCarthy and his followers, all looking to carve out political futures for themselves, exploited a growing American fear of Soviet communism by making reckless, random, almost invariably groundless accusations wherever they went. Among McCarthy's earliest victims were Owen Lattimore, a State Department China expert and Johns Hopkins University professor, and John S. Service, another State Department employee. Before the Tydings Committee, McCarthy pressed his case that these two men were essentially Soviet agents. He never presented concrete evidence, but the mere accusations were sufficient to instill suspicion about these men and numerous others whose appearances before the committee followed. Often, the accusation was no more than an allegation of being "soft" on communism, a stance, according to McCarthy, that was responsible for the "loss" of China to Mao Zedong and the Chinese Communist Party after World War II.

The junior senator from Wisconsin seemed undaunted and even unfazed by the failure of the Tydings Committee to definitively brand Lattimore and Service as communists. Propelled by his willingness to accuse, he won the chairmanship of the Senate Subcommittee on Governmental Operations, from which he personally launched investigations of the Voice of America and the US Army Signal Corps. The nation was stunned—but fearful—when McCarthy accused George C. Marshall, World War II army chief of staff, former secretary of state, architect of the Marshall Plan (for which he received the Nobel Peace Prize), and, finally, Truman's secretary of defense, of being a traitor. McCarthy blamed him for the "loss" of China in a "conspiracy so immense and an infamy so black as to dwarf any previous venture in the history of man."

McCarthy and his lieutenants, most notably an oily young lawyer named Roy Cohn, launched investigations of a variety of prominent celebrities, including Hollywood stars, writers, and producers. The Hollywood witch hunt and similar campaigns undertaken against other industries were especially destructive because the mere accusation of communist affiliation or sympathies was sufficient to ruin the career of the accused. But as his heedless campaign rolled on, Senator McCarthy became increasingly oblivious to the changing realities around him. Even after his own Republican party won control of the White House and Congress in the 1952 elections, he persisted in attacking the government, claiming now that it was "infested" with communists.

Then, in the spring of 1954, he took aim at his most formidable target, charging that the US Army itself had been infiltrated. Hitherto reluctant to intervene, arguing that McCarthy would surely self-destruct, President Dwight D. Eisenhower, a career military officer who led the Allies in the European campaign in World War II, could not tolerate the blackening of *his* army's reputation. He sought reports and quickly discovered that, at the behest of Roy Cohn, McCarthy had tried to coerce army officials into granting preferential treatment for a former aide, Private G. David Schine. Ike sent this information to Congress and quietly encouraged the creation of a committee to investigate McCarthy's machinations.

The so-called Army–McCarthy hearings were televised between April and June 1954, and the nation was both fascinated and disgusted by what it saw. McCarthy appeared not as a great crusader against godless communism but as a reckless bully who sprayed accusations as from a fire hose. The bottom fell out on day 30 of the hearings, June 9, 1954. Joseph Welch, legal counsel for the army, challenged Roy Cohn to deliver McCarthy's list of 130 subversives in defense plants to the FBI and the Department of Defense "before the sun goes down." Seeking to evade the challenge, McCarthy told Welch that he should check on Fred Fisher, a young attorney in Welch's Boston law firm. Fisher, McCarthy said, had once belonged to the National Lawyers Guild, an organization the US attorney general had called "the legal bulwark of the Communist Party."

Welch told McCarthy that Fisher had indeed revealed to him his membership in the Guild. What of it? Referring to his gratuitous attack on Fisher, an effort to avoid producing evidence of defense plant infiltration, Welch turned on McCarthy. Before the assembled television cameras, he declared, "Until this moment, Senator, I think I never really gauged your cruelty or your recklessness. . . . Senator, may we not drop this? We know he belonged to the Lawyer's Guild . . . Let us not assassinate this lad further, Senator; you've done enough. Have you no sense of decency, sir? At long last, have you left no sense of decency?"

From that moment, Joseph McCarthy was a broken man. Discredited publicly, he was subsequently censured by the Senate. An alcoholic, he began drinking fiercely and was dead three years later—of acute hepatitis, "cause unknown." The press attributed his liver ailment to drink. With his ignominious end came an end to four years of preying on America's fears, four years of attacks on due process of law.

The Supreme Court's Decision in *Brown v. Board of Education* Outlaws Racial Segregation (1954)

Up through the early 1950s, racial segregation in public schools was universal in the South and often the norm in other regions of the United States. The legality of this segregation rested largely on the "separate but equal" doctrine enunciated in *Plessy v. Ferguson*, an 1896 Supreme Court decision upholding racial segregation of public facilities provided that the separate facilities for blacks and whites were equal in quality. Applied to public education, the theory was that maintaining separate schools for blacks and whites was legal provided that, within a given district, the schools for blacks and whites were equal in quality and resources offered. In reality, most black schools were far inferior to their white counterparts. Moreover, in the broader social context, they could never be equal.

Against this background, *Brown v. Board of Education* was litigated. An African American third grader named Linda Brown in Topeka, Kansas, had to walk one mile through a railroad switchyard to get to her all-black elementary school, even though a white school was just a safe seven-block walk away from her home. When the principal of the white school refused to enroll Brown, her father, Oliver Brown, approached the Topeka branch of the National Association for the Advancement of Colored People (NAACP). Other black parents joined Brown in asking the NAACP to request an injunction to forbid the segregation of Topeka's public schools. Before the US District Court for the District of Kansas during June 25–26, 1951, the NAACP argued that segregated schools sent a message to black children that they were inferior to whites; therefore, the schools were inherently unequal, as an expert witness for the NAACP, Dr. Hugh W. Speer, testified. The Topeka Board of Education countered that because segregation in Topeka and elsewhere was pervasive, segregated schools realistically prepared black children for the segregation they would experience as adults.

Although the district court agreed with the NAACP that segregation "has a detrimental effect upon the colored children," the court decided that the precedent of *Plessy v. Ferguson* nevertheless allowed separate but equal school systems for blacks and whites. Absent a Supreme Court ruling overturning *Plessy*, the district court believed itself "compelled" to rule in favor of the Board of Education. This ruling threw the door wide open to a Supreme Court appeal, which Brown and the NAACP brought on October 1, 1951. Their case was combined with others challenging school segregation in South Carolina, Virginia, and Delaware. The case was first argued before the high court on December 9, 1952, by NAACP chief counsel and future Supreme Court justice Thurgood Marshall. When the court failed to reach a decision, Marshall reargued it on December 7–8, 1953. This time, the court delivered a decision, on May 17, 1954, based on whether or not segregated schools deprived black children of equal protection of the law. Chief Justice Earl Warren wrote,

> We must consider public education in the light of its full development and its present place in American life throughout the Nation. Only in this way can it be determined if segregation in public schools deprives these plaintiffs of the equal protection of the laws. . . . Compulsory school attendance laws and the great expenditures for education both demonstrate our recognition of the importance of education to our democratic society. . . . In these days, it is doubtful that any child may reasonably be expected to succeed in life if he is denied the opportunity of an education. Such an opportunity, where the state has undertaken to provide it, is a right which must be made available to all on equal terms.
>
> We come then to the question presented: Does segregation of children in public schools solely on the basis of race, even though the physical facilities and other "tangible" factors may be equal, deprive the children of the minority group of equal educational opportunities? We believe that it does. . . .

We conclude that, in the field of public education, the doctrine of "separate but equal" has no place. Separate educational facilities are inherently unequal.

Believing it important to deliver a unanimous opinion, Warren decided not to include a remedy in the May 17, 1954, ruling. A year later, the Supreme Court issued an "Enforcement Decree," putting lower federal courts in charge of implementing the *Brown* decision "with all deliberate speed." The decision opened the door to ending all racial segregation of public accommodations—not just schools but also businesses that serve the public—and this, in turn, led to racial equality as the general standard in all business, including, most importantly, housing. The era of Jim Crow was coming to an end in America.

Dr. Jonas Salk Successfully Tests a Polio Vaccine (1955)

By the middle of the twentieth century, Americans had won two world wars, had rescued a war-ravaged Europe from starvation and Soviet tyranny, and had created the greatest economy the world had ever known. Yet the 1950s—to borrow the title of a long poem by W. H. Auden—were an "Age of Anxiety." For all they had accomplished, Americans were plagued by two great fears. One was annihilation by the nuclear weapons they themselves had invented to win World War II. The other was polio.

Also known as infantile paralysis because most of its victims were children, polio was sometimes fatal but more often crippling—creating disabilities ranging from impaired movement to lifelong paralysis of the legs to a more complete paralysis, extending to the involuntary muscles by which human beings draw the breath of life itself. Children stricken to this degree were condemned to a lifetime in "iron lungs," the massive respirators of the era.

Thus as 1955 verged into summer, American parents looked forward not to having their children home from school, taking a vacation, and enjoying the beach or the municipal swimming pool but to worry over a disease at its most contagious during the warm months. Indeed, in many places, families avoided crowds, beaches were sometimes closed for the season, and public swimming pools shuttered.

What America's parents did not know is that 1955 would prove to be a year of hope and breakthrough.

Jonas Salk was born in New York City in 1914, the son of a first-generation American father of eastern European Jewish parentage and a mother who immigrated from Russia when she was twelve. The family was not wealthy, but young Jonas was put in a public high school for the gifted and went on to enroll at the City College of New York (CCNY)—a low-priced public institution both highly competitive and highly regarded. He earned a bachelor's degree in chemistry and enrolled in the medical school of New York University, which, unlike Columbia and Cornell, did not have a restrictive quota on the enrollment of Jews.

At NYU, Salk became interested in medical research, especially in the area of vaccines. He took an elective course in immunology under Dr. Thomas Francis at the University of Michigan, where the first killed-virus vaccine against influenza had been developed. Salk then returned to New York, graduated, and accepted a residency at Mount Sinai Hospital, this time working in Dr. Francis's laboratory there. He continued to study viral vaccines using killed viruses. The University of Michigan breakthrough had put the lie to the prevailing theory that, while vaccines prepared from attenuated or killed bacteria were often effective in immunizing against bacterial infections, immunization against viruses required live-virus vaccines—despite the dangers of inoculating patients with viable viruses.

After serving his residency, Salk took his background in killed-virus vaccines to his new position as head of a viral research laboratory at the University of Pittsburgh. His top priority was developing a killed-virus vaccine against polio, and his research in this field was supported by the March of Dimes Foundation, which had been founded in 1938 by President Franklin D. Roosevelt as the National Foundation for Infantile Paralysis. (FDR, of course, had had been stricken in adulthood by what was universally assumed to be polio, which left him a paraplegic. Many modern physicians believe it more likely that he was actually a victim of Guillen-Barré syndrome.)

Salk began testing a killed-virus vaccine for polio in 1954, made rapid progress, and, in 1955, the Food and Drug Administration found it safe and effective. Production of the vaccine began immediately, and the first doses were made available by the summer. Within a remarkably short time, the Salk vaccine was in universal use throughout the United States, a required vaccination for virtually all children of school age. In 1962, Dr. Albert Sabin developed a live-virus alternative, which could be administered orally rather than by injection. Despite resistance against using live virus, the Sabin vaccine became widely used. Nevertheless, Sabin's fame never eclipsed that of Salk, who was given the credit for having rid America and the world of one of its cruelest, most devastating, and most terrifying diseases.

The Birth Control Pill Is Approved (1960)

Based on the historical record, people have been trying to have sex without producing babies at least since 3000 BC, when accounts show that condoms were being made from fish bladders, animal intestines, and linen sheaths. By the sixteenth century in Europe, men were using linen condoms "impregnated" (so to speak) with chemicals to kill sperm. Vulcanized rubber condoms and diaphragms appeared in 1838—but, thirty-five years later, the US Congress passed the Comstock Act (1873) prohibiting the use of the US mails to distribute these and other birth control devices as well as information and advertisements about birth control. Margaret Sanger (neé Higgins), born in Corning, New York, in 1879, one of eleven children whose mother died young, became an avid socialist and an advocate of birth control—in defiance of the Comstock Act and mainstream social morality. In 1916, she even opened the first birth control clinic in America. Sanger endured persecution and prosecution for her advocacy, and in a 1938 case against her, a judge lifted the federal ban on birth control, thereby ending the era of Comstock. In 1948, the sixty-nine-year-old Sanger became a cofounder of the International Committee on Planned Parenthood, which was renamed the International Planned Parenthood Foundation in 1952. Sanger was the organization's first president, and in the early 1950s lobbied Katharine McCormick, a biologist, feminist, and heir to much of the McCormick International Harvester fortune, to fund the work of Gregory Goodwin Pincus.

A Harvard-based biologist, Pincus studied hormonal biology, concentrating his research on how steroidal hormones affected the reproductive systems of mammals. He investigated the potential of hormone therapy both to treat infertility and, at Sanger's behest, to produce a human oral contraceptive using synthetic progesterone. Sanger took McCormick to Pincus's laboratory, the Worcester Foundation for Experimental Biology, where he and the Chinese American reproductive biologist Min Chueh

Chang were working on the contraceptive. Impressed, McCormick started with a $10,000 donation but soon began contributing between $150,000 and $180,000 annually, partly through Planned Parenthood. Ultimately, Katherine McCormick contributed $2 million to the research—about $18 million in today's dollars.

Pincus and McCormick enlisted the clinical expertise of Harvard professor of gynecology, Dr. John Rock, renowned as an expert in the treatment of infertility. Rock agreed to supervise the clinical research with women. Rock was already using oral dosages of estrogen and progesterone to treat infertility by initially suppressing ovulation so that he could regulate hormone levels to increase the chances of successful conception. Pincus determined that higher doses of progesterone would consistently suppress ovulation—and thereby prevent conception and pregnancy. He and Chang worked with pharmaceutical companies to obtain compounds with progestogenic activity that would enable them to synthesize progesterone. They focused on norethisterone from the Synthex company and on Searle's noretynodrel and norethandrolone. Dr. Rock began his studies at the end of 1954 and narrowed the field to Searle's noretynodrel for the first formal contraceptive trials in women.

Rock's trials allowed Pincus and Chang to tweak their formula, removing, adding, and then balancing mestranol with the noretynodrel to prevent mid-cycle "breakthrough" bleeding in the women who were being treated. After the completion of the trials in 1956, the combination of noretynodrel and mestranol was given the proprietary name Enovid.

Enovid's first contraceptive trial was conducted in Puerto Rico (which had no laws against contraception and had a well-developed network of birth control clinics) in April 1956 and then in Los Angeles, beginning in June of the same year. The Food and Drug Administration approved Enovid in June 1957—not for contraception but for the treatment of menstrual disorders. The FDA did not clear it for contraception until 1960, but by 1965, one out of every four married women in America under forty-five used what was universally referred to as "The Pill." By 1967, some thirteen million women were using it worldwide. By 1984, the number reached fifty to eighty million, and today more than one hundred million women use the pill.

It hit drugstore shelves at the cusp of what would soon be called the Sexual Revolution, a widespread assault on American sexual puritanism but also a platform for the phase of American feminism popularly called Women's Liberation and the Women's Movement. "The Pill," which removed a principal consequence of extramarital sex, was the catalyst for profound cultural change in the United States and much of the world.

US Spy Planes Find Nuclear Missiles in Cuba (1962)

John F. Kennedy ran against Dwight Eisenhower's vice president, Richard M. Nixon, in 1960. JFK promised a new direction for the United States, a "New Frontier," he called it, and yet he inherited from the Eisenhower administration a plan to use anti-Castro Cuban exiles in an invasion of Cuba intended to foment a popular revolution to overthrow the Soviet-aligned government there. The result was a humiliating defeat at the Bay of Pigs (April 17–20, 1961), in which Fidel Castro's military easily nipped the revolution in the bud—largely for lack of popular support. Shortly after this, on August 31, 1961, in a Berlin divided between the democratic West and the Communist-aligned Eastern Bloc, construction of a wall between the western and eastern zones of the city began. Clearly, the Soviet Communist world and the American democratic world were coming into collision.

The precarious situation of Berlin, together with the catastrophe of the Bay of Pigs, weighed heavily on the president's mind on October 16, 1962, when he was shown reconnaissance photographs taken by high-flying U-2 "spy" planes, revealing construction of a Soviet SS-4 medium-range ballistic missile (MRBM) launch site at San Cristóbal in western Cuba. The SS-4 could deliver a nuclear warhead to US East Coast cities (including New York and Washington) and even urban centers in the Midwest.

The situation was almost unthinkable. How to deal with Soviet nuclear weapons on the doorstep of the United States—without, in the process, yielding on the one hand to nuclear blackmail by retreating from Berlin or, on the other hand, fighting a thermonuclear war that would cost millions of lives—or worse?

President Kennedy reacted to the crisis by secretly assembling under his brother Attorney General Robert F. Kennedy a fourteen-member "Executive Committee" (EXCOMM) of the National Security Council.

A US Navy Lockheed P-3A-20-LO Orion surveillance aircraft flies over the Soviet cargo ship *Metallurg Anosov* and destroyer USS *Barry* (DD-933) during the naval "quarantine" of the Cuban Missile Crisis. US NAVY NATIONAL MUSEUM OF NAVAL AVIATION

He tasked its members with formulating options for a response that would remove the threat without touching off Armageddon. EXCOMM offered five alternatives:

1. Make no response.
2. Rally international diplomatic pressure to compel the Soviets to remove the missiles.
3. Bomb the missile installations and destroy them.
4. Invade Cuba.
5. Set up a naval blockade of Cuba to interdict, board, and inspect ships suspected of carrying missiles or personnel and turn them back. Since a blockade was technically an act of war, it could be more innocuously described as a "quarantine."

The US military high command—the Joint Chiefs of Staff—unanimously recommended combining options 3 and 4, a massive air raid immediately followed by an amphibious invasion. The military advisers believed—and were willing to bet—that the Soviet Union would not go to nuclear war to save Cuba.

Rejecting the first option—doing nothing—President Kennedy also objected to the military's recommendation for two reasons. First, even if the air raid destroyed every single missile before any could be launched—a very doubtful outcome—and if the follow-on invasion was also successful, the Soviets could retaliate in Europe, probably against Berlin. In the worst case, they could launch an ICBM (Intercontinental Ballistic Missile) or long-range bomber attack directly against the United States. It would be a nuclear/thermonuclear retaliation. And even if the Soviets acted only against Berlin, the United States would have little choice but to respond in Europe. This also would likely lead to a nuclear/thermonuclear exchange.

Worse—yes, there was worse—if the US Air Force failed to destroy all the missiles (many were hidden), at least some would be launched and hit US targets with nuclear warheads. This would require an all-out US nuclear response against Soviet targets. Once again, a civilization-killing World War III would result.

Kennedy also rejected launching an air attack without a follow-up invasion, because he believed the raid would goad the Soviets into overrunning Berlin. Moreover, if the Soviets moved against Berlin after the United States started bombing Cuba, Kennedy believed that US allies, including those in NATO, would accuse America of having foolishly thrown away Berlin because they were unwilling to peacefully resolve the crisis in Cuba.

By process of elimination, only option 5, the naval quarantine, remained. Of all the options short of inaction, it was least likely to provoke World War III.

By the time the decision was reached, new U-2 reconnaissance revealed more missiles deployed in four separate sites. Kennedy decided that he needed to proceed with the quarantine, but he also ordered preparations for the air raid. The entire 1st Armored Division and five infantry divisions were sent to Georgia for quick deployment, and the Strategic Air Command (SAC) positioned its nuclear-armed B-47 Stratojet bombers at civilian airports within striking range of Cuba. Much larger nuclear-armed B-52 Stratofortresses were also sent aloft, poised to attack Cuba as well as the Soviet Union.

At seven o'clock on the evening of October 22, the president delivered a somber televised address to the nation in which he announced the discovery of the missiles as well as the government's intention to take all steps necessary for defense. His speech left no doubt that the world was on the brink of all-out thermonuclear war.

The fate of humankind itself now depended on how Soviet vessels coming to Cuba with supplies and, presumably, more missiles or other war-related materiel, reacted to the US naval quarantine. In the meantime, EXCOMM member George Ball sent a cable to the US ambassadors to Turkey and NATO informing them that President Kennedy was considering offering to withdraw obsolescent US nuclear-armed Jupiter missiles from Turkey in exchange for the withdrawal of Soviet missiles from Cuba. He sent the message in the clear (unencrypted) in the hope and expectation that the Soviets would intercept it. By making the Jupiter missiles part of an exchange deal, Kennedy offered Soviet premier Nikita Khrushchev a means of saving face at home. The withdrawal of missiles from Cuba would look like a reasonable bargain, not a defeat.

On October 24, the first Soviet cargo ships approached the quarantine line—and turned back. Secretary of State Dean Rusk sighed gratefully, "We're eyeball to eyeball, and I think the other fellow just blinked."

Yet, day by day, the missiles that had already been delivered were still being erected. President Kennedy pondered ordering an invasion. The military was poised, but EXCOMM prevailed on him to await Khrushchev's response to the back-channel offer of exchanging withdrawal of the Jupiters from the Turkish-Soviet border area for the missiles in Cuba.

At nine o'clock on the morning of October 28, Khrushchev made a Radio Moscow broadcast aimed at JFK and the world. "The Soviet government," the premier said, "has issued a new order on the dismantling of the weapons which you describe as 'offensive' and their crating and return to the Soviet Union." President Kennedy announced that he considered the premier's decision to be "an important and constructive contribution to peace" and added that the United States would make a statement to the United Nations declaring that it would "respect the inviolability of Cuban borders, its sovereignty" and never attempt to invade.

After thirteen days, World War III had been flirted with and avoided. Kennedy had engineered a major American victory in the Cold War, but it left the entire world shaken. Total annihilation was always close at hand.

Betty Friedan Publishes *The Feminine Mystique* (1963)

It was billed as "the book that defined the problem that has no name," and it became an immediate blockbuster best seller in 1963. The publication of *The Feminine Mystique* meshed with, even as it encouraged, the return of women to a job market expanding with opportunities in the burgeoning service sector, which was just beginning to displace manufacturing in the American economy by the 1960s. The decade ushered in a surge of consumerism, which sent women into the workplace to earn additional income for their families. A consumer-driven economy could not be sustained on the traditional single-breadwinner income. At the same time, greater numbers of women were getting college degrees and were no longer content with remaining exclusively home makers. Besides, the breakthrough availability of the birth control pill meant that the workplace really could take precedence over the nursery.

Born Betty Naomi Goldstein, Friedan was one of a rising generation of college-educated women. She graduated in 1942 from Smith College with a BA in psychology and went on to do graduate work at the University of California, Berkeley. She moved to New York City and worked as a journalist until 1947, when her marriage to Carl Friedan (divorced 1969) made her mostly a conventional homemaker for the next decade—although she always kept her hand in the world of journalism, frequently contributing articles to magazines.

Friedan reflected on her own life, outwardly successful, yet inwardly never fully satisfying. She decided to find out if her experience represented more the rule than the exception. In 1957, Friedan composed and circulated a questionnaire to her Smith classmates. It was aimed at determining what they had done since leaving college and how they felt about it. For she had begun to hear random stories of discontent, and she started

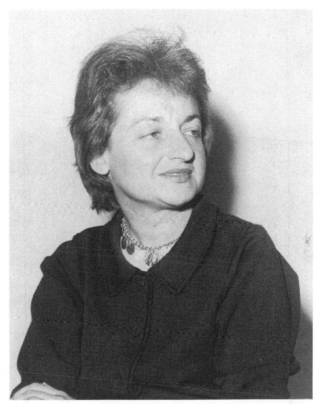

Betty Friedan's bestselling *The Feminine Mystique* launched the "Women's Liberation" movement in the 1960s. *PHOTOGRAPH BY FRED PALUMBO*, WORLD TELEGRAM, *COLLECTION OF THE LIBRARY OF CONGRESS*

referring to this as the "problem that has no name." The Smith responses confirmed her anecdotal evidence. Most of the women who responded to her questionnaire, affluent, outwardly successful, having made "good marriages" and borne families, were, in fact, profoundly dissatisfied with their lives.

Friedan dug deeper, determined to get to the root of this discontent. The result was *The Feminine Mystique*, an exploration of the sense of worthlessness many women—by most measures socially "well adjusted"—felt because they had subordinated or entirely submerged themselves in intellectual, economic, and emotional reliance on a husband. Friedan's book explored how American society enforces and reinforces, both overtly and more subtly, the subordination and limitation of women. All of this was fascinating and provocative, but the bombshell was that the generalized social oppression was inculcated in women as well as in men from a very early age and figures as the "normal" social state that any "normal" woman should be content to live. Regardless of education and social status, marriage and family were meant to be wholly fulfilling and satisfying—at least for "normal, healthy" women. This latter belief, a mythology of women's "normal" role and identity, was what she identified as the "feminine mystique," thereby giving a name to the hitherto unnamed problem.

Friedan's book struck a resounding and resonant chord among women and gave her both the impetus and the credibility to cofound the National Organization for Women (NOW), a civil-rights organization dedicated to achieving equality of opportunity for women. As the group's first president, Friedan led it in campaigns to abolish gender-classified employment ads, to increase the role of women in government, to encourage or mandate childcare centers for working mothers, and to make birth control and abortion more generally available. In 1970, Friedan resigned the NOW presidency but remained active in the women's movement, even organizing a dramatic nationwide Women's Strike for Equality on August 26, 1970, the fiftieth anniversary of women's suffrage. She also took leadership of the effort to obtain ratification of the Equal Rights Amendment (ERA), an endeavor under way since Alice Paul introduced the ERA in 1923. Its sum and substance are contained in Section 1: "Equality of rights under the law shall not be denied or abridged by the United States or by any state on account of sex." The ERA passed the Senate and the House on March 22, 1972, and was sent to the states for ratification, but failed to gain approval by the thirty-eight-state, three-fourths majority required. An original seven-year ratification deadline was extended but also expired three votes short of ratification. Efforts to revive the amendment continue.

In 1971, Friedan became a founder of the National Women's Political Caucus and two years later was made a director of the short-lived First Women's Bank and Trust Company. Betty Friedan died in 2006 at the age of eighty-five, but *The Feminine Mystique* continues to be widely read and enormously influential.

John F. Kennedy Is Assassinated in Dallas (1963)

Dwight David Eisenhower, the five-star general who had led the Allies to victory in the European theater of World War II, was elected by a wide margin as the thirty-fourth president of the United States in 1952 and served two terms. Tremendously popular, he enjoyed bipartisan support and was a symbol of American postwar confidence—some would say complacency. It was widely expected that his vice president, Richard M. Nixon, would sail to victory in 1960. But the Democrats fielded forty-three-year-old US Senator John Fitzgerald Kennedy, a candidate who embodied everything people liked about the rising generation of post-postwar America. Nixon represented the Eisenhower-era status quo, which many voters thought was just fine. Kennedy offered what he called the "New Frontier," and he asked Americans to break out of the status quo, to aspire to a new idealism. Besides, where Nixon had a reputation for deceit (he had already earned the epithet "Tricky Dick") and political cynicism, Kennedy embodied hope and passion and a new sophistication. By a very narrow popular vote margin—34,220,984 to 34,108,157—Kennedy defeated Nixon.

He had an uneasy time with a Congress that often opposed him—especially since Southern Democrats objected to a liberal northeasterner who was at least mildly receptive to the Civil Rights movement then in its early years—but he did manage to usher into law a number of pioneering programs and bold actions, including the establishment of the Peace Corps, the acceleration of the US space program (setting the goal of putting a "man on the moon" before the end of the decade), and the creation of the Alliance for Progress with Latin American countries. His record on support for Civil Rights, including passage of a comprehensive Civil Rights Act, was somewhat more timid and tentative, and his role in the bungled 1961 Bay of Pigs invasion of Castro's Cuba was downright humiliating. Nevertheless, his handling of the Cuban missile crisis in October 1962, which brought the United States and the Soviet Union to the very brink of thermonuclear war, was brilliant, heroic, and nuanced.

Kennedy escalated American involvement in the Vietnam conflict, which had first involved the United States during the administrations of Truman and Eisenhower. He committed his administration to supporting South Vietnam's baroquely corrupt President Ngo Dinh Diem, only to become complicit in CIA operations to overthrow and even assassinate him. Yet, in the end, Kennedy seemed to be inclining toward withdrawal from Vietnam, which he had come to regard as more of a civil war than an aspect of the Cold War between Communist China and the Soviet Union on the one hand and the Western democracies on the other.

Most of all, however, there was a mystique about John F. Kennedy, whose good looks, wit, vigor, and youthful style made people proud to call him their president. Around him a kind of cult of personality grew, and while he was admired even in some Republican-aligned circles for his handling of the economy (which was favorable to business), he continued to fall short of winning congressional support for Civil Rights, anti-poverty legislation, increased spending on education, and a program of medical care for the elderly.

There was a certain aura of ambivalence looming over the White House. All of that changed suddenly at 12:30 p.m., November 22, 1963, in Dallas, Texas.

The president decided to visit Dallas in the hope of healing strained relations between the liberal and conservative wings of his party. Advance word was that JFK was not particularly welcome in Texas, but Dallas crowds gave him a warm reception. As his motorcade made its way past downtown's Dealey Plaza, three shots rang out from the sixth floor of the Texas School Book Depository. President Kennedy was fatally wounded in the neck and head, and Texas governor John Connolly, riding in the limousine's jump seat in front of the president, was seriously wounded in the chest.

Later in the day, the suspected assassin, Lee Harvey Oswald, who had lived for some time in the Soviet Union and had distributed pro-Castro leaflets, was arrested by the Dallas Police after he had shot and killed a Dallas officer. Incredibly, much of the action that accompanied and followed the assassination was broadcast both in live and filmed television news coverage. The nation was riveted in horror and disbelief. Even more incredibly, on Sunday, November 25, two days after the assassination, Oswald himself was gunned down in the basement garage of Dallas Police Headquarters as he was being transferred to prison. The murder, which was broadcast live on national television, was committed by a local nightclub owner and fringe organized crime figure, Jack Ruby.

Almost immediately, there were rumors of conspiracy, coup d'etat, Soviet or Cuban involvement, and even the complicity of the Mafia. On the day of the assassination, there was fear that the crime was an overture to a sneak attack by the Soviet Union. Lyndon Johnson, Kennedy's vice president, was sworn in aboard Air Force One before leaving Dallas for Washington—with Kennedy's widow and his casketed body on board. Soon after returning to Washington, Johnson appointed a presidential commission, headed by Chief Justice Earl Warren, to investigate the assassination. The new president was determined to scotch the wildest of the conspiracy theories.

After a ten-month investigation, the Warren Commission found that Lee Harvey Oswald was the lone assassin—despite some eyewitness reports and forensic evidence that led many Americans to believe the Warren Commission was either wrong or deliberately covering up a conspiracy. Indeed, the manufacture of Kennedy assassination conspiracy theories became a popular culture industry that has yet to cease production. In 1976, Congress itself formed a special committee in the House of Representatives and produced startling new revelations about the CIA and FBI. Breaking with the Warren Commission findings, the committee concluded that a conspiracy was likely.

While disputes over the assassination continued, the effect of Kennedy's sudden "martyrdom"—as the tragic event was often called—became the inspiration for Lyndon Johnson's "Great Society" package of sweeping social reforms. Johnson portrayed himself as carrying out the slain president's wishes and achieved passage of the Civil Rights Act of 1964 and the Voting Rights Act of 1965 in addition to the most ambitious welfare programs since FDR's New Deal. Among these were Medicare and Medicaid and a general "War on Poverty." For millions of Americans, the Great Society was primarily Kennedy's legacy, and he became the mythic embodiment of the ideal American chief executive.

Lyndon B. Johnson Sets His Goals for a "Great Society" (1964)

Lyndon B. Johnson (LBJ) had come of age politically during Franklin D. Roosevelt's Depression-era New Deal, and, as vice president in the Kennedy administration, he regretted JFK's inability to push through Congress welfare legislation approaching the scale of FDR's ambitious program. The Kennedy assassination thrust Johnson into the White House and gave him leverage to craft a social program and promote it as the unfinished legacy of the martyred thirty-fifth president.

When he ran for election in his own right in 1964, Johnson defined his social program in direct opposition to the small-government conservatism of his Republican opponent, Arizona senator Barry M. Goldwater. During the campaign, Johnson unabashedly called on his fellow Americans to build with him a "Great Society," one that "rests on abundance and liberty for all." Like "New Deal," the phrase "Great Society" stuck, becoming the general label for a series of laws passed in Johnson's elective term. It was a decision to further develop the American welfare state.

In 1964, the nation's electorate resoundingly rejected what was then the far-right conservatism of Goldwater and the GOP. LBJ won 486 electoral votes and 43,127,041 popular ballots to Goldwater's 52 and 27,175,754— 61.1 percent versus 38.5 percent. With him came a Democratic sweep of Congress, and, together, president and Congress embarked on a period of social legislation that rivaled the Roosevelt years.

Civil rights were the cornerstone of Johnson's Great Society. In 1964, Congress passed a Civil Rights Act, which desegregated such public accommodations as restaurants, hotels, and theaters, and banned job discrimination on the basis of race. It was followed in 1965 by the Voting Rights Act, aimed at ensuring that African Americans would not be denied their constitutional right to vote in elections at all levels—especially in the Jim Crow South. Three years later, the Civil Rights Act of 1968 barred discrimination on housing based on "race, color, religion, or national origin."

Concepts of racial justice were at the heart of the Great Society, but passage of a 1965 law creating the Medicare program, which partially subsidized the medical expenses of all Americans over the age of sixty-five regardless of need, transcended issues of race. In 1966, subsidized medical coverage was expanded to include welfare recipients in a program called Medicaid.

Great Society legislation was also directed at educational reform. The 1965 Elementary and Secondary Education Act provided federal funds to poor school districts across the country, and the Higher Education Act of 1965 furnished tuition assistance to college and university students, ensuring that millions who before could not afford to attend might now earn a college degree—increasingly the ticket into the American middle class.

Great Society legislation created the Department of Housing and Urban Development, the Department of Transportation, the National Endowments for the Humanities and the Arts, and the Corporation for Public Broadcasting. Environmental legislation in 1964 included a law creating the National Wilderness Preservation System and the Land and passage of the Water Conservation Act of 1964. The National Trails System and the National Wild and Scenic Rivers System were created in 1968.

In 1964, Johnson declared a "War on Poverty," and Congress passed that year the Economic Opportunity Act, which created the Office of Economic Opportunity to oversee a multitude of community programs, including the Job Corps, the Volunteers in Service to America (VISTA), the Model Cities Program, Upward Bound, the Food Stamps program, and Project Head Start.

But it was another war, the ever-expanding conflict in Vietnam, that ultimately defeated the War on Poverty and curtailed other Great Society initiatives. Although bold legislation was passed, the economic demands of Vietnam meant that most Great Society programs were inadequately funded. The landmark Civil Rights legislation survived, as did the very popular Medicare and Medicaid, but others faltered and many programs were scrapped after Richard M. Nixon captured the White House in 1968.

Johnson surely had a vision for America and, arguably, an even more compelling vision for the personal legacy he wished to create. In the end, however, his increasingly monomaniacal and dissembling commitment to the Vietnam War undid much of the Great Society and marked him less as a great humanitarian than as a war monger, who could not be trusted to tell the truth. Both the Vietnam War and the War on Poverty lost public support, and both suffered due to the resulting reduction in funding. Today, while Social Security and some other New Deal–era welfare programs survive, only Medicare and Medicaid remain as functioning monuments of an abortive but profound experiment in creating an American welfare state.

Congress Passes the Civil Rights Act of 1964 (1964)

A centerpiece of the "Great Society" package of legislation and initiatives promoted by the administration of Lyndon Johnson came into being when the president signed the Civil Rights Act on July 2, 1964. It banned racial discrimination in all public accommodations—hotels, theaters, and restaurants—outlawed racial discrimination by employers and unions, and withdrew or withheld federal funds from state programs that discriminated because of race, color, religion, or national origin.

Declining to abolish slavery when the nation was founded in the name of liberty, equality, and justice was not an inadvertent omission. It was a choice—a choice that spawned a civil war, followed by a bitter and deeply flawed effort at "Reconstruction," followed by many decades of racial injustice and unrest, which have been addressed only occasionally by major legislation. The return of GIs, black and white, from World War II brought the "unrest" to a boiling point, especially in the big cities.

Although he was a leader keenly aware of the differences between right and wrong, President Harry S. Truman was also a politician politically reluctant to propose federal civil rights legislation. Nevertheless, he ordered the racial desegregation of the military in 1948, which was a limited yet dramatic step toward integration on a larger social scale. Democrat Truman's successor, Republican Dwight D. Eisenhower, was even less politically inclined to introduce sweeping civil rights legislation, but during his administration the Supreme Court ordered the nation's schools desegregated in its 1954 *Brown v. the Board of Education* decision.

Encouraged, African American activists nationwide, but especially in the South, began testing racial barriers. The Montgomery bus boycott (1955–1956) led to a Supreme Court decision that barred segregation in

President Lyndon B. Johnson signs the 1964 Civil Rights Act as Martin Luther King Jr. and others look on. PHOTOGRAPH BY CECIL STOUGHTON, WHITE HOUSE PRESS OFFICE

public transportation systems and brought the Reverend Martin Luther King Jr. to the forefront of the Civil Rights movement. In 1961, more than 70,000 participated in sit-ins in 112 southern cities, pressing for the desegregation of restaurants. "Freedom Rides" tested the federally ordered desegregation of interstate transportation, primarily on long-distance buses, throughout the South. In August 1963, more than two hundred thousand people marched on Washington to demand racial equality and on August 28 heard Dr. King deliver his historic "I Have a Dream" speech from the steps of the Lincoln Memorial.

The passage of the Civil Rights Act the following year was the culmination of the executive and judicial activity as well as the popular movement. The act did not immediately produce social equality and equal protection of the laws for African Americans or anyone else. Repression at the state and local levels continued, the FBI put King under covert surveillance, and internal disputes sometimes threatened to tear apart the

Civil Rights movement from the inside. Peaceful social protest declined by the late 1960s, and urban rioting increased.

Yet the substance of a quotation King borrowed from the nineteenth-century American abolitionist clergyman Theodore Parker seemed to be proving true: "The arc of the moral universe is long, but it bends toward justice." The social changes that produced the Civil Rights Act of 1964 left a lasting imprint on American government, culture, and society. Racism endured—and endures—but the most egregious forms of discrimination and the social acceptance of bigotry ended. African Americans ran for and won political office, including, in 2008 and again in 2012, the presidency. Colleges and universities, even in the South, recruited black students instead of banning them. Television and other media featured more African American stories and actors. Employers nationwide instituted affirmative action programs.

De jure (law-based) segregation essentially ended, but de facto (actual) segregation remained pervasive both in the North and South, especially in housing and in public school systems, whose enrollments were based on local housing patterns. Income inequality and disparities of wealth remained, and African American unemployment persistently exceeded that of other racial groups. The rate of black incarceration remained persistently higher than that of other groups, as did the rate of crime and violence. The moral arc had surely been bent by passage of the Civil Rights Act of 1964. Yet it also remained long.

Congress Passes the Tonkin Gulf Resolution (1964)

Lyndon Johnson inherited a war in Vietnam that was growing in scope and intensity. He sent out vague peace feelers to Hanoi, which were rebuffed, whereupon his secretary of defense, Robert McNamara, urged air strikes against North Vietnam. Military advisers wanted more, arguing that only a large infusion of American ground troops would put iron into the spine of the Army of the Republic of South Vietnam (ARVN), the South Vietnamese army. LBJ was inclined to agree but, facing a general election against Republican senator Barry Goldwater of Arizona, a conservative hawk who advocated a very aggressive Vietnam policy, including bombing the Northern capital, Hanoi, Johnson wanted to portray himself as the peace candidate in contrast to Goldwater. Accordingly, he put the bombing campaign on the shelf, along with troop increases. When, on November 1, two days before the general election, Viet Cong briefly overran Bien Hoa Air Base, killing four US Air Force airmen, wounding seventy-six others, and wrecking aircraft and buildings, Johnson deferred any reprisal decision.

The summer before the election had brought LBJ extraordinary war powers in Vietnam. These he now held in his pocket, pending the election.

On August 2, 1964, the US Navy destroyer *Maddox*, on a reconnaissance mission in the Gulf of Tonkin, off the coast of North Vietnam, reported itself under attack, "in international waters," by North Vietnamese patrol boats. *Maddox* withdrew to South Vietnamese territorial waters and was joined by another destroyer, USS *Turner Joy*. The reported "battle" produced no US casualties and negligible damage to *Maddox*: a single ding made by the impact of a single machine-gun bullet. Two days later, on August 4, US Navy patrol craft intercepted what radio operators interpreted as communications signaling another

North Vietnamese naval attack. The intelligence was relayed to *Maddox* and *Turner Joy*, which went on high alert. When a radar operator identified blips that appeared hostile, the two destroyers unleashed a two-hour barrage in the direction and at the range of the radar contacts. Although no one on either ship sighted an enemy, the radar contacts were relayed to the White House. Johnson, McNamara, and their aides put the August 4 report together with the gunfire exchange of August 2, and on the evening of August 4, President Johnson appeared on all three national television networks to describe the attacks and retaliatory measures he had authorized. He described the August 4 incident as an attack "by a number of hostile vessels . . . with torpedoes," not just machine guns. After the president addressed the nation, Secretary McNamara testified to Congress that the North Vietnamese attacks had been entirely unprovoked, even though he knew (but did not reveal to Congress) that the *Maddox* was employed on a "signals intelligence" mission inside "hostile" waters—not, as claimed, *international* waters. McNamara thus lied to Congress about the August 2 attack, which was neither unprovoked nor in international waters. As for the August 4 "attack," he told Congress that the administration possessed "unequivocal proof" that it had occurred. There was no such proof, and McNamara knew it.

Based on the administration's lies, Congress formulated the so-called Gulf of Tonkin Resolution, authorizing the president "to take all necessary steps, including the use of armed force, to assist [any signatory of the Southeast Asia Collective Defense Treaty (SEATO)] requesting assistance in defense of its freedom." A few legislators expressed alarm over giving the president a "blank check" to conduct a war without consulting with Congress, but the resolution was passed by both houses of Congress on August 7, 1964.

President Johnson neatly folded his "blank check," tucked into his pocket, and cashed it only after he had achieved election in November. Almost immediately after the election, faced with withdrawing from the war or escalating it, LBJ sent in twenty-two thousand fresh troops. By 1965, 75,000 Americans were fighting in Vietnam; by 1966, 375,000; by the next election, over half a million. US forces in Vietnam reached a peak of 542,000 under Johnson and, as the cost of the war exploded, the

Great Society fell victim. By 1966, popular opposition to the war grew, reaching its peak in January 1968 following a massive coordinated attack of Viet Cong and North Vietnamese Army forces in the Tet Offensive, which overran much of South Vietnam. On March 31, 1968, President Johnson addressed the nation on television and announced, "I shall not seek, and I will not accept, the nomination of my party for another term as your President." On May 10, 1968, the United States forced its puppet regime in South Vietnam to meet North Vietnamese delegates for peace talks in Paris.

The Vietnam War would continue under President Richard M. Nixon and, after his resignation, President Gerald R. Ford, until April 30, 1975. It ended in abject defeat for South Vietnam and the United States, as the nation was unified under a single Communist government. US military dead totaled 58,318; including South Vietnamese forces and other US allies, the death toll was between 318,568 and 377,311. North Vietnamese military dead have been estimated between a half million and 1.5 million, with unknown numbers of civilian dead.

Ronald Reagan Speaks of "A Time for Choosing" (1964)

In 1964, most Americans knew Ronald Reagan as a journeyman film actor, whose best-known roles were as George Gipp, the doomed "Gipper" in 1940's *Knute Rockne, All American*, a biopic about the legendary coach of the Notre Dame football team; a young man who awakens from surgery in *King's Row* (1942), discovers he is now a double amputee, and asks, "Where's the rest of me?"; and a psychology professor paired with laboratory chimp in *Bedtime for Bonzo* (1951). When his film career faltered, Reagan became the host of television's *General Electric Theater* and a corporate spokesman, who toured GE plants, delivering inspirational speeches.

Less well known was his activism in the Screen Actor's Guild (SAG), of which he served as president from 1947 to 1952 and again in 1959. During the late 1940s, he and his first wife, Jane Wyman, were covert FBI informants who provided the names of movie industry figures they believed were communist sympathizers. Reagan later testified publicly to the House Un-American Activities Committee. Through the 1940s, he was a "Roosevelt Democrat" but moved closer to the right end of the political spectrum, becoming a Republican in 1962.

As an actor, Ronald Reagan never reached the top, but he was a man who had good reason to believe that the American Dream had been his. Raised poor in small-town Illinois, he nevertheless got a college education (at Eureka College in Eureka, Illinois), graduated in 1932, and realized one of his early ambitions—to become a radio sports announcer. After working at several regional stations, he moved to Hollywood in 1937 and became a successful actor, mostly in B pictures. His work in SAG drew him into politics, and although he supported the Senate candidacy of Democrat Helen Gahagan Douglas against

Republican Richard Nixon in 1950, he became increasingly disillusioned with the Hollywood left wing. His work for General Electric involved making numerous speeches, many of which he wrote. While they were nonpartisan, they were strongly pro-business, and in 1952 and 1956, he endorsed Dwight D. Eisenhower for president of the United States and then, in 1960, Richard M. Nixon.

"I didn't leave the Democratic Party," he often said. "The party left me." In the 1950s, this expressed the sentiments of many Americans, and in 1961 the American Medical Association hired Reagan to make a phonograph recording condemning Medicare—the concept for which was introduced in 1961—as "socialized medicine." His credentials as a Republican conservative established, he was tapped to speak at the 1964 GOP national convention. Although the speech nominating Barry Goldwater—by the standards of the time a far right-wing conservative—was delivered by Richard Nixon, Reagan's speech, titled "A Time for Choosing," was presented much closer to the election, on October 27, 1964, as part of a prerecorded television program, *Rendezvous with Destiny,* intended to rally voters to cast their ballots for Goldwater.

The speech presented Goldwater's conservative ethos, especially the "American" virtues of minimal government—a government essentially opposite that which Roosevelt had built and Lyndon Johnson proposed to expand. "The Founding Fathers," Reagan said, "knew a government can't control the economy without controlling people. And they knew when a government sets out to do that, it must use force and coercion to achieve its purpose. So, we have come to a time for choosing." It was a choice "between a left or right, but I suggest there is no such thing as a left or right. There is only an up or down. Up to man's age-old dream—the maximum of individual freedom consistent with law and order—or down to the ant heap of totalitarianism."

The speech succeeded in raising a million dollars for Goldwater on what was essentially the eve of the election but failed to capture the presidency for the Arizona senator. Yet it launched the political career of Ronald Reagan. Two years later, he answered the GOP's call to run for California governor. He won, serving as governor from 1967 to 1975. He failed in his 1976 primary challenge against Gerald Ford for the presidency but, four years later, defeated Jimmy Carter in the Democrat's bid for a second term. The Reagan presidency transformed what had often been a left-leaning nation into one driven by a hard-right, small-government, pro-business, pro-military ideology. Reagan became the anchor of Republicanism—until the surprise election of Donald J. Trump in 2016.

Bloody Sunday Happens in Selma (1965)

Alabama's state Constitution functionally disenfranchised most African Americans—and some poor whites—by requiring would-be voters to pay a poll tax and pass tests of literacy and understanding of the Constitution. During the late 1950s and early 1960s, activists made efforts to register African Americans. Blocked by state and local officials, the Ku Klux Klan, and others, local activists called for help in early 1963 from the Student Nonviolent Coordinating Committee (SNCC), whose organizers were subsequently assaulted and threatened with death. After an African American church in Birmingham was bombed on September 15, 1963—a crime in which four black girls were killed—African American students in Selma staged sit-ins at local segregated lunch counters. Some three hundred were arrested during two weeks of protests.

Still, voter registration efforts pressed ahead, but state officials repeatedly and arbitrarily denied most of the applications. On July 6, 1964, four days after President Johnson signed the Civil Rights Act of 1964, SNCC activist John Lewis led fifty black citizens to the Selma courthouse to register to vote. All were arrested by County Sheriff Jim Clark. Three days later, Judge James Hare issued an injunction forbidding any gathering of three or more people under the sponsorship of civil rights organizations or leaders. Amid growing frustration, the Selma Voting Rights Campaign officially began on January 2, 1965, when Martin Luther King Jr. addressed a meeting in Brown Chapel A.M.E. Church in defiance of the Judge Hare's injunction. The Southern Christian Leadership Committee (SCLC) and SNCC expanded voter registration drives and led protests in Selma and nearby black communities. While this activity was taking place, on January 15, King called President Lyndon Johnson, who agreed to begin pushing for passage of a Voting Rights Act.

On January 18, King appeared at a "Freedom Day" demonstration and was assaulted by a member of the National States Rights Party. In the meantime, arrests of African Americans who attempted to register to vote continued. At last, on January 25, a US district judge ordered that at least one hundred people must be permitted to wait at the courthouse without being arrested. Sheriff Jim Clark began arresting all registrants beyond the hundred-person limit while also effectively holding the others back.

The volume and scope of protests increased both locally and nationally, with pickets marching around the White House. At this point, Malcolm X addressed three thousand students at the Tuskegee Institute and essentially challenged King's nonviolent approach. At long last, however, on February 4, President Johnson issued a public statement supporting the Selma voter registration campaign, and a federal judge issued an injunction suspending Alabama's literacy test and ordered Selma to take at least one hundred applications per registration day. On February 9, Dr. King met with US attorney general Nicholas Katzenbach, Vice President Hubert Humphrey, and, briefly, with President Johnson. Johnson promised to deliver a message "very soon." Still, little progress was made in registering black voters, and King pushed more urgently for passage of a Voting Rights Act.

On February 18, 1965, during a march to the Perry County courthouse in Marion, Alabama, a town near Selma, Alabama State Trooper James Fowler pursued, shot, and fatally wounded a protestor, Jimmie Lee Jackson, who had sought refuge in a café. To protest the killing, Marion's black community decided to stage a march, which Martin Luther King Jr. agreed to lead on Sunday, March 7, from Selma to the Alabama state capital, Montgomery. There they planned to make a direct appeal to Governor George Wallace, calling for an end to police brutality. Wallace responded by refusing to allow the march. King responded by going to Washington to meet with President Johnson. This, however, required delaying the march until March 8. The Selma protestors believed the postponement would be seen as a surrender. They decided to march, without King, on March 7.

Arriving at the Selma city limit, at the Edmund Pettus Bridge, the marchers were confronted by a phalanx of state troopers. The marchers began to cross the bridge and were ordered to disperse. Instead of waiting to see if the order would be obeyed, the troopers attacked the marchers, who had halted and bowed their heads in prayer. The troopers fired tear gas and then waded into the marchers, beating them with their batons. At this, many demonstrators fled—only to be pursued into a black housing project. Here the troopers wielded their batons against demonstrators and housing project residents alike. This police action was dubbed "Bloody Sunday" not only by the Civil Rights movement but also generally by the national press.

To protest Bloody Sunday, King led a return march to the Pettus Bridge on March 9. Once again, state troopers attacked. This time, they killed one marcher, and King ordered a withdrawal. President Johnson interceded, allowing King to complete a march from Selma to Montgomery on March 25, 1965. This march and the two preceding it prompted many demonstrations nationwide. It also spurred President Johnson to deliver to Congress his most important speech on civil rights, in support of passage of the Voting Rights Act of 1965, which was signed into law on August 6.

North Vietnam Launches the Tet Offensive (1968)

Most Americans turned against the war in Vietnam in 1967. In 1965, polls showed that President Lyndon Johnson enjoyed an 80 percent approval rating. By 1967, it was down to 40 percent, a decline due almost exclusively to the Vietnam War. Johnson responded by waging his own war at home, a "media offensive" that brought his top man in Vietnam, General William Westmoreland, back to Washington to present his military achievements in the war. By the numbers, it could be argued that the United States was winning. The best estimates were that the North Vietnamese Army (NVA) could infiltrate about seven thousand troops down the Ho Chi Minh Trail into South Vietnam every month and that, monthly, the Viet Cong could recruit 3,500 troops within South Vietnam. Yet US and Army of the Republic of Vietnam (ARVN) forces claimed 8,400 Communist losses per month. By the summer of 1967, they claimed 12,700, meaning that the North's losses outpaced reinforcement. Moreover, while the Northern insurgents had closed 70 percent of South Vietnam's roadways and waterways in 1965, by the beginning of 1967, 60 percent were open.

But the numbers notwithstanding, there was no end to the war in sight. By the end of 1967, most Americans had concluded that the Vietnam War was stalemated. When President Johnson told his people that there was "light at the end of the tunnel," the ever-increasing US casualty roll created what was being called a "credibility gap" between what the administration claimed and what the public believed.

In this period of accumulating American popular doubt, Hanoi launched a massive series of offensives. The first were just over the Demilitarized Zone (DMZ), the border between North and South. Attacks throughout South Vietnam began on January 30, 1968, on Tet,

US Marines move through the ruins of the South Vietnamese hamlet of Dai Bo after several days of intense fighting during the Tet Offensive. US GOVERNMENT PRINTING OFFICE

a Vietnamese lunar holiday. Northern forces hit major cities and military bases from Quang Tri and Khe Sanh near the DMZ in the northern region of South Vietnam to Quang Long near the country's southern tip. Even the brand-new US embassy in Saigon (today Ho Chi Minh City) was targeted, and airmen were pressed into the defense of Tan Son Nhut Air Base. Up north, Viet Cong cut off the US Marine outpost at Khe Sanh starting on the first day of Tet, January 30. The base was held under heavy siege until mid-March. During this span, B-52s and fighter bombers flew over 24,400 sorties, dropping 100,000 tons of ordnance in defense of the beleaguered marines. Airlift operations defied heavy enemy antiaircraft fire to keep the isolated marines supplied, the supplies parachute-dropped or simply shoved out of low-flying C-123 and C-130 aircraft.

Without question, the Tet Offensive was costly to US and ARVN forces, and American news media made that abundantly clear. Yet it was far costlier to the NVA and VC. Of an estimated eighty-four thousand attackers, as many as forty-five thousand were killed. By any strictly military standard, the US-ARVN defense against Tet was a triumph. The North believed they could break the fighting spirit of an already badly demoralized South Vietnam. Yet Tet had precisely the opposite effect. In the immediate aftermath of the offensive, some 15,000 ARVN deserters voluntarily *returned* to the army, and 240,000 South Vietnamese young men rushed to volunteer for military service. Almost all the initial gains made by the Northern forces were reversed throughout the South, typically within days of the initial onslaught. As for body count, some 15,515 Communist fighters were killed during January 28–February 3, whereas 416 US and 784 ARVN troops (as well as 3,071 South Vietnamese civilians) died. Thus, nearly fifteen NVA/VC troops fell for every US/ARVN soldier killed in the opening phase of the offensive. Far more dire for the North, the costly offensive failed to trigger the general southern uprising its planners had banked on. This may have been due less to the mood of the South Vietnamese people than to the sheer velocity with which the Allied forces pushed back the North Vietnamese.

But in America, the three-week offensive was a devastating psychological victory for North Vietnam. It persuaded many Americans, including politicians and policy makers, that the war was unwinnable. With American casualties having risen from 780 per month during 1967 to 2,000 a month in February 1968, it was very difficult to believe official military pronouncements that Tet was not a defeat.

Tet had the effect of hardening American public opposition to the war, and it sharply divided legislators, with "hawks" (war supporters) on one side and "doves" (peace advocates) on the other. When a somewhat distorted news story broke in March, announcing that General Westmoreland was asking for two hundred thousand more men to be committed to the Vietnam War, a spasm of outrage gripped the public. Antiwar demonstrations became increasingly frequent, bigger, and more boisterous. By the middle of March 1968, public opinion polls revealed that 70 percent of the American people favored a phased withdrawal of

US forces from Vietnam starting immediately. In response, at the end of that month, President Johnson initiated a process designed to take the United States out of the war. Although the president did not give Westmoreland anything approaching the number of troops he requested, US ground strength in Vietnam would reach a high of 536,000 by the end of 1968 before the start of a general withdrawal and reduction.

Reverend Martin Luther King Jr. Is Assassinated (1968)

Annus mirabilis is a traditional Latin phrase to describe a "wonderful year," a year of joyful wonders. But 1968 was starting off as the very opposite, a year of horrors, *annus horribilis*. The shocking Tet Offensive began 1968 in Vietnam, prompting Secretary of Defense Robert McNamara to privately declare in February that the war was clearly unwinnable. On March 12, Senator Eugene McCarthy, an outspoken opponent of the war, came close to defeating President Lyndon Johnson in the New Hampshire primary. Encouraged by this, four days later, Robert Kennedy, brother of John F. Kennedy and Democratic senator from New York, declared his candidacy for the Democratic nomination. On March 31, LBJ stunned the nation by announcing the withdrawal of his own candidacy. Before the first quarter of 1968 had ended, it was clear that America was in danger of coming apart.

Two days before Johnson's announcement, on March 29, Martin Luther King went to Memphis, Tennessee, to support a strike by African American sanitary workers. They wanted wages equal to those paid to white employees but, even more, they demanded safer working conditions—Echol Cole and Robert Walker, two sanitation workers, having been crushed to death by dangerous compactors. On the evening of April 3 in Memphis, King delivered his stirring—and haunting—"I've been to the mountaintop" address. "Well, I don't know what will happen now," he said. "We've got some difficult days ahead. But it really doesn't matter with me now, because I've been to the mountaintop. And I don't mind. Like anybody, I would like to live—a long life; longevity has its place. But I'm not concerned about that now."

He spoke of how the Lord allowed him "to go up to the mountain. And I've looked over. And I've seen the Promised Land. I may not get

Martin Luther King Jr. photographed on March 26, 1964, four years before his assassination. LIBRARY OF CONGRESS

there with you. But I want you to know tonight, that we, as a people, will get to the Promised Land. So, I'm happy, tonight. I'm not worried about anything. I'm not fearing any man. Mine eyes have seen the glory of the coming of the Lord."

The next day, April 4, at 6:01 in the evening, King was standing on the balcony of his room at the Lorraine Motel when he was cut down by a single rifle shot. Emergency surgery failed to save him, and he was pronounced dead at St. Joseph's Hospital at 7:05. No sooner did the news hit the airwaves than, in more than one hundred cities across the country, African American neighborhoods erupted in violence. When Robert Kennedy, now a presidential candidate, heard the news, he was in Indianapolis, having spoken at two Indiana universities earlier in the day. He was scheduled to speak at campaign rallies in the city, including one in an African American neighborhood. He was warned to cancel for fear of riots. Instead, he made his appearance, and he began by quietly and calmly informing the gathering that King had been killed. He shared his own experience of loss, and he encouraged his audience to embrace Dr. King's ethos of nonviolence. In contrast to the many other black urban communities that night, the Indiana capital remained peaceful.

James Earle Ray, a career criminal specializing in the robbery of gas stations and stores, escaped from the Missouri State Penitentiary on April 23, 1967. He allegedly used a rifle to fire at King from a flop house window across the street from the Lorraine Motel. He then fled first to Toronto, where he obtained a Canadian passport, and on to London and Lisbon, where he obtained a second Canadian passport. The FBI, which had quickly identified Ray as the prime suspect in the assassination, tracked him on his return from Lisbon to London, where, on June 8, he was arrested at Heathrow Airport. He confessed to the assassination, pleaded guilty, but while in prison recanted his confession and claimed that he had been set up in an assassination conspiracy. Ray's appeals to change his plea and secure a trial were supported by members of the King family, including King's widow, Coretta Scott King, who believed that her husband had been the victim of a larger conspiracy. Ray died in prison of liver disease on April 23, 1998, his appeals having failed.

As for 1968, the *annus horribilis* continued. For disaffected African Americans, King's murder loomed as a terrible symbol of American injustice. Two months later, Robert Kennedy fell victim to another assassin, and, come summer, the Democratic National Convention—which might well have seen the nomination of RFK, exploded into riots.

Robert F. Kennedy Is Assassinated (1968)

History is both the story what was and of what might have been. How different would post–Civil War America have been if Abraham Lincoln had not fallen victim to John Wilkes Booth? How different would America, mired in Vietnam and torn by civil strife, have been if Robert F. Kennedy had lived to become president?

RFK—as the younger brother of JFK came to be called—served as attorney general of the United States in the administration of his brother and, briefly, during the administration of Lyndon Johnson. Although Bobby Kennedy was more than an attorney general, serving his brother as his closest and most trusted adviser and in particular playing a key role during the Cuban Missile Crisis of October 1962, he earned a place in history as attorney general for his strong stance against organized crime and for his bold advocacy of the Civil Rights movement. Even more than the president himself, Robert Kennedy pushed for sweeping new Civil Rights legislation, including the Civil Rights Act and Voting Rights Act, which did not come into being until the Johnson administration in 1964 and 1965, respectively. Like his brother, Robert Kennedy had both the appeal of youth and appealed to youth. His was the voice of resolute idealism, which exhorted his fellow citizens to be their best selves.

As a champion of Civil Rights, minority rights, and an activist role of government in addressing the needs of the poor, he made friends and enemies. He was also headstrong, authoritarian, and even imperious. These traits alienated those who disagreed with him and led him to challenge the long-held authority of others, including FBI director J. Edgar Hoover, his unwilling subordinate in the Justice Department. At times as well, RFK's zeal for justice assumed the character of a personal vendetta, most famously in his relentless pursuit of a conviction against mob-affiliated Teamster Union President Jimmy Hoffa, who remarked to associates after the assassination of President Kennedy, "Bobby Kennedy is just another lawyer now."

Lyndon Johnson was never an intimate of the Kennedy circle. He had been tapped as vice president in an effort to capture at least some of the Southern vote. Once he had served that function, he was typically left out of the major decisions. While he and the president had tolerably cordial relations, there was not even the pretense of such cordiality between LBJ and RFK. Even before Robert Kennedy resigned from the Johnson cabinet, it was painfully obvious to the new president that the younger Kennedy was trying to devise a way to challenge him for the 1968 nomination. When RFK aligned with the antiwar movement, Johnson became frankly enraged.

Indeed, LBJ had much to fear from Bobby Kennedy as a challenger. And when Eugene McCarthy's strong showing in the 1968 democratic primary in New Hampshire revealed Johnson's vulnerability, Robert Kennedy felt emboldened to declare his candidacy. In quick succession, he won both the Indiana and Nebraska primaries. There can be little doubt that, once Kennedy was in the race, Johnson began eyeing the exit. With Vietnam having become a reason to hate Johnson, with his bond of popular trust broken, Johnson had no desire to be humiliated by a Kennedy victory. On March 31, he announced his withdrawal from candidacy in an election that had become a referendum on both his character and the nation's continued involvement in Vietnam.

The great prize that was the California primary was wide open after LBJ bowed out. Kennedy won and, shortly after midnight on June 5, smilingly addressed his supporters in the ballroom of the Ambassador Hotel in Los Angeles. He stepped down from the podium and left the ballroom through the hotel kitchen, which was the quickest way to the press room. As he squeezed through a narrow kitchen hall, Kennedy turned to shake hands with a young busboy, Juan Romero, just as self-proclaimed Palestinian nationalist Sirhan Sirhan opened fire with a .22-caliber revolver, hitting Kennedy at pointblank range three times and wounding five others nearby. Romero kneeled beside the stricken man, cradling his head in his arms, awaiting aid as others, including RFK supporters journalist George Plimpton, former decathlete Rafer Johnson, and former professional football player Roosevelt "Rosey" Grier, disarmed Sirhan and wrestled him to the floor. Emergency neurosurgery was performed, but Robert F. Kennedy died at Good Samaritan Hospital, some twenty-six hours after the shooting.

And so another horror marked 1968, and to this day, Americans are left to wonder what if Kennedy had survived to run against Richard M. Nixon. Would Vietnam have ended quickly? Would ending it have made RFK a one-term president? Would the cause of civil rights have been accelerated by the greater fulfilment—on the ground—of the Civil Rights Act of 1964 and the Voting Rights Act of 1965? Would the Great Society have been revived?

We can only speculate. What is incontrovertible is that the assassination of Robert Kennedy turned an already violent year into one that was thoroughly chaotic and nearly incomprehensible. The possibility of bringing the nation together seemed very dim.

Democratic National Convention Erupts in Riots (1968)

The assassination of Robert Kennedy left the Democratic Party with one antiwar candidate in contention for nomination at the Democratic National Convention, held in Chicago during August 26–29. But Eugene McCarthy, though widely admired, fell short of the Kennedy charisma and was less in tune with the youth culture so pervasive in the late 1960s. He managed to command just 23 percent of the delegates as the convention opened. The party mainstream rallied behind Vice President Hubert H. Humphrey—more liberal than LBJ, yet by no means an antiwar candidate. He quickly accumulated a commanding lead for the nomination.

To give Humphrey his due, he was an early and passionate advocate of civil rights, a prime mover in the founding of the Peace Corps in 1961, and an ardent champion of the Civil Rights Act of 1964. On the other hand, he had been a vocal opponent of communism during the 1950s and was sponsor of the infamous Title II of the Internal Security Act of 1950, which provided for the "emergency detention" of communists and subversives. He even called for legislation to make membership in the Communist Party a felony. (Robert F. Kennedy had served from December 1952 to July 1953 as assistant counsel to the US Senate Permanent Subcommittee on Investigations, serving no less than redbaiting Senator Joseph McCarthy. RFK's supporters readily forgave this, however, if they were even aware of it.)

As LBJ's vice president, Humphrey began to oppose escalation of the Vietnam War. Clearly conflicted, candidate Humphrey pushed for prosecuting the war to its conclusion—in short, staying the course with the Johnson program. As antiwar Democrats saw it, the party was nominating a continuation of the current war policies. This drew some ten thousand antiwar and civil rights protestors to Chicago during the convention.

The protestors commandeered two of the city's stately lakefront green spaces, Grant Park and Lincoln Park, as campgrounds. Their intentions, they declared, were peaceful—but disruptive. They did not want the process of nominating Hubert Horatio Humphrey to go easily. The occupants of the parks ran the antiwar gamut, from relatively moderate to boisterously radical. Among the latter were members of the Youth International Party (known as Yippie), led by Abbie Hoffman and Jerry Rubin, and the National Mobilization Committee to End the War in Vietnam (MOBE), an umbrella organization that included many Yippies as well as Students for a Democratic Society (SDS) and others.

The presence of counterculture "hippies"—a new word at the time—along the lakefront commanded a great deal of media attention leading up to the convention, and on August 22, when police officers shot and killed a seventeen-year-old youth (who was not associated with the protests) during a stop for a curfew violation (the boy allegedly drew a pistol that misfired), protests erupted from the groups still assembling at the parks. Although no violence resulted, the demonstrators exuberantly mocked the police as "pigs" and proposed to run a pig—named Pigasus (after Pegasus, the winged horse of Greek mythology)—as their presidential candidate. Tensions quickly ratcheted up and there were sharp clashes between baton-wielding police, intent on enforcing eleven o'clock park curfews, and demonstrators. Both sides exaggerated the scale of the violence, but, without doubt, heavy police use of tear gas gave the scene the appearance of a battleground.

Police later claimed that ten thousand protestors rioted on August 25, the night before the convention. Protestors, in turn, claimed to have been attacked by one thousand officers. An official Chicago Police Department report listed 152 officers as wounded—though the reported "wounds" included the likes of a split fingernail. Medical volunteers among the protestors reported treating five hundred civilians. Yet the total number of injured treated in Chicago hospitals during the entire convention week was just 101. There were no fatalities.

The Sunday night fracas set the tone for the week of the convention. Television crews covered every "confrontation"—as the clashes were invariably termed. It was easy to get the impression of civil war on the streets of Chicago. Unmistakable, however, was the fact that the police were often gratuitously violent. The demonstrators made the most of this, chanting for the cameras, "The whole world is watching! The whole world is watching!"

In the convention venue itself at the International Amphitheatre, located in the heart of an urban ghetto forty blocks south of the lakefront parks, delegates denounced what Senator Abraham Ribicoff of Connecticut called "Gestapo tactics on the streets of Chicago." But, in the end, protests failed to scuttle the Humphrey nomination—though they may well have helped to ensure victory for his Republican opponent. Weeks earlier, in accepting his own nomination, Richard Nixon denounced the violence that plagued "the nation with the greatest tradition of the rule of law."

The Stonewall Uprising in New York City Begins the Gay Liberation Movement (1969)

Like other gay bars on or near Christopher Street in New York City's Greenwich Village, the Stonewall Inn at 51 and 53 Christopher Street was frequently the target of police harassment during the 1960s. Raids on the bars in this area occurred about once a month. The raid against the Stonewall, which started at 1:20 a.m. on Saturday, June 28, 1969, began no differently from many others. Four plainclothes officers and two uniformed beat cops, accompanied by Detective Charles Smythe and Deputy Inspector Seymour Pine, entered the bar and called out, "Police! We're taking the place!"

The routine was to line up the patrons, check their identification, and have female police officers take customers dressed as women to the bathroom to verify their gender. Any men dressed as women would be arrested. But not this night.

On this night, those in drag refused to go with the officers. Soon, all the men who were lined up refused to show their identification. Taken aback, the police decided to bring everyone down to the station house. Patrol wagons were summoned. By the time the first of these arrived, a crowd had gathered around the Stonewall and soon grew (according to Inspector Pine) by a factor of ten. The bar patrons were quiet as they were loaded into the first patrol wagon, but the crowd began shouting "Gay power!" and someone started singing the Civil Rights anthem "We Shall Overcome." What had begun as bemused observation among the spectators grew increasingly hostile. Word was passed outside that patrons inside the Stonewall were being beaten. This ignited several scuffles, which rapidly escalated into a riot, which ultimately morphed into three days of raucous protest and much publicity.

In the aftermath of Stonewall, a gay rights movement began to coalesce and go public. A Gay Liberation Front was created, and within six months of the "riots," the Gay Activists Alliance was formed. It was not so much that Stonewall started the gay rights movement as it served as a rallying event that brought many gay men and women, hitherto keeping low profiles, into the light. They engaged with a movement and asserted their right to live as they pleased.

The following year, on June 29, 1970, the first annual Christopher Street Liberation Day was celebrated. This included a Gay Pride March in New York and others in Chicago and Los Angeles. A Gay Pride movement quickly became national. Through self-assertion and self-declaration, American gays were liberating themselves from a shame and condemnation that had been imposed from without as well as within. They joined African Americans and women in declaring their right not only to a positive social and political presence and identity but also to a proud self-identity.

Neil Armstrong Sets Foot on the Moon (1969)

Close to the start of the decade, the thousand days of the John F. Kennedy administration were marked by the young president's vigor, idealism, and aspirational presence. The United States seemed new, fresh, and young again, and when President Kennedy addressed a large crowd at Rice University Stadium, in Houston, Texas, on September 12, 1962, near the site of the new Manned Spacecraft Center then under construction, the nation listened. He began by citing William Bradford: "Speaking in 1630 of the founding of the Plymouth Bay Colony," the president pointed out, Bradford observed, "that all great and honorable actions are accompanied with great difficulties, and both must be enterprised and overcome with answerable courage."

Kennedy warned that the "exploration of space will go ahead, whether we join in it or not, and it is one of the great adventures of all time, and no nation which expects to be the leader of other nations can expect to stay behind in this race for space." He spoke of setting sail on "this new sea because there is new knowledge to be gained, and new rights to be won, and they must be won and used for the progress of all people," and then he made the boldest of bold declarations:

We choose to go to the moon. We choose to go to the moon, we choose to go to the moon in this decade and do the other things, not because they are easy, but because they are hard, because that goal will serve to organize and measure the best of our energies and skills, because that challenge is one that we are willing to accept, one we are unwilling to postpone, and one which we intend to win, and the others, too.

Many were inspired but few, if they were honest about it, thought this mission was possible—certainly not within a single decade and not by a

Neil Armstrong, the first human being to set foot on the moon, works at an equipment storage area on the Lunar Excursion Module (LEM). It is one of the few photographs that document Armstrong during the "moonwalk." NASA

nation that was, at the moment, a distant second in a "space race" with the Soviet Union. The United States had entered this race in 1958 when the National Aeronautics and Space Administration (NASA) was created—a year *after* the Soviets launched the first successful artificial earth satellite, Sputnik I. Four years after this, the Soviets launched the first manned satellite, carrying Cosmonaut Yuri Gagarin, who made an orbital flight on April 12, 1961. Less than a month later, on May 5, NASA's Project Mercury sent Alan B. Shepard into space on a fifteen-minute suborbital flight. It was not until some nine months after this, on February 20, 1962, that John Glenn became the first American to orbit Earth.

The first US manned flights, all part of Project Mercury, were followed by Project Gemini, whose two-man crews were, in effect, rehearsing for a lunar mission, with maneuvers that included space walks and docking procedures. On January 27, 1967, a ground test of the vehicle for the moonshot ended in catastrophe when fire swept the cabin of *Apollo 1*, killing astronauts Virgil I. "Gus" Grissom, Ed White, and

Roger B. Chaffee. Despite this, the Apollo program made great strides over the next two and a half years, and on July 20, 1969, at 4:17 p.m. Eastern Daylight Time, Apollo 11 astronauts Neil Armstrong and Edwin ("Buzz") Aldrin, having separated their Lunar Excursion Module (LEM) *Eagle* from the Apollo command module (flown in lunar orbit by Michael Collins), became the first human beings to land on the moon—indeed, to land on any place other than Earth.

The landing was broadcast worldwide and viewed live by an estimated six hundred million. Armstrong set foot on the lunar surface first, proclaiming, "That's one small step for [a] man, and one giant leap for mankind." He was soon joined by Aldrin, and the two gathered lunar rock samples and performed various experiments before blasting off in the LEM and successfully docking with the command module, which took them back to Earth—thereby fulfilling President's Kennedy's mandate for America.

The event united America—and, indeed, much of humanity—for a brief and precious moment at the end of a decade that had brought much division, fear, violence, and even despair. It reminded Americans that their nation was capable of great things, which it would, in turn, share with the world.

The Woodstock Festival Becomes an Icon of 1960s American Youth Culture (1969)

Mention Woodstock to a baby boomer, and there is a good chance you'll be told in response: "I was there!" Millions have been saying it since the late summer of 1969—but, in fact, no more than about 400,000 actually attended. True, that was some 350,000 more than the 50,000 expected, but the cultural impact of the event was so pervasive, powerful, and, in a word, iconic that millions claim to have borne witness. It was an event that marked a generation.

Woodstock was not the world's first rock music festival. Most historians of rock 'n' roll identify the festival staged at the Monterey County Fairgrounds in northern California during June 16–18, 1967, as the first. Woodstock and others followed its example over the next two years. Rock festivals both drew and repelled many. The baby boom generation—or that portion of it who identified themselves as hip (so hip, they called themselves "hippies")—was attracted. Those who identified as what President Richard Nixon called the "silent majority," the mass of middle-class white America over thirty, were wary at best and appalled at worst. They hated the new music, and they saw the outdoor festivals as orgies of sex and illicit drug use—which, to an important degree, they were. Beyond this, some in that silent majority feared that the festivals were emblematic of the decay of American society, the America that had passed through the crucible of the Great Depression and World War II, the American cohort that would later be dubbed "the Greatest Generation." The self-reliant dual ethos of hard work and patriotism, some feared, was melting into amoral laziness or, even worse, revolutionary anarchy.

Some of the early outdoor festivals were ugly. Drugs and sex there were, but so were genuine public nuisances: noise, traffic jams, and major sanitation problems. Festival promoters were typically inexperienced or

Snapshot of some of the four thousand people who attended the Woodstock music festival. PHOTO BY PAUL CAMPBELL, PUBLISHED ON WIKIMEDIA COMMONS

carnival barkers who threw shows together with little preparation and promises they knew they could not keep. No-show acts were the rule as much as the exception. At worst, concertgoers, feeling ripped off, reacted with anger expressed in vandalism and violence.

Woodstock promised something different. Posters—widely reproduced even today—advertised an "Aquarian Exposition"—a reference to the "Age of Aquarius," an astrological epoch supposedly heralding a utopian revelation of truth and expansion of consciousness. The hit song of Broadway's *Hair: The American Tribal Love-Rock Musical,* "Aquarius" celebrated this secular Second Coming. The most popular posters characterized the event as "3 Days of Peace & Music."

The amazing thing was that, for the most part, Woodstock delivered on what was promised. It was planned for a site outside of Wallkill, near Woodstock, New York, but the local zoning board served the promoters with a permit revocation just four weeks before the advertised show dates, August 15–17, 1969. There was a mad scramble for a new site, which was found outside of Bethel, New York, when Max Yasgur, a hard-up dairy farmer in urgent need of cash, rented out his spread. Since the posters had been distributed and the advertising circulated, there was no way that the name was going to be changed. So, "Woodstock" the Bethel festival remained.

As it turned out, the cultural timing for Woodstock was perfect. The promoters had been set up to deal with fifty thousand paying attendees. When four hundred thousand give or take showed up, the promoters were ill-equipped to check tickets. After the first few hours of the festival, they let all comers in—and, what is more, did so ungrudgingly. This gave Woodstock the feeling of a free event.

Overwhelmed as well were local police and other authorities. The rural location—Bethel was a town of fewer than three thousand—had few police officers or anyone else capable of providing protection and other services. Remarkably, the "anarchists," "hippies," and "loafers" policed themselves. Fans who happened to have medical training volunteered themselves to render emergency first aid, especially in the minor epidemic of overdoses, hangovers, and bad acid trips. Food was hardly in abundance. Nor was drinkable water. Portable toilets were rushed in, but there weren't enough in the entire Northeast to accommodate nearly a half million human beings. And then the weather turned terrible as the rains came down in proverbial buckets, transforming the Yasgur farm into a field of soupy mud.

No one seemed to care. They didn't even care that, having come to hear the greatest rock musicians ever gathered in one place, the vast majority of the crowd were far too far from the stage to hear them or even really see them. Yet the magic was present. It had to do with the music, yes, but, even more, it was about a disaster that failed to happen. It was about a spontaneous outbreak of peace, love, and understanding among a vast impromptu population.

Woodstock came one month after the Apollo 11 mission to the moon—the first great unifying event of 1969 that seemed to counter the divisive terrors of the year before. The music festival took the moonshot's optimism in a more popular and, if anything, universal direction, above and beyond the assassinations, riots, and Vietnam War killing machine. It made 1968 look like the past, not the future.

It proved to be a future hardly utopian in fact. This was made most immediately apparent when, in December 1969, promoters hoped to replay Woodstock with a rock festival at Altamont Speedway near San Francisco, California. The turnout was great—three hundred thousand fans—but violence scarred the event. The Rolling Stones, who gave a free concert, chose to hire some Hells Angels to provide security. A dubious decision, it soon proved tragic. When a young African American man in the crowd was seen to draw a handgun, the Angels descended upon him and stabbed him to death. In the melee, three others were also killed. The American years to come would offer both good and bad, as years always do, but Altamont seemed to bring a bitter end to the American Age of Aquarius.

ARPANET, Precursor to the Internet, Is Launched (1969)

There is a scant handful of life-transforming inventions that can be pinned to a particular person and a particular date. The telephone was invented by Alexander Graham Bell in 1876. The incandescent electric light was invented by Thomas Edison in 1879. But the great majority of profound developments in technology, the ones that produce the most dramatic and enduring impacts on culture and commerce, are not the work of a single time or a single inventor. Such a development is the Internet, the electronic nervous system of our world. Indeed, the Internet is less an invention than it is a contemporary state of being: the interconnectedness of millions of computers and computer networks, an ever-evolving web, which bears greater resemblance to some vast organism than it does to a piece of electronic machinery.

The Internet has been very well established since the beginning of the 1990s. That is, by the last decade of the twentieth century, the Internet had created a new dimension of reality, "cyberspace," a "virtual" reality, an apparently dimensionless realm in which data, ideas, images, and thoughts are created, transmitted, exchanged, shared, and modified, and in which a vast volume of commerce, including buying, selling, lending, and advertising, is transacted.

Today, when we speak of the "Internet" what we really mean is the World Wide Web (WWW), which, unlike the Internet, did have a single inventor, the British computer scientist Tim Berners-Lee. He was working at the European Organization for Nuclear Research (CERN) in the 1980s and was frustrated by the lack of true interconnectivity among the many computers on the organization's network. Berners-Lee was determined to find a way not only to work with many incompatible computer and software systems spread out over a wide geographical area but also to make working with them easy, routine, and transparent. He decided that he needed a way to convert every information system so that it all looked like part of a virtual information system that everyone could access. Whereas the Internet is a physical network-of-networks, a material infrastructure, the system Berners-Lee invented, the WWW, is a virtual information space. It is accessed via the Internet, but instead of consisting of numerical addresses of computers, it is a system of what Berners-Lee called uniform resource locators (URLs), which can be keyed to and accessed via hypertext links. Hypertext—which Berners-Lee also invented—is a way of linking keywords in one text or dataset to related information in another. Hypertext enables, enhances, and facilitates information sharing over the WWW, which runs on the Internet.

The WWW makes the Internet truly useful, but it came into existence because of the Internet, which not only had no one inventor, it is also not even an invention. But, of course, it did have an origin, which came about in 1969, when the US Department of Defense created ARPANET. The Advanced Research Projects Agency Network was a computer-mediated communications network designed to link US military forces together while also connecting them with a network of nonmilitary institutional, contractor, and governmental computers. ARPANET was the first large computer network, a means of transmitting and sharing data among a variety of computers in a variety of settings.

Almost immediately after ARPANET was in place, university researchers from outside the defense field hopped aboard to gain access to the data and research stored on remote computers. They did not regard this as a free ride but contributed their own data to the network so that with each new user ARPANET expanded and ramified.

When ARPANET was set up, computers were large devices that required a room of their own and had to be operated by trained technicians and programmers. After the desktop-sized personal computer (PC) was introduced in 1981 and became equipped with a modem, enabling it to receive and transmit data via telephone lines, the ARPANET mushroomed very far beyond its original purpose and confines. The result was dubbed the Internet, and it began to go everywhere the PC went: to school, to the office, and at home. No government agency, no corporation, no academic institution could contain it. The Internet became a new forum, a new town hall, a new library, a new marketplace, and, ultimately, a new platform for society and civilization. Although it transcended national borders, the origin and nucleus of the Internet was and remains the United States.

Sesame Street Debuts on Public Television, Becoming an Instant Media Landmark in Culture and Education (1969)

In a 1961 speech to the National Association of Broadcasters, Newton Minow, chairman of the Federal Communications Commission (FCC), invited his listeners "to sit down in front of your television set when your station goes on the air—and keep your eyes glued to that set until the station signs off. I can assure you that you will observe a vast wasteland."

That phrase, "vast wasteland," hit home. People were indeed tired of inconsequential programming, and they worried that the "boob tube" was "rotting the brains" of their children. Even more, educators were especially discouraged that the powerful technological wonder called television was full of wasted potential. Marshall McLuhan, an influential media theorist of the 1960s, predicted that television would interconnect the peoples of the world, transcending international borders and political divisions to create a global village. Instead, it seemed to be aimed exclusively at the village idiot.

In 1966, a young television producer named Joan Ganz Cooney met with Carnegie Foundation vice president Lloyd Morrisett to create a children's television show intended to realize the full potential of the medium. Parents were concerned that their children were becoming passive TV addicts. Cooney and Morrisett decided to find a way to "master the addictive qualities of television and do something good with them." Their idea was to use TV to jumpstart the early education of children, to prepare them for school.

They spent two years researching the field and, in 1968, founded the Children's Television Workshop (CTW), funded with a combined $8 million from the Carnegie Foundation, the Ford Foundation, and the US government. Their objective was to create and produce a new children's television show unlike any other. It was called *Sesame Street*, and it debuted on public television on November 10, 1969. Aimed at preschoolers, its programming was based on original laboratory and formative research. Despite much skepticism, it was received mostly with praise, except from some conservative pundits, who objected to what they saw as its permissive and liberal bent. Most important, it enjoyed high ratings from the very beginning. The viewer numbers were far beyond the modest draw public—or "educational"—television usually commanded. Today, *Sesame Street* is broadcast in more than 120 countries.

Over the years, *Sesame Street* evolved and expanded. Under the conservative administration of Ronald Reagan, in 1981, federal funding for the program was withdrawn, whereupon CTW created new revenue sources, including a magazine, a book division, extensive product licensing, and income from international broadcasts. Freed from government control, *Sesame Street* also expanded the content of its programming. While a preschool "curriculum" remained in place, the show began to address such topics as ethics, emotions, and relationships. The emphasis became increasingly diverse in ethnic, racial, and social terms, with the emphasis always on tolerance and openness.

While the focus of *Sesame Street* was on innovative content for mainly preschool children, the creators were always determined to exploit the full potential of the television medium. Thus, the show emphasized a strong visual style, a quick pace, inventive music, and a large dose of humor. Live action was interspersed with animation. While many television "experts" warned that the attention of children could not be held throughout a sixty-minute program, CTW structured the entire series with considerable continuity yet segmented into short sequences with strong narrative direction and a rich variety of characters. The controlling metaphor was that Sesame Street was indeed a *street*, a neighborhood block, with a cast of distinctive residents, which included a unique puppet population called the Muppets, created by master puppeteer Jim Hansen. Each show continually counterpointed live actors, puppets, and animation—and it often incorporated celebrities that the children would recognize.

Behind all the variety and creativity was the notion that, if television could hold a child's attention, it could educate that child. After the first few episodes, it was apparent that *Sesame Street's* mastery of mass media, child psychology, sound teaching, and an elevated level of common decency and empathy was a powerful, positive cultural force. It was a stride toward the "global village" McLuhan had predicted.

Richard Nixon Creates the Environmental Protection Agency (1970)

Richard M. Nixon did a lot of things no one expected from a conservative Republican who had rocketed to political prominence in the 1950s as a zealous anti-communist. Against the odds, he became the thirty-seventh president of the United States in 1969. He wound down the ground war in Vietnam while invading neutral Cambodia and bombing that country as well as Laos and North Vietnam. He was a pro-business fiscal conservative, who nevertheless rocked the global economy by taking the United States off the gold standard. He took a hard line against communism, even as he boldly opened diplomatic relations with Communist China. He proclaimed himself the law-and-order president even as he put himself above the law by using his office to sabotage and undermine political opponents, including the entire Democratic Party and its major candidates. He rallied what he called the conservative "silent majority" against liberal intellectuals and "hippies," yet he gave this leftist constituency—which was most certainly not *his* constituency—what many of them clamored for: a massive federal commitment to the environmental movement through the creation of the Environmental Protection Agency.

This last action vies with his breakthrough to China as Nixon's most dramatically unexpected move. He is given credit for having played a key role in launching what has been rightly called the "environmental decade" of the 1970s. While it is true that the environmental legislation of this period was the product of congressional initiative and pressure from environmental and consumer groups, "conservative" Nixon, like "liberal" Lyndon Johnson before him, freely, even enthusiastically, endorsed the environmental movement. Through Congress, he was also instrumental in establishing a Commission on Population Growth and the American Future, and he acceded to environmentalists' demands to block construction of an Everglades jetport and to halt construction on the Cross-Florida Barge Canal project. Nixon signed into law the sweeping National Environmental Policy Act (NEPA) and he established the Council on Environmental Quality (CEQ) as well as the most visible federal environmental administrative unit, the Environmental Protection Agency (EPA). Together, the Nixon-era measures constitute the most important body of conservation law ever enacted—in the United States and, quite possibly, the world.

President Nixon signed the NEPA legislation in January 1970. It declared "a national policy which will encourage productive and enjoyable harmony between man and his environment [and] enrich the understanding of the ecological systems and natural resources important to the Nation." The law required each federal agency to prepare an estimate of environmental impact (an "environmental impact statement") before taking any action that might harm the environment, and it established the Council on Environmental Quality, an executive agency that set long-term policy, advised the president, and monitored the environmental impact statement process.

Six months after NEPA was signed into law, President Nixon established the EPA, which started with a staff of 6,673 and an annual budget of $1.28 billion, growing to $5.6 billion by 1980. The president also established an advisory council representing industry to convey business concerns over emerging environmental regulation and, through the Office of Management and Budget (OMB), set up a system of "quality of life" reviews of environmental regulation.

In truth, despite the epoch-making environmental legislation enacted during his administration, President Nixon was hardly an unconditional and ardent environmentalist. As early as the summer of 1971, in the wake of the legislation he had endorsed, he expressed serious reservations concerning the economic impact of wholesale environmental regulation. In August, the president responded to a memo a staffer had prepared concerning the "negative economic impact of . . . the environmental movement." The president wrote, "I completely agree. We have gone overboard on the environment—& are going to reap the whirlwind for our excesses." He even ordered White House counsel John Ehrlichman to "get me a plan for cooling off the excesses." Subsequently, the president came to blows with his creation, the EPA, over its move to ban the use of the pesticide DDT, and in 1972 he vetoed the Federal Water Pollution Control Act Amendments because of their nearly $25 billion price tag. Congress overrode the veto, and the legislation became popularly known as the Clean Water Act, which the Natural Resources Defense Council called "one of the strongest environmental laws ever written."

His reservations and backslidings on environmental issues prompted many Nixon critics to claim that the president's endorsement of the legislation was largely motivated by a desire to appease national unrest by diverting attention from the seemingly endless nightmare of the Vietnam War. Whether this was the case or not, Vietnam became the scene of the Nixon administration's single greatest offense against the environment. All war, of course, is destructive to life, but Vietnam saw the use of a new defoliant called Agent Orange, a dioxin compound designed to deprive the enemy of concealing camouflage by denuding vast tracts of jungle. Not only did this intended effect of Agent Orange damage the environment, its unanticipated side effects continue to pose long-term consequences for plant life, wild life, and human life, including nervous disorders and cancer among some Vietnam veterans.

As for the EPA, it has suffered attacks and diminution under various Republican administrations, most recently that of Donald J. Trump. He appointed as EPA administrator Scott Pruitt, who, as Oklahoma's attorney general had sued the EPA at least fourteen times. Pruitt, who resigned on July 5, 2018 under a storm of ethics controversies, rejected the scientific consensus that human-caused carbon dioxide emissions are a primary contributor to global climate change, regarded his tenure as the head of the EPA as a conservative mandate to blunt or even dismantle the agency.

President Richard M. Nixon Takes the United States off the Gold Standard (1971)

Everyone knows that Richard Nixon inherited the Vietnam War from his predecessor, Lyndon Johnson. Less widely recognized is the economic legacy LBJ passed down to Nixon. Johnson struggled mightily to fund both his "Great Society" welfare programs and the ever-expanding Vietnam War. He insisted that the United States was prosperous enough not only to foot the bill for an expanded war but also to continue to financing the Great Society without raising taxes. Inflation, however, reduced domestic demand for goods, and the trade surplus of 1964 had by 1968 evaporated. As dollars piled up in offshore markets, upward pressure on the gold price mounted. America's gold reserves were dwindling, and any trigger event might cause a panic in the global market capable of provoking a run on those imperiled reserves. The Arab-Israeli "Six-Day War" in June 1967 was that trigger, and the United States found itself on the hook to supply 50 percent of the gold required to keep the global price of the metal stable. The Senate repealed a law requiring that Federal Reserve notes be backed 25 percent by gold. This allowed the US Treasury to access *all* of the nation's remaining gold stock, some $12 billion—already down from the $22 billion 1959 high. The next logical step was to increase taxes and cut spending before the gold was exhausted, forcing the price of the basis of the planet's major currencies to explode upward, setting off massive inflation. Instead, on March 14, 1968, LBJ closed the international gold pool, which set off a worldwide dumping of the dollar for other currencies.

Johnson cut the cord connecting the US dollar with London's global free market in gold. By the time Richard Nixon was sworn in on January 20,

1969, US gold reserves had dwindled to $10 billion, whereas short-term dollar liabilities held by foreign central banks totaled some $20 billion. In other words, the United States could not cover with gold the dollar debt it owed to foreign nations and interests. The Vietnam War plus the Great Society had overdrawn the American bank account. Nations now began to exit the so-called Bretton Woods system, which managed the monetary systems of the United States, Canada, Western Europe, Australia, and Japan. Early in 1971, West Germany withdrew from Bretton Woods, boosting the German economy but causing the US dollar to drop sharply against the Deutsche Mark. Next, Switzerland and France redeemed their dollars for gold, prompting Congress to recommend devaluation of the dollar to protect it against "foreign price-gougers." In August 1971, Switzerland withdrew from the Bretton Woods system altogether.

On August 13, 1971, Federal Reserve chairman Arthur Burns, newly appointed treasury secretary John Connally, and Paul Volcker, future chairman of the Federal Reserve and, at the time, undersecretary for International Monetary Affairs, secretly met at Camp David with President Nixon and a dozen other top economic advisers. Secretary of the Treasury Connally, the former Texas governor who had survived grievous wounds received in the assassination of John F. Kennedy, urged Nixon to permanently shut the "gold window"—the gold exchange—and thereby end the Bretton Woods system once and for all. To preempt the inflation that would result from cutting the dollar loose from gold, Connally recommended freezing wages and prices for ninety days and, to forestall a run on the dollar, he wanted to impose an immediate 10 percent surcharge on all imports. He believed these steps would stabilize the economy and reduce both the 6.1 percent unemployment rate and the 5.84 percent inflation rate.

Nixon agreed. On August 15, he closed the gold window and imposed the ninety-day freeze on wages and prices—the first time the federal government had intervened in this way since the days of rationing in World War II. He also announced a 10 percent import surcharge. The dollar—to the value of which all other major currencies were pegged—was cut loose from gold and allowed to float freely.

Most Americans enthusiastically approved the step—at least at first. The Dow Jones averages jumped 33 points on the Monday following Nixon's speech announcing the change. At the time, it was a record one-day gain. President Nixon ended the import surcharge in December, and in March 1973, the fixed exchange rate system officially became a floating exchange rate system.

Then came the long term.

As the months went by, the departure from gold triggered stagflation, an especially brutal economic situation in which inflation is high while the growth of the economy is stagnant. It was slow growth *and* high unemployment. Still, voters widely accepted the break with gold as a "necessary" response to an international economic crisis. By December 1974, unemployment hit 7.2 percent and kept rising, reaching a ruinous 9 percent in May 1975. Inflation rates averaged 5.7 percent in 1970, falling to 4.4 percent and 3.2 percent in 1971–1972, when President Nixon introduced the wage and price freezes, but the number hit 6.2 percent in 1973 (when the controls were lifted) and stood at 11 percent for 1974, having peaked in December of that year at 12.3 percent. The brave new world without gold to steady global currencies was becoming a frightening and difficult place, and, untethered from the yellow metal, the superpower influence of the United States was subjected to unprecedented questioning and challenges.

Nixon's Plumbers Are Nabbed at the Watergate (1972)

Going into the 1972 reelection campaign, every indication was that Richard Nixon would sail to a second term. Everyone associated with the campaign was confident of this—with one exception, the candidate himself. Writers of history and biography have delighted in the "character" of the thirty-seventh president. A complex, even tortured figure, he was a man profoundly uncomfortable in his own skin, self-confident in his public persona, yet self-conscious and self-doubting in private. The word often heard in connection with him was *paranoid*.

The Watergate scandal began on the night of June 17, 1972, when Washington, DC, police officers responded to a call from a security guard at the Watergate office and residential complex. Five "burglars" were arrested there—all employees of the Nixon campaign's Committee to Re-elect the President, an organization better known by its remarkable acronym, CREEP. At the Watergate, they had broken into the offices of the Democratic National Committee (DNC) headquarters. It was soon revealed that the "burglars" were not at the DNC headquarters to steal office supplies and petty cash but to bug the telephones and photograph political documents outlining the Democratic campaign strategy.

In the slowly unfolding course of the break-in investigation, it was revealed that this gang had a name. They were known as the "Plumbers," a unit covertly created inside the Nixon White House to "fix leaks" in the wake of the Pentagon Papers revelations—the leaking and publication (in the *New York Times, Washington Post*, and other national papers) of the secret history of US involvement in Vietnam. The Plumbers consisted of anti-Castro Cuban refugees (veterans of the Bay of Pigs), former FBI agents, and a former CIA agent who had helped plan the Bay of Pigs. One of the ex-FBI men, G. Gordon Liddy—a right-wing extremist who liked to quote Nietzsche in the original German—and the former CIA man, E. Howard Hunt—who left the CIA to write pulpy spy novels— were in charge of the group. Both worked directly for CREEP and had been on the official White House payroll.

Although *Washington Post* reporters Bob Woodward and Carl Bernstein began covering the Watergate affair from the very beginning, the stories did not damage Nixon's reelection campaign. He was returned to office in a landslide. But, thanks largely to Woodward and Bernstein's dogged reporting, Watergate became the scourge of Nixon's second term. The stories prompted the Senate to form a select committee to investigate the scandal, which they did—in special televised hearings. Not since the Army–McCarthy hearings of 1954 had television coverage of a congressional proceeding so riveted the nation's attention. It soon became clear to viewers that Nixon, his aides, and his reelection committee conspired to sabotage the campaigns of the Democratic challengers and then acted to obstruct justice by impeding the Watergate investigation.

Richard M. Nixon Resigns
the Presidency (1974)

Slow to simmer, public outrage over the growing Watergate scandal boiled over in May 1973. Nixon responded by appointing a special prosecutor for what was now called the Watergate case. A distinguished Harvard law professor, Archibald Cox worked in collaboration with a federal grand jury under the direction of Judge John Sirica. When the investigation revealed that White House conversations and phone calls had been covertly tape-recorded on a secret system Nixon had installed, Cox asked the grand jury to subpoena that evidence. Cornered, Nixon refused to produce the tapes, citing national security and executive privilege. When Cox persisted in pressing the subpoena, Nixon ordered Attorney General Elliott Richardson to fire Cox. Richardson defiantly resigned rather than carry out the order. Nixon then ordered Deputy Attorney General William Ruckelshaus to fire Cox. He likewise resigned on the same evening, Saturday, October 20, 1973. Nixon then prevailed upon Solicitor General Robert Bork, who obediently dismissed Cox. The series of events went down in history as the "Saturday Night Massacre," which stunned America, convincing most of the public of Nixon's complicity in Watergate. Backed further into a corner, the president immediately appointed a new special prosecutor, Leon Jaworski, who promptly resumed the legal battle for possession of the tapes.

By July 1974, the grand jury Jaworski convened named the president as an unindicted coconspirator in the obstruction of justice, which prompted the House Judiciary Committee to adopt three articles of impeachment. Nixon, whose presidency was now limping along, released edited transcripts of the tapes, which were rejected by the Judiciary Committee. It demanded full compliance with the subpoena. A new, expanded subpoena was issued, and when Nixon refused to comply, Jaworski

Richard M. Nixon, having resigned as president of the United States, boards Army One, the helicopter that took him from the White House and into private life. PHOTO BY OLLIE ATKINS, WHITE HOUSE PRESS OFFICE

appealed to the Supreme Court, which ruled against the president's claim of executive privilege. In late July 1974, Nixon relented and released the tapes. Despite an 18½ -minute erasure, the recordings made clear that

Nixon had entered into a criminal conspiracy to obstruct justice. The most damaging taped sequence—the so-called smoking gun—revealed Nixon's agreement that the director of the CIA and the deputy director of the FBI should ask Acting FBI Director L. Patrick Gray to halt the bureau's Watergate investigation. On August 5, this "smoking gun tape" was released to the public, whereupon lingering support for the president instantly evaporated.

The Watergate scandal would seem to vindicate the position of those who believed Nixon was an "imperialist" chief executive with an insatiable appetite for power. Henry Kissinger said of the affair that destroyed the Nixon presidency, "It was a Greek tragedy. Nixon was fulfilling his own nature. Once it started it could not end otherwise." To get down to cases, White House crimes uncovered by the congressional investigation included the fact that former Nixon attorney general John Mitchell, in his capacity as Nixon's reelection campaign manager, had controlled secret monies used to finance "dirty tricks" intended to sabotage the Democratic party; that major corporations had made millions of dollars in illegal campaign contributions; that Nixon promised the Plumbers clemency and even bribes in return for their silence; that L. Patrick Gray, Nixon's nominee to replace the recently deceased J. Edgar Hoover as FBI director, had illegally turned over FBI records on Watergate to White House counsel John Dean; that Mitchell and CREEP finance chairman Maurice Stans took bribes; that the White House possessed illegal wiretap tapes; that Nixon directed the CIA to instruct the FBI not to investigate Watergate; and that, during 1969 and 1970, Nixon had secretly bombed Cambodia without the knowledge of Congress.

Amid these grim allegations, on the night of August 7, 1974, Senators Barry Goldwater and Hugh Scott and Congressman John Jacob Rhodes met with Nixon in the Oval Office. Scott and Rhodes were the Republican leaders in the Senate and House, respectively; Goldwater was brought along as an elder statesman. The three lawmakers told Nixon that his support in Congress was gone. Rhodes told Nixon that he would face certain impeachment when the articles came up for vote in the full House. Goldwater and Scott told the president that there were enough votes in the Senate to convict him, and that no more than fifteen senators were willing to vote for acquittal.

Realizing that he had no chance of remaining in office and that public opinion was against him, Nixon decided to resign, becoming the first American president to do so. In a nationally televised address from the Oval Office on the evening of August 8, 1974, Richard Nixon said, in part, "I would have preferred to carry through to the finish whatever the personal agony it would have involved, and my family unanimously urged me to do so. But the interest of the Nation must always come before any personal considerations. . . . I have never been a quitter. To leave office before my term is completed is abhorrent to every instinct in my body. But as President, I must put the interest of America first. America needs a full-time President and a full-time Congress, particularly at this time with problems we face at home and abroad. To continue to fight through the months ahead for my personal vindication would almost totally absorb the time and attention of both the President and the Congress in a period when our entire focus should be on the great issues of peace abroad and prosperity without inflation at home. Therefore, I shall resign the Presidency effective at noon tomorrow. Vice President Ford will be sworn in as President at that hour in this office."

Gerald Ford—who had been appointed to the vice presidency after the elected vice president, Spiro T. Agnew, resigned in disgrace and pleaded guilty to income tax evasion—preemptively pardoned Nixon for all offenses he had committed (or might have committed) during his presidency. Nixon thus became the only Watergate conspirator who escaped conviction.

AIDS First Clinically Observed in the United States (1981)

In 1981, a bewildering cluster of patients with a very rare infection, Pneumocystis carinii pneumonia (PCP), came to the attention of public health officials. The only thing these patients had in common, aside from their clinical problem, was that they were either gay or intravenous drug users. None had a previous history of earlier impaired immunity. A short time after patients with PCP appeared, numerous gay men showed up at their physicians' offices complaining of skin lesions. It was a cancer known as Kaposi's sarcoma (KS). Before long, both PCP and KS appeared all over the United States, always among gay men or intravenous drug users. The US Centers for Disease Control and Prevention (CDC) began monitoring what it identified as an outbreak.

Not only did the CDC researchers have to figure out the cause of the outbreak, they also needed a name for the disease that underlay the symptoms. Lymphadenopathy was one name—but it described a lymphatic symptom, not a disease. Kaposi's sarcoma was another, but it was also a symptom or sign of a disease rather than a disease in itself. The CDC tried calling it "4H disease," since it affected heroin users, homosexuals, hemophiliacs, and Haitians, but that soon faded, and the acronym "GRID" emerged in the popular media, standing for gay-related immune deficiency. When it was confirmed that the disease was not confined to the gay community, however, the CDC settled on AIDS, for acquired immune deficiency syndrome.

"AIDS" was more accurate than GRID in that it did not imply that the new disease was exclusive to gay men, but, nevertheless, the illness quickly acquired a homophobic social stigma. Some believed it was the result of the "promiscuous" gay lifestyle and the nature of gay sex. When it was pointed out that infected blood transfer can also spread the disease, some responded that heroin users (who often shared blood-contaminated needles) deserved what they got—though, of course, those who required medically necessary intravenous blood transfusions were also vulnerable to infection. There was, furthermore, a widespread panic that AIDS could be spread by the most casual of contact. So much as touching an infected person, sharing a towel or an article of clothing, and eating at the same table could be lethal, many believed. At this time, the Reagan administration, which had cut back many welfare and public health programs, turned a blind eye to what was rapidly becoming a bewildering and terrifying plague that hit the male gay community hardest. This indifference at the highest levels of government persisted even after more and more cases were diagnosed in heterosexual men, in women, and in children.

As the 1980s wore on, it became increasingly clear in the gay community that gay men had to help themselves because nobody else was going to. Such grassroots organizations as Gay Men's Health Crisis (GMHC) and AIDS Coalition to Unleash Power (ACT UP) aggressively pressured government officials, accusing the Reagan administration of failing to respond to a public health emergency because the epidemic was perceived to be confined to socially marginal groups, namely homosexuals and intravenous drug abusers. President Ronald Reagan, renowned as the "Great Communicator," failed to mention AIDS in public until April 1987, a full six years after the CDC determined that an epidemic was under way. Thanks to AIDS activists, federal funding did grow, from $5.6 million in 1982 to more than $2 billion by 1992.

By the late 1980s and into the 1990s, high-profile celebrities— among them Princess Diana in England—campaigned for increased AIDS research funding. To this day, however, there is neither a cure nor a preventative vaccine. Major progress in treatment has been made, however, with antiretroviral medications slowing the course of the disease so dramatically that many who are infected with human immunodeficiency virus (HIV), the virus that can develop into AIDS, may now look forward to normal or near-normal life expectancies. Left untreated, survival time after infection averages eleven years.

Socially, AIDS has largely emerged from the early hysteria, and those with HIV are readily accepted into society. As yet incurable, the disease can be managed, and the shunning and discrimination associated with disease in the 1980s has been replaced, in significant measure, by empathy and understanding.

Motorola Releases the DynaTAC 8000X, First Commercial Cellular Telephone (1983)

The earliest form of electrical communication, the telegraph, was introduced in a practical way in 1844, when Samuel F. B. Morse transmitted the message *What hath God wrought?* between Baltimore and Washington. Transformative breakthrough though it was, the telegraph had one great limitation: unless you could afford your own transmitting and receiving station and connection (and few businesses and even fewer individuals could), messages had to be sent and received at centralized telegraph offices. Thus, telegraphy was not person-to-person communication but station-to-station messaging. Alexander Graham Bell's telephone, patented in 1876, quickly evolved into a device approaching person-to-person communication—provided that the people communicating both had access to telephones, either at their homes or places of business. In a sense, then, it was not so much person-to-person as it was communication from place to place.

The first practical demonstration of wireless telegraphy—radio—by Guglielmo Marconi in 1896 potentially freed communicating parties from physical connection; indeed, ship-to-shore radio communication was introduced early in the twentieth century. In 1918, the German national railroad system began testing wireless telephony on military trains. This was extended to civilian trials in 1924, after World War I, and went into regular operation in 1926. World War II brought the next breakthroughs: handheld radios, walkie-talkies. The war also brought systems that linked radios installed in vehicles and handheld walkie-talkies to regular telephone connections.

After the war, in 1946, Bell Labs of the United States introduced Mobile Telephone Service (MTS), which routed calls through a live operator, allowing wireless telephone communication between vehicles and ordinary telephones in offices and houses. The invention of the transistor allowed electronics to be made much smaller and use much less power than vacuum tube technology. This, in turn, brought the introduction of various miniaturized mobile and handheld phones from the late 1950s through the 1960s.

Still, the radio telephone was not yet a mass technology. During the 1960s and 1970s, various radio telephone systems were created, but there was little standardization, and the cost of equipment and service was prohibitive for many. None of the systems used handheld devices. All were installed exclusively in vehicles—until April 3, 1973. That is when Motorola executive and researcher Martin Cooper made the first mobile phone call from a handheld device, which resembled a walkie-talkie with a keyboard "dial." Yet one great technological stumbling block remained. Mobile phones, whether vehicle-mounted or handheld, had to stay within the coverage area serviced by one base station for the duration of the call. There was no way to hand off a call between broadcast areas, or "cells," as they were called.

In 1979, an analog—nondigital—system capable of handing off mobile calls from one broadcast cell to another debuted in Japan. Two years later, such systems appeared in Norway and Sweden as well. In the United States, the Advanced Mobile Phone System (AMPS), a version of this analog system, was activated in October 1983.

It was already obsolete. In March 1983, Motorola introduced the DynaTac 8000X, the first commercial *digital* cellular telephone—that is, a handheld phone capable of handing off calls from cell to cell digitally, which made calls much more secure and practical than those transmitted and received with analog technology. Weighing in at about two pounds, the DynaTac was aptly nicknamed "the brick," and its price, $3,995 ($10,091.39 in 2018 dollars), put it well beyond the mainstream market.

Launched on the first US 1G network by Ameritech, the phone worked—although its rechargeable battery yielded a talk time of just thirty-five minutes on a full charge, which required ten hours of plugged-in recharge time. Despite the cost, the limited talk time, and the narrow availability of service, high-end consumers clamored for the device. Being continuously connected to the main office, head-quarters, clients—whomever—never being wholly out of touch, conferred a tremendous competitive edge for everyone from salespeople, to stockbrokers, to commodity traders, to lawyers, to spies. The demand signaled that developing a truly mass-market cell phone and infrastructure would be tremendously profitable. In 1990s, the cell phone market exploded. Each year, the phones were smaller and cheaper, and the service network steadily expanded. Added to voice communication was SMS messaging. By the close of the decade, so-called smartphones began to appear, which integrated Internet technology, and cell phones increasingly entered the mainstream. By the beginning of the twenty-first century, the BlackBerry became the business smartphone of choice, and in 2007 Android smartphones (from various makers) and the Apple iPhone appeared, both taking consumers by storm and steadily over-taking BlackBerry in the market.

By 2007, it was clear that the smartphone had transformed more than communications. Civilization itself had turned a corner. By 2017, the United States had an estimated 224.3 million smartphone users, and it is believed that there are more than two billion users worldwide—each potentially connectable with the others.

The Berlin Wall Falls (1989)

At the Yalta Conference among Franklin D. Roosevelt, Winston Churchill, and Joseph Stalin held from February 4 to 11, 1945, as victory in Europe neared, the Allies agreed to divide Germany for purposes of occupation into three western sectors (controlled by the United States, the United Kingdom, and France) and one eastern sector, controlled by the Soviet Union. Since the German capital, Berlin, was deep within the Soviet sector, it, too, would be divided, with the Western powers controlling the western zones and the Soviets the eastern zone. The Soviets agreed to recognize a corridor between the western Germany and western Berlin for purposes of communication, supply, and movement. Despite this agreement, the political division made life difficult for residents of West Berlin, especially as Cold War friction intensified between West and East.

One side of the divided city soon appeared very different from the other. Aided by the United States, West Berlin quickly recovered from the devastation of World War II and became a vibrant and prosperous European city. In contrast, much of East Berlin remained in ruins and, even where rebuilt, became a typically grim city of the "Soviet bloc." The Easterners could see how much better the Westerners lived. As a result, many left the East for the West, creating a brain drain of skilled professionals, a more general labor shortage, and a major embarrassment in the ongoing values and propaganda contest between capitalist democracy and communist collectivism. When Soviet—and, later, East German—authorities blocked immigration to the West, many East Berliners found ways to steal across. At last, in 1961, the new East German government built a wall along the demarcation between East and West Berlin, a brick, concrete, and barbed wire barrier overseen by armed guards with orders to shoot to kill anyone attempting to scale or otherwise breach the wall. It was a tangible symbol of East German coercive power, tyranny, and the

The Berlin Wall, November 10, 1989. The red graffiti text at the top, "Irgendwann fällt jede Mauer," translates as "Sooner or later every wall falls." PHOTO BY FREDERIK RAMM, PUBLISHED ON WIKIMEDIA COMMONS

denial of liberty. It was also a vivid reminder of the ever-present potential for nuclear Armageddon between the forces of East and West. During 1961–1989, some 140 people were killed or died while attempting to escape from East Berlin to the West. An unknown number of people either successfully scaled the wall or tunneled beneath it.

The Berlin Wall was not about containment alone. It was a means by which Soviet Premier Nikita Khrushchev challenged the young American president John F. Kennedy. The wall dared him to oppose Soviet hegemony over the Eastern Bloc. Kennedy defied the existence of the wall by traveling to Berlin in June 1963, where, on the twenty-sixth, twenty-two months after the wall had been erected, he delivered a speech expressing America's solidarity with the people of West Berlin.

"Today, in a world of freedom, the proudest boast is 'Ich bin ein Berliner,'" Kennedy declared—"I am a Berliner." He continued, "All free men, wherever they may live, are citizens of Berlin, and therefore, as a free man, I take pride in the words 'Ich bin ein Berliner!'"

On June 12, 1987, with a substantially more liberal leader, Mikhail Gorbachev, having assumed power in the Soviet Union, President Ronald Reagan also came to the Berlin Wall and made a memorable speech: "General Secretary Gorbachev, if you seek peace, if you seek prosperity for the Soviet Union and Eastern Europe, if you seek liberalization, come here to this gate. Mr. Gorbachev, open this gate. Mr. Gorbachev, tear . . . *down* . . . this . . . wall!"

It did not happen immediately, the destruction of the brick and mortar barrier, but Gorbachev's reforms and outreach to the West were nevertheless breakthroughs—so remarkable that, within two years, the wall seemed the product of an empty gesture, one that had outlived both its symbolic power its usefulness as a barrier. The Cold War was clearly coming to an end as European communism and the Soviet Union itself tumbled into sharp decline. In June, the Hungarian government tore down an electrified fence along its border with Austria. This allowed East Germans to enter Hungary, pass through, and easily migrate to the west. By November, people on both the eastern and western sides of the wall began attacking it with sledge hammers, crow bars, and other tools, tearing it down bit by bit by hand. On June 13, 1990, the East German government officially began demolition.

Despite a last-gasp KGB-led coup d'etat against him, Gorbachev disbanded the Communist Party created by Lenin and Trotsky during the 1917 Russian Revolutions and then abdicated his position as head of the USSR, resigning as president on December 25, 1991, and turning over governing power to Boris Yeltsin. With this, the Cold War ended, and the prospect of World War III between the Soviets and the United States seemed to vanish. US president George H. W. Bush spoke of a "new world order" over which the United States, the world's only remaining superpower, presided. What Bush did not reckon on was the emergence of a new threat, mainly from outside Europe, as a war began to crystallize between the Christian-dominated West and the Muslim-dominated Middle East. A new ideological polarity was taking shape, in which the United States would play a central role.

Federal Officers Lay Siege to the "Branch Davidian Compound" in Waco, Texas (1993)

The fall of the Soviet Union and end of fifty years of Cold War somehow failed to bring a feeling of victorious unity to the American homeland. On the contrary, during this decade, the climate of American democracy was often bitter, angry, and violent. The issues, typically, were political—but only vaguely so. They boiled down to a general distrust and resentment of government—this government, any government. Various "fringe" groups sprang up across the country. Some called themselves "militias." Others, including the Branch Davidians, were religious in nature and, typically, millenarian, believing humanity to be living in the "end times," with a harsh Judgment Day imminent as prelude to the Second Coming.

The Branch Davidians were led by one David Koresh and had a compound at the Mount Carmel Center Ranch in the community of Axtell, Texas, some thirteen miles northeast of Waco. Religious freedom is, of course, guaranteed by the Constitution, but agents of the federal Bureau of Alcohol, Tobacco, Firearms and Explosives (ATF) had reason to suspect that the Koresh group was stockpiling illegal weapons. There were also stories emerging of child abuse within the compound. The ATF obtained a search warrant for the compound as well as arrest warrants for Koresh and several Davidian members. When the ATF attempted to raid the ranch and serve the warrants, Koresh and his group resisted and an intense gun battle broke out. Four government agents and six Branch Davidians were killed, a standoff developed, and for the next fifty-one days the FBI laid siege to the compound.

On April 19, 1993, the FBI decided to end the siege with an attack. It began with a volley of tear gas, to which the Branch Davidians responded

An aerial view of the Branch Davidian compound near Waco, Texas, before its partial but lethal destruction by fire during an FBI assault. FEDERAL BUREAU OF INVESTIGATION

(according to law-enforcement officials) by setting fire to their own compound. The conflagration killed more than eighty Davidians, including twenty-four children. Across the nation, millions witnessed both the February 28 shoot-out and the April 19 inferno, which was covered live by television news crews.

The origin of the fire remained a subject of intense controversy. For six years, the FBI held that the Davidians had set the fire, and then, in August 1999, FBI officials, who had steadfastly denied using munitions capable of igniting a blaze, finally admitted that agents had used some incendiary tear gas cartridges. The very next year, however, an internal Justice Department investigation concluded that it was unquestionably the Branch Davidians who had ignited the blaze. Furthermore, the investigators found that the FBI did not shoot at Davidians during the fire. The investigation did little to persuade a core of conspiracy theorists, who continued to believe that the assault was the result of a federal law enforcement conspiracy.

It was all too easy for members of the public to write off the Waco siege and assault as the products of religious fanaticism. But the Waco tragedy and a siege and shoot-out at Ruby Ridge, Idaho (August 21–31, 1992), were cited as the primary motivations behind an act of terrorism more bewildering than either Waco or Ruby Ridge.

At 9:04 on the morning of April 19, 1995, a Ryder rental truck packed with highly explosive ammonium nitrate fertilizer and other materials exploded with devastating force outside the Alfred P. Murrah Federal Office Building in Oklahoma City. One side of the office tower collapsed, killing 168 men, women, and children, who were at play in the building's day care center. The chief perpetrator of this crime was a young US Army veteran, who had fought in the Gulf War, Timothy McVeigh. He had been one of the millions who saw live coverage of the shoot-out and inferno near Waco. As he watched those events unfold, he was already stirred to outrage by the FBI's bloody shoot-out and arrest white separatist "militia" activist Randy Weaver at Ruby Ridge, Idaho. What the government now did to Koresh and his followers was the last straw. McVeigh vowed to act, taking vengeance against the government that had killed people who felt and acted the same way as he did.

With fellow army vet Terry Nichols, McVeigh conspired to bomb the Murrah Building. There was no strategic reason for this. It was neither a military headquarters nor a center of federal law enforcement. The CIA had no offices there. But McVeigh and Nichols convinced themselves that it was a symbol of federal tyranny, and that was reason enough to attack.

McVeigh never expressed remorse for perpetrating what remains the deadliest act of domestic terrorism in the United States. In June 1997, he was found guilty on eleven counts of murder. He was sentenced to death and executed by lethal injection at the Federal Penitentiary in Terre Haute, Indiana, on June 11, 2001—the first federal execution since 1963. Nichols, who had turned state's evidence, was found guilty on December 23, 1997, of the lesser charge of involuntary manslaughter and conspiracy.

He was sentenced to life imprisonment. Mainstream America was now left to ponder the existence and the consequences of what was being called "homegrown" terrorism. Having defeated the Soviet Union and achieved preeminence among nations, it felt to some as if the United States hardly knew itself anymore as the greatest threat to the American democracy seemed to come from within.

Terrorists Attack the United States (2001)

At 8:45 a.m. (EDT) on the morning of September 11, 2001, a Boeing 767 passenger jetliner, American Airlines Flight 11 out of Boston, struck the north tower of the World Trade Center in lower Manhattan, explosively penetrating the building as if it were a guided missile.

The gaggle of morning TV shows was interrupted by live coverage of the disaster, cameras focused on the impenetrable black smoke issuing from the gaping wound torn in the gleaming silver skin of the 110-story skyscraper. Broadcast of these images and accompanying commentary began a mere three minutes after the impact. The nation's eyes, ears, and emotions were thus focused on the scene when a second 767 (United Airlines Flight 175) sliced into the south tower of the World Trade Center at 9:03. With cameras already trained on the towers, America and much of the world saw it happen in real time. There was no mistaking the situation now. These were not terrible accidents. The United States was under attack.

President George W. Bush was not in the White House but in Florida, reading *The Pet Goat* to a class of second graders in Sarasota. His chief of staff, Andrew Card, was in a room nearby when he heard the news. Waiting for a pause in the reading, he walked into the classroom and whispered in the president's ear. Mr. Bush said nothing, asked no questions, and gave no orders. He resumed following along as the children read aloud, and it was 9:30 before he announced on television that the nation had suffered "an apparent terrorist attack." Thirteen minutes later, at 9:43, a Boeing 757 (American Airlines Flight 77) barreled into the Pentagon, US military headquarters. At 10:05, in New York, the south tower of the World Trade Center collapsed. Nothing like it had ever been seen, not on television, not in real life. One hundred ten stories of steel, concrete, and humanity were consumed, swallowed, in seconds. Five minutes later, at 10:10, the quiet of rural Somerset County, Pennsylvania, was torn by the explosive impact of United Airlines Flight 93, which blasted into the black earth an even blacker crater. After another eighteen minutes, in New York, the north tower of the World Trade Center collapsed.

The nation's shock would be long sustained, but its collective bewilderment did not last long. Well before the day ended, the same mass media that covered the immolation of the World Trade Center reported that the airplane downed in Pennsylvania had been on course for the White House or the US Capitol. Before the day was over, Americans were also told that all four aircraft had been hijacked by terrorists who used them, filled as they were with passengers and thousands of pounds of jet fuel, as powerful weapons. Almost immediately, it was revealed that the terrorists were members of al-Qaeda (Arabic for "The Base"), an organization of perhaps ten thousand Islamist jihadists fighting what they deemed a holy war against Israel, the West, and especially the United States. Al-Qaeda was led by Osama bin Laden, a Saudi multimillionaire who lived under the protection of the radical Islamic Taliban government in Afghanistan. All this came to light so quickly because, it turned out, the American government was keenly aware of bin Laden and al-Qaeda, both of which had been the subject of a Presidential Daily Briefing (PDB) titled "Bin Laden Determined to Strike in US" and shown to the president on August 6, 2001. The forewarned government's apparent failure to prepare was never adequately accounted for.

The death toll from what many were calling America's second Pearl Harbor was set at 2,893 lives lost at the World Trade Center, 189 killed at the Pentagon, including the 64 passengers and crew of Flight 77, and 40 killed in the crash of Flight 93 in Pennsylvania. In 2004, a specially constituted "9/11 Commission" concluded that federal officials at every level had been unprepared "in every respect" to stop the suicide hijackings. But on September 12, 2001, President Bush was quick to remark, "We have just seen the first war of the twenty-first century," and eight days after this, on September 20, he announced in a speech to Congress that the United States would attack the Taliban in Afghanistan unless it surrendered "all the leaders of al-Qaeda who hide in your land." The war that was begun against Afghanistan on October 7, 2001, has, as of 2018, entered its seventeenth year and is by far the longest war the United States has ever fought.

At the president's urging, Congress also rushed to expand the investigative powers of US law enforcement agencies. The most sweeping legislation was the USA PATRIOT ACT, passed by the Senate on October 11, 2001, and the next day by the House. Among other things, it provided measures against money laundering used to finance international terrorism, expanded provisions for federal wiretaps and surveillance, authorized immunity against prosecution for the providers of government-requested wiretaps, authorized so-called sneak-and-peek searches and surreptitious search warrants and seizures, empowered law enforcement to examine public library records to determine who has been reading what, and instituted a foreign student monitoring program. The law's provisions have been repeatedly reauthorized since 2001.

The summer of 2002 saw heated debate about where what was now being called the "war on terrorism" should be taken next. A coterie of neoconservatives, or "neocons," in the Bush administration—with Vice President Dick Cheney, Secretary of Defense Donald Rumsfeld, and Deputy Secretary of Defense Paul Wolfowitz foremost among them—persuaded the president to make a case for invading Iraq, which they identified as the linchpin of the Middle East. Overthrow its dictator, Saddam Hussein, and transform Iraq into a democracy, they argued, and the entire region would become a US ally. Over the objections of many, who pointed out that there was no direct connection between Iraq and 9/11, President Bush took the nation to war in Iraq on March 20, 2003. Saddam Hussein was overthrown and subsequently executed, but civil war ensued, and combat continues into the present—although principal US forces were withdrawn on December 18, 2011, the war having officially lasted eight years, eight months, and twenty-eight days. For the first two decades of the twenty-first century, the United States has been a nation at war.

Human Genome Project Is
Completed (2003)

DNA, deoxyribonucleic acid, is a thread-like chain of organic molecules called nucleotides that carry the genetic instructions by which all living organisms grow, develop, function, and reproduce. The substance was isolated in 1869 by a German scientist, Freiderich Miescher, but it was not until 1953 that Francis Crick and James Watson at Cambridge University discovered the double-helix molecular structure of DNA, which explained, essentially, the core secret of life itself.

This breakthrough, it turned out, was just the beginning. The next step was to map out the genetic material in the chromosomes of any organism—its "genome." In the case of an organism as complex as a human being, researchers would have to sequence some three billion units of DNA—an epic task.

Why do it?

If the DNA could be sequenced, or "mapped," it would become possible to locate a particular gene within the genome, to identify and find other genes in the same region, and then correlate many diseases with specific genes. Once this was accomplished, a path would be open by which gene therapies could be developed to cure, prevent, or eliminate a large variety of diseases.

Mapping the human genome became one of the great quests of the late twentieth century and early twenty-first. It was not only a scientific quest, a search for understanding human life on a level never before reached, it was also an opportunity for almost unimaginable profit. A US government-funded endeavor, the Human Genome Project (HGP), began in 1990 under the auspices of the Department of Energy and the National Institutes of Health. The goal was to complete the mapping within fifteen years, but within just ten years, in 2000, a so-called working draft of the genomic map was announced.

On April 6, 2000, however, a privately funded, for-profit American corporation, Celera Genomics, announced that it had already completed mapping the entire human genome. Celera published its work on February 15, 2001, and the government-funded Human Genome Project published its own draft the very next day.

The photo finish of the private and government efforts were the end products of a landmark scientific endeavor that was nevertheless burdened by great controversy. When genetic researcher Craig Venter launched Celera Genomics in 1998, he announced that his company intended to seek patent protection on the sequencing of some two hundred to three hundred genes. As work progressed, however, Celera filed preliminary patent applications on 6,500 whole or partial genes. Venter assured the scientific community that his company would publish all its findings, but he cautioned that it would not permit free redistribution or commercial use of the data. This set off a debate at the highest levels of government. At last, in March 2000, President Bill Clinton announced that the human genome sequence could not be patented by the US Patent Office and that it should be made freely available to all researchers.

The decision was widely greeted as a triumph for open-source scientific inquiry, but, predictably, the decision caused Celera's stock to plummet, a fall that sent shockwaves throughout the entire biotech sector trading on NASDAQ. In a mere forty-eight hours, biotech stocks lost some $50 billion in market capitalization. Yet, in the end, they more than recovered. By making the research of Celera and the government project universally available, many investors and firms rushed into genetic research focused on targeted gene therapies. Although exclusive possession of genome maps was effectively outlawed, patents on individual products—drugs and other genetically based therapies—enabled by the genomic map were allowed. This opened infinite avenues for profit on such products as genetic tests that reveal the predisposition to various illnesses, including breast cancer, cystic fibrosis, liver diseases, and others, and on research and cures for many cancers, Alzheimer's disease, and countless additional disorders. At the same time, the contribution of the human genome map to the understanding of evolution and of life itself, especially through the comparative analysis of DNA sequences from different organisms, is almost incalculable—certainly the equivalent, say, of the discoveries of Copernicus, Galileo, and Newton.

The announcement of what was essentially the "final" draft of the genome map was made on April 14, 2003 (although this actually covered only the most active portion of the genome within the cell nucleus, euchromatic DNA, which represented about 92 percent of the human genome). For some people, the announcement of this final version was more disturbing than thrilling. The notion of manipulating the genome stirred both intense excitement in genetic research and intense controversy. Without question, gene therapies promised a rolling revolution in medicine, on a par with the development of vaccines and antibiotics. Yet the prospect of reshaping life at its most basic levels challenged the intellectual, ethical, and spiritual barriers that have traditionally walled off science and technology from the realms of morality and religion.

As the American Revolution brought into the world the potential of democracy's great benefits and its formidable challenges to the old order, so the American revolution in science created by the work of Celera and the Human Genome Project created both new possibilities and new moral, spiritual, and political conundrums.

Facebook Is Launched (2004)

Born in White Plains, New York, in 1984, Mark Zuckerberg was the son of a psychiatrist mother and a dentist father. He showed an early interest in computers and natural creativity as a programmer. As the parents of children who demonstrate an early genius for the violin or the piano might hire a prominent music teacher, Zuckerberg's folks engaged a software developer to tutor their eleven-year-old. Not long afterward, young Zuckerberg began creating commercially viable software, including a program he called Synapse, which learned a user's musical taste and purchasing habits through AI. Both AOL and Microsoft expressed interest in the program—and in employing Zuckerberg. Instead, he enrolled at Harvard in 2002, majoring in psychology but also studying computer science. The two fields intertwined in his imagination, and in October 2003 he created FaceMash, a website that allowed Harvard students to evaluate the attractiveness of one another through rankings. FaceMash was an overnight sensation but was shut down by the Harvard administration, which threatened to expel its creator for appropriating photographs of Harvard students without their permission.

Despite its forced demise, FaceMash led to the creation of TheFacebook, intended to be a kind of universal directory of everyone with a Harvard email address. It was a way to network with the entire university by creating a profile in which you could upload a photo, share your interests, and connect. It also created a visualization of your personal Harvard network. Within a month, half of the student body had signed up. Zuckerberg, however, was sued by three Harvard seniors who had hired him to create a social network called HarvardConnection. The suit was not settled until 2008, when the three plaintiffs were awarded 1.2 million shares in the now-prospering Facebook company.

TheFacebook quickly grew beyond the confines of Harvard, with membership open to virtually all American and Canadian universities by

Facebook founder Mark Zuckerberg during a speaking engagement on April 30, 2018. PHOTO BY ANTHONY QUINTANO, PUBLISHED ON WIKIMEDIA COMMONS

the end of 2004. Zuckerberg left Harvard to move, with his new company, to Palo Alto, California, ground zero of Silicon Valley. Investments poured in from prominent venture capitalists, and in August 2005, "TheFacebook" became, simply, Facebook. In September, Facebook expanded its membership to high school students—and, its first foray beyond the student community, to employees of Microsoft and Apple.

Having left Harvard for a semester, Zuckerberg crossed the Rubicon and formally dropped out. The reach of Facebook continued to expand, going beyond the United States and Canada to Australia, New Zealand, Mexico, the United Kingdom, and Ireland. In September 2006, Facebook was opened to everyone—in the world—over thirteen years of age who had a valid email address.

The aggressive monetization of the Facebook platform began in May 2007, when it opened its Marketplace, which let users post classifieds to sell products and services. This year also saw the launch of the Facebook Application Developer platform, which enabled developers to create applications and games that integrated with Facebook. While personal profiles remained Facebook's major draw, the company began avidly recruiting businesses to use the site. Before 2007 ended, more than one hundred thousand companies had signed up, and Facebook was on its way to becoming the world's largest advertising vehicle.

Facebook was all about connecting. This meant that users self-created immense bodies of data about themselves—their location, their interests, what they bought, and what they wanted to buy. America had long been the epicenter of mass media, which broadcast everything from ads to ideas to millions and even billions of users. Broadcast media is essentially one-way communication. A television or radio station or network broadcasts its content to everyone with a TV or radio. The Internet and the World Wide Web that inhabited it stepped beyond one-way mass communication to interactive massive communication. More than any other platform on the Web, Facebook exploited the interactivity, connecting users with one another—and connecting companies with consumers who, because they revealed so much about themselves on the platform, were readily converted into customers.

In 2012, Facebook floated its IPO and in 2013 joined the Fortune 500 at number 462. As of January 2018, Facebook had 2.2 billion monthly active users—out of a planet populated by an estimated 7.63 billion. Many of these users, doubtless, treat the platform casually. But many also live virtual lives on it. They transact business, they buy and sell products and services, they communicate with one another, and they share huge tranches of their lives with hundreds or even thousands of people they have never physically met. They also get their knowledge of the world—their news—from it.

Facebook has attempted to flag "fake news" and to ban harmful or malicious pages (including some controlled by terrorist organizations), but the platform in many ways remains a free-for-all. This offers the vast benefits of tremendous freedom, but it also presents a boundless digital arena for mischief and worse. During the 2016 US presidential election, for instance, a UK-based, Russia-affiliated data firm, Cambridge Analytica, used an app that the Moldavan-born data scientist Aleksandr Kogan, lecturer at Russia's St. Petersburg University, developed to covertly "scrape" Facebook, collecting the personal details of some eighty million users. These details, in turn, were used to create ads and fake news stories specifically crafted to persuade targeted Facebook users to vote for Donald Trump in preference to Hillary Clinton. In effect, the Facebook platform had been hijacked by the Russian government in a sophisticated digital psyops campaign intended to put into the White House the Kremlin's preferred candidate.

Facebook is the archetypal Internet application. It uses the full potential of this technology to overcome most of the "frictions" that have inhibited communication and commerce throughout history—time, distance, the mechanics of producing and disseminating information (or disinformation), and the formidable obstacles and clumsy processes that get between the lonely and those seeking connection, sellers and buyers, cheaters and cheated, thieves and victims. With unprecedented access to virtually unlimited sources of information has come the possibility of great discoveries, remarkable strides in education, political transformation, and the opening of vast stores of knowledge, wisdom, stupidity, good, evil, truth, and lies. As the 2016 US election demonstrated, Facebook has the power to transform the fortunes and fate of nations.

Lehman Brothers Collapses, Triggering a Global Financial Crisis (2008)

Until it filed for Chapter 11 bankruptcy on September 15, 2008, Lehman Brothers, founded in 1850, was among the most storied of global financial firms on Wall Street. It was blue chip, gilt-edged, and proverbially rock solid. But in the months, weeks, days, and hours before it filed, clients poured out of Lehman like the audience in a theater suddenly engulfed by flame. Its share value plummeted and then evaporated. The credit rating agencies savaged it. And its bankruptcy, when it came, was the largest in US history, with bank debt of $613 billion and bond debt of $155 billion against assets valued at $639 billion.

Lehman was one of a handful financial titans experts dubbed "too big to fail," meaning that its collapse, however unimaginable, would be so catastrophic to the rest of the economy that the government would have to jump in to prevent potential failure. Under the conservative Republican administration of George W. Bush, however, the government did not jump in, and global markets immediately careened downward. Over the next several months, day after day, hour after hour, one new crisis developed after another as American and world economies verged on collapse. What happened was compared to the Wall Street crash of 1929 and the Great Depression that followed. Except, this time, it was called a "meltdown," like a nuclear reactor gone rogue and approaching the verge of mushroom cloud annihilation.

It had all begun with something called the subprime mortgage crisis. Deregulation of the financial sector during the Clinton and Bush years loosened mortgage lending requirements. Lenders began making many subprime loans, writing mortgages for people with poor credit or inadequate income and little possibility of paying off the loan. The result was an increasingly high default rate.

This was bad enough, but what turned it into a full-blown crisis was "securitization." Investment companies began bundling large numbers of mortgages into new financial instruments called mortgage-backed securities. The bundles were given deceptively high ratings by the standard securities rating agencies and therefore sold as comparatively low-risk investments. Doubtless, some mortgages in a given bundle were sound, but many were not—and no agency could possibly evaluate each mortgage (there might be thousands) in a bundle. In the deregulated climate, underwriting criteria were loose or nonexistent. Moreover, mortgage brokers, eager for commissions, often encouraged prospective homeowners to inflate their income statements. A well-intended federal law, the Community Reinvestment Act, designed to help low- and moderate-income Americans get mortgages, also encouraged lenders to make riskier loans. Beyond this, many subprime loans were sold by their makers so that they finally accrued to Fannie Mae and Freddie Mac, two government-sponsored publicly traded enterprises that financed the secondary mortgage market. In effect, the government implied a guarantee of the loans. This created what economists call a "moral hazard" for American taxpayers, upon whom, ultimately, much of the burden for defaulted loans fell. It was as if all Americans had unwittingly cosigned millions of bad loans.

Before the meltdown, high mortgage approval rates created a high demand for homes, which, in turn, increased home prices, including the value of existing homes. This led many homeowners to borrow against their homes, cashing out what appeared to be a huge windfall representing the difference between the home's cost at purchase and its current high price. A bubble quickly inflated—only to burst beginning in August 2006 as delinquencies and defaults climbed steeply, peaking at the start of 2010. During this time, home prices sharply declined so that many borrowers, including those who had taken out home equity loans, found themselves "underwater," their debt substantially exceeding the new value of their homes.

At the same time, the mortgage-backed securities were rapidly devalued. Apparently low-risk, sure-thing investments became high-risk junk practically overnight. The many banks that held most of these securities now suffered liquidity crises. In a bid to prevent their collapse, the federal government assumed control of Freddie Mac and Fannie Mae on September 7, 2008. A week later, Lehman Brothers filed for bankruptcy, and it looked to be certain that Merrill Lynch, reinsurance giant AIG, UK-based banking and insurance company HBOS, Royal Bank of Scotland, and other major firms (Bradford & Bingley, Fortis, Hypo Real Estate, and Alliance & Leicester) would follow Lehman.

In this climate of sheer terror, on September 16, the day after the Lehman bankruptcy, the US government announced an $85 billion bailout of AIG. It was the first of trillions the government poured out. Arguably, these unprecedented expenditures averted economic Armageddon, but it did little to quickly unfreeze frozen credit markets, which meant that housing prices fell even more sharply and the bottom dropped out of stock markets across the planet. Foreclosures, evictions, layoffs, and unemployment became realities of life, with major declines in consumer wealth. Another Great Depression did not set in, but the economic picture during 2008–2012 was dubbed the Great Recession and, if anything, hit Europe even harder than the United States, creating a sovereign-debt crisis. Depending on one's feelings about the nature and role of government, the crisis was interpreted either as a cautionary tale about the dangers of too little government—the failure to regulate the free market—or as a warning about too much government, the inevitably spendthrift ways of "big government." This great American debate continues—often with irrational, even tribal ferocity.

Barack Obama Is Elected the Nation's First African American President (2008)

The election of 2000, pitting Democratic vice president Al Gore against Republican Texas governor George W. Bush, was so closely fought in the electoral college that the decision between the two candidates came down to a few hundred votes cast in Florida. The election there was marred by disputed counts and recounts and an antiquated punch-card ballot system that left many votes in doubt. In the end, a combination of a Supreme Court decision and the goodwill of the candidates decided the contest in favor of Bush. He therefore entered office under a cloud. But when the terror attacks of September 11, 2001, struck, the nation did as it has always done. It rallied behind the president, across party lines. Overnight, Bush's approval rating spiked from slightly more than 50 percent to a lofty peak of 90 percent, only to decline steadily until the commencement of the Iraq War in March 2003, when it rose from below 60 percent to just above 70 percent before resuming a downward slope as the war proved increasingly complex, costly, and fruitless. Then, in August 2005, when Hurricane Katrina tore across Florida and slammed into the Gulf Coast, submerging New Orleans under some twenty feet of water, Bush's approval descended further. Under his administration, the federal response to the disaster was itself disastrous. A vacationing president left management of the hurricane to the Federal Emergency Management Agency (FEMA), the funding of which had been drastically cut on his watch and the direction of which had been put in the hands of Michael Brown, a Bush supporter whose prior leadership experience had been as the Judges and Stewards Commissioner for the International Arabian Horse Association from 1989 to 2001. Finally came the economic meltdown of 2007–2008, in the face of which President Bush seemed as feckless as he had appeared during Katrina.

The official White House photographic portrait of Barack Obama, forty-fourth president of the United States. PHOTO BY PETE SOUZA

The 2008 election pitted Republican John McCain and running mate Sarah Palin against the first African American nominated by a major party as its presidential candidate, Democrat Barack Obama, and his running mate, Delaware senator and veteran politician Joe Biden.

As home real estate prices tanked in the subprime mortgage crisis and securities markets derived from mortgages likewise collapsed as mortgage lenders and major banks faltered and even failed and as three major US automobile manufacturers careened toward bankruptcy, the presidential campaign took on an urgency that had been missing from the elections of 2000 and 2004. Both candidates, Democrat and Republican, campaigned against George W. Bush as much as they did against one another. In the end, John McCain could not disassociate himself from the incumbent, and a majority of the American electorate clearly craved change. Although many pundits opined that the nation was "not ready" for an African American president, Barack Obama defeated McCain 66,882,230 votes (53 percent) versus 58,343,671 (46 percent), taking 365 electoral votes to McCain's 173.

2008 clearly brought a change election, and Barack Obama was an inspiring, eloquent candidate, who ran a campaign driven by the words *Hope* and *Change*. They were precisely the words most Americans wanted to hear in 2008. The eager, even desperate, expectation of the American people, those who voted for him and surely many who did not, was that they might be inspired by a president again. Many Americans were justly proud of having finally journeyed beyond the nation's long heritage of a racial division born from an eighteenth- and nineteenth-century legacy of slavery and a twentieth-century history of Jim Crow laws and other manifestations of racial injustice. Some even spoke of having achieved a "post-racial America."

There was a certain patriotic and moral euphoria in the air. But this new era of good feelings did not last long. It was quickly apparent that many in America had not entered anything resembling a post-racial state of consciousness. It was also apparent that many in the Republican Party intended to oppose the new president on principle and as a matter of course—not merely debating him and his policies but working to confound and defeat them. One wing of the GOP even signed onto a new conspiracy theory, which held that Obama was not even a "natural born" citizen of the United States, that the story of his birth in Hawaii was an elaborate fraud, and that his real birthplace was Kenya, his father's country of origin. In 2010, Newt Gingrich, onetime speaker of the house and now an out-of-office gadfly some called the intellectual leader of the GOP, asked in an interview published in the conservative *National Review*, "What if [Obama] is so outside our comprehension, that only if you understand Kenyan, anti-colonial behavior, can you begin to piece together [his actions]?" He called the president "fundamentally out of touch with how the world works" and described him as having "played a wonderful con, as a result of which he is now president."

Among those who embraced what was being called "birtherism," the belief that President Obama had been born outside of the United States, was a celebrity real estate developer and formerly unsuccessful presidential candidate, Donald J. Trump. "Why doesn't he show his birth certificate?" Trump asked on ABC's *The View* in 2011. "I want to see his birth certificate," he later told Fox News's *On the Record*. And in 2012, on NBC's *Today Show*, he declared, "I'm starting to think that he was not born here." Barack Obama was soon internationally respected, but many Americans, it seemed, found it impossible to acknowledge this man as *their* president. They decided that they wanted "*their* country back."

Donald Trump Defeats Hillary Clinton to Become the Forty-Fifth President of the United States (2016)

Like all working democracies, the United States, born in revolution, remains a revolutionary nation. After eight years of wasteful war punctuated by an incompetent response to natural disaster in Katrina and capped by economic meltdown, voters demanded the revolution our four-year election cycle offers. On the Democratic side, Hillary Clinton and Barack Obama battled it out in a bitter primary. Both candidates embodied an element of change: Clinton, if elected, would be the first female American president; Obama, the first African American. But Clinton, US senator from New York and wife of the forty-second president, ran on her credentials as an experienced political leader, whereas Obama, a freshman senator from Illinois, ran on the promise of "hope and change." Perceived as the genuine change candidate, Obama captured the nomination and defeated Republican John McCain—who, despite his efforts to define himself in contrast to outgoing incumbent George W. Bush, did not persuade the electorate that he offered the change most voters wanted.

Obama was greeted with great expectations but also great resistance. The 2010 midterms brought Republican majorities to both houses of Congress, and while Obama was returned to office for a second term, the nation faced the election of 2016 more deeply divided than ever. The Republicans offered the largest primary field in American history—seventeen major candidates, the least likely of whom was one Donald J. Trump, a man most accurately described (at the time) as a celebrity real estate developer best known to most of the nation as the star of a popular reality TV series called *The Apprentice* and a spin-off, *Celebrity Apprentice*. He had flirted with presidential politics in the past but was discounted

The official White House photographic portrait of Donald Trump, forty-fifth president of the United States. PHOTO BY SHEALAH CRAIGHEAD

by the mainstream of both major political parties as far too inexperienced and extreme to have a realistic shot at the candidacy, let alone the election. He came with a great deal of baggage: multiple marriages, multiple bankruptcies, a reputation as a playboy, and a tendency to shoot from the hip with outrageous comments.

Even as, one by one, the sixteen other primary hopefuls fell away, the establishment of both parties and the mainstream media persisted in denying even the possibility of a Trump candidacy. As the field narrowed, some Republicans even declared themselves "Never Trumpers," swearing they would not support this wholly inexperienced extremist—who was more interested in tearing down the established order than in building something new, who was long on bluster and short on facts—even if he was somehow nominated.

But a GOP nomination? *That*, most insisted, would never happen. For the Republican Party to nominate a political novice, a walking scandal, a "carnival barker" (as some called him), would be to commit collective suicide as a serious party. Of genuine political debate, precious little was heard during the primaries. Instead, Trump, a self-promoter whose specialty was branding, launched a series of ad hominem assaults, in which former Florida governor Jeb Bush became "Low-energy Jeb," Texas senator Ted Cruz "Lyin' Ted," and Florida senator Marco Rubio "Li'l Marco." Counterpointed to this schoolyard-level rhetoric was Trump's utterly simple message, "America is being cheated by the world, and American politicians are cheating the 'forgotten man'"—by which candidate Trump meant working-class white America. The candidate campaigned under the slogan "Make America Great Again," which was emblazoned on baseball caps (available at the official Trump online shop for $25 each), and which implied that the way forward was a return to a past in which most Americans were white, Christian, and "ordinary" folks rather than elite intellectuals. Trump's opponents persistently refused to recognize that the candidate they dismissed as a showman and a con man had tapped into a vein of urgent American populist sentiment.

In the meantime, the Democratic primary race came down to a contest between Hillary Clinton, who had served in President Obama's cabinet as secretary of state, and Bernie Sanders, senator from Vermont, an Independent running as a Democrat. Sanders generated a great deal of enthusiasm, especially among younger voters, who found his liberal, even socialist brand of populism highly appealing. They viewed Clinton, in contrast, as an agent of the status quo. Yes, she was a *woman* running for president, but she was also a Clinton, not just well connected but entangled with special interests. The great lesson of her 2008 primary contest against Obama was that opposing *change* with *experience* was a losing strategy. Instead of learning the lesson, Clinton ran on the very promise that had failed her eight years earlier. Moreover, she was hobbled by the scandals of her husband's presidency and the taint of crony capitalism, her own defensiveness in the face of Republican charges concerning her reputed failure to keep diplomats safe in war-torn Libya, her use of a private email server for official State Department communications, and the apparent disappearance of some thirty thousand emails reputedly on that server. The Republican-controlled Congress conducted several investigations during the campaign itself.

In the end, Trump and Clinton emerged as the nominees. Polls gave Trump virtually no chance of victory, although pundits did note the enthusiasm of Trump's minority of supporters. As for Clinton, her supporters rarely exhibited anything approaching enthusiasm. Their vote for her was a vote against Trump.

October, days before the election, brought two "October surprises." One was the revelation of a 2005 video outtake from an episode of TV's *Access Hollywood*, which recorded Trump boasting to TV host Billy Bush that he routinely kissed and groped women at random. "I don't even wait. And when you're a star, they let you do it. You can do anything. Grab them by [their private parts]."

The resulting scandal, dubbed "Pussygate" in echo of "Watergate," brought a renewed chorus of appraisals that the Trump candidacy was dead. Instead, the Trump scandal was rapidly overshadowed by a resurgence of the Clinton email controversy. On July 5, 2016, FBI director James Comey had announced the bureau's recommendation that no charges be filed against her, but he nevertheless observed that "Clinton or her colleagues . . . were extremely careless in their handling of very sensitive, highly classified information." Suddenly, on October 28, eleven days before the election, the director informed Congress that the FBI was investigating some additional Clinton emails that had come to light as the result of an unrelated case.

Democrats and Never Trumpers feared that this announcement would throw the race to Trump. But they continued to take comfort in polls that still showed a "solid" Clinton lead. Election night brought a different result. Although Clinton won the popular vote by three million ballots, she lost the electoral vote, 227 to 304.

It will be years, of course, before history passes its verdict—almost always a divided one—on the candidacy let alone the presidency of Donald Trump. What was immediately apparent is that the "progressive" and "post-racial" America that elected Barack Obama chose to take a step back to nativism, populism, and isolationist nationalism. The election of a brash reality TV star was perhaps the ultimate expression of government in a democracy. The people voted for the candidate with whom they both felt—and for years had experienced through the media—a direct connection. Their hope, presumably, was that this would bring beneficial change.

It may. Yet polls suggested that a majority of Americans, after two years of the Trump presidency, saw the administration less as an expression of democracy than as a challenge to it. Of course, "polls" had also predicted that Donald Trump could never be elected.

Russia Is Accused of "Meddling" in the US Presidential Election (2016)

On January 6, 2017, the US Office of the Director of National Intelligence issued an "Intelligence Community Assessment Assessing Russian Activities and Interference in Recent US Elections" (ICA 2017-01D). Its "Key Judgments" were as follows:

Russian efforts to influence the 2016 US presidential election represent the most recent expression of Moscow's longstanding desire to undermine the US-led liberal democratic order, but these activities demonstrated a significant escalation in directness, level of activity, and scope of effort compared to previous operations.

The report went on to assess that "Russian President Vladimir Putin ordered an influence campaign in 2016 aimed at the US presidential election. Russia's goals were to undermine public faith in the US democratic process, denigrate Secretary Clinton, and harm her electability and potential presidency." The Intelligence Community further assessed that "Putin and the Russian Government developed a clear preference for President-elect Trump" and "aspired to help" his "election chances when possible by discrediting Secretary Clinton and publicly contrasting her unfavorably to him."

"Moscow's approach," the intelligence report observed, "evolved over the course of the campaign based on Russia's understanding of the electoral prospects of the two main candidates. When it appeared to Moscow that Secretary Clinton was likely to win the election, the Russian influence campaign began to focus more on undermining her future presidency." The Russian influence campaign followed a Russian messaging strategy that blends covert intelligence operations—such as cyber activity—with overt efforts by Russian Government agencies, state-funded media, third-party intermediaries, and paid social media users or "trolls." Russia, like its Soviet predecessor, has a history of conducting covert influence campaigns focused on US presidential elections that have used intelligence officers and agents and press placements to disparage candidates perceived as hostile to the Kremlin. To achieve its ends, Russian "intelligence services conducted cyber operations against targets associated with the 2016 US presidential election, including targets associated with both major US political parties."

The Intelligence Community assessed "with high confidence that Russian military intelligence" used the persona of a hacker calling himself Guccifer 2.0 to acquire sensitive data—including emails from the Democratic National Committee—which it gave to a website called DCLeaks.com. At some point, we now know, WikiLeaks, the international organization that publishes secret information, obtained this leaked material and released it very broadly.

The Intelligence Community also revealed that "Russian intelligence obtained and maintained access to elements of multiple US state or local electoral boards. DHS [Department of Homeland Security] assesses that the types of systems Russian actors targeted or compromised were not involved in vote tallying." Nevertheless, "Russia's state-run propaganda machine contributed to the influence campaign by serving as a platform for Kremlin messaging to Russian and international audiences." The intelligence report concluded with a warning that "Moscow will apply lessons learned from its Putin-ordered campaign aimed at the US presidential election to future influence efforts worldwide, including against US allies and their election processes."

Candidate Trump and, subsequently, President Trump consistently expressed doubt that Russia had meddled in the election. Nevertheless, the FBI launched an investigation into the interference and the involvement, if any, of the Trump campaign in the Russian efforts. On May 9, 2017, President Trump fired FBI director James Comey, citing the recommendation of Attorney General Jeff Sessions and Deputy Attorney General Rod Rosenstein founded on Comey's mishandling of the investigation of Secretary of State Hillary Clinton's emails. Remarkably, however, on May

11, the president told newscaster Lester Holt in a nationally broadcast NBC News interview, "When I decided [to fire Comey], I said to myself, I said, 'You know, this Russia thing with Trump and Russia is a made-up story.'"

The revelation in the Holt interviews was widely interpreted as a confession that the real reason for dismissing Comey was to end the Russian investigation. But the dismissal did no such thing. The investigation continued under Robert Mueller III, who was appointed "special counsel" by Deputy Attorney General Rosenstein (Attorney General Sessions having recused himself from the Russia investigation because he had been an official in the Trump campaign). As of the fall of 2018, Mueller's investigation has indicted, convicted, or obtained guilty pleas from thirty-two people and three companies—that the public knows of. Of this group, four are former Trump advisors, twenty-six are Russian nationals, the three companies are Russian. The four Trump aides have all pleaded guilty. The Mueller investigation also referred some investigations to other parts of the Justice Department. This resulted in two more guilty pleas. Among those who pleaded guilty was Michael Flynn, who not only was part of the Trump campaign but also served in the administration, as National Security Advisor. Paul Manafort pleaded not guilty to numerous charges unrelated to the campaign; however, he was employed by the Trump campaign for some five months, including as campaign chairman from June 20, 2016, to August 19. Manafort, whose connections with the Kremlin were of long-standing, participated on June 9, 2016, with candidate Trump's son Donald Trump Jr. and son-in-law, Jared Kushner, in a meeting with a Kremlin-connected Russian attorney Natalia Veselnitskaya and several others, including Russian nationals, in a meeting at Trump Tower in New York. The meeting focused on damaging information concerning Hillary Clinton, which the Russian government reputedly held and was willing to share with the Trump campaign. Manafort was convicted on August 21, 2018, of five counts of tax fraud, two counts of bank fraud, and one count of failing to report foreign bank accounts. Seeking to avoid a second trial on additional charges, he pleaded guilty on September 14, 2018, to two counts of conspiracy and agreed to cooperate with Special Counsel Mueller's investigation.

Thus, the Trump presidency, already highly controversial, labored day after day, month after month, in the shadow of a scandal revolving around questions concerning the possible complicity of the president and his campaign with a hostile Russian government in manipulating the US general election of 2016. Such questions in and of themselves were unprecedented in American history, and the prospect of an American president colluding with a foreign power to win office was all but unthinkable—until President Trump met in Helsinki, Finland, on July 16, 2018. Standing next to Russian president Vladimir Putin at a joint press conference, the American president expressed doubt concerning the unanimous conclusion of the US intelligence community, that Russia had interfered in the 2016 election, and embraced the Russian president's denial of "election meddling." Many Americans expressed outrage, and a few, like former CIA director John O. Brennan, made references to treason, calling Trump's "press conference performance . . . nothing short of treasonous. Not only were Trump's comments imbecilic, he is wholly in the pocket of Putin." Brennan asked, "Republican Patriots: Where are you???" While some GOP lawmakers expressed concern, most retained confidence in the president, even as Special Counsel Mueller continued to investigate Russian meddling and the role of Americans, including members of the Trump campaign, in it.

Amid a New Nationalism, the United States Withdraws from the Paris Climate Accords (2017)

In 1899, the American geologist Thomas Chrowder Chamberlin theorized that major changes in climate could result from changes in the concentration of carbon dioxide in the atmosphere. The climate change of greatest significance in recent times has been so-called global warming. In 1967, Syukuro Manabe working with Richard Wetherald at the Geophysical Fluid Dynamics Laboratory of the National Oceanic and Atmospheric Administration (NOAA) in Washington and Princeton, New Jersey, used mainframe computers to make the first detailed calculation of what was being called the greenhouse effect. The two researchers concluded that the doubling of atmospheric carbon dioxide from the level current in 1967 would result in approximately 2°C increase in global temperature. Subsequent studies over the years have detailed how the increase of carbon dioxide and other so-called greenhouse gases will inevitably warm the planet. Global warming melts the planet's snowpack and glaciers, significantly raising the level of the world's oceans and thus threatening low-lying and coastal areas with floods or submergence. A warmer planet produces more extreme—and damaging—weather, and, as the oceans get hotter, they become more acidic, threatening a significant portion of sea life, including species important as food.

Throughout the world in the late twentieth century and into the twenty-first—and nowhere more than in America—both the existence and causes of climate change have been intensely debated. Internationally, the scientific consensus concerning the existence of the phenomenon is overwhelming. The nature of the causes is subject to more scientific debate. While it is recognized that certain biological processes, natural variations in solar radiation the earth receives, and geological processes—including plate tectonics and volcanic eruptions—all contribute to climate change, questions remain as to which processes contribute the most. In addition, almost all climate scientists believe that certain human activities, mostly associated with industrial civilization, are among the primary causes of ongoing climate change. Again, however, the degree of these human impacts versus those in nature remains undetermined, but human impacts are widely believed to be very significant.

On April 22, 2016, the United States became one of the 195 signatories and 178 national parties to the Paris Agreement under the United Nations Framework Convention on Climate Change. Each country that is party to the agreement determines, plans, and regularly reports on its contributions to mitigate climate change. There is no mechanism of enforcement or force, and the agreement does not bind a country to whatever measures and timetable it sets. The importance of the accord is primarily as a universal declaration that climate change is a clear and present danger to life as well as the economic well-being of all people on the planet and that it is in the common interest of humanity to urgently address the issues involved. The overall aim of the Paris Agreement is to keep the increase in average global temperature below the 2°C above pre-industrial levels.

Accession to the Paris Agreement by the United States during the Obama administration was considered a victory for both the US environmental movement and the global environment, since the United States is second only to China as a carbon dioxide emitter, responsible for 14.3 percent of emissions, compared to China's 29.4 percent. Nevertheless, in 2017, President Donald Trump announced the withdrawal of the United States from the agreement, effective on the earliest possible date, November 4, 2020 (in accordance with Article 28 of the agreement).

President Trump's withdrawal fulfilled a campaign promise and is consonant with his claim that leaving the agreement will benefit US businesses and workers. He condemned the agreement as generally undermining the US economy and putting the nation "at a permanent disadvantage." Leaving the agreement was essential, he claimed, to what he called his "America First" policy.

While many Republican politicians approved the withdrawal, most Americans—including political leaders from both major parties, business leaders, religious leaders, and scientists—condemned withdrawal from the agreement. In an unprecedented step, the governors of sixteen US states and the territory of Puerto Rico created a bipartisan US Climate Alliance committed to upholding the objectives of the Paris Agreement despite the federal withdrawal. Environmentalism has become an aspect of the American identity even apart from official federal policy.

Index